UNABOMBER

The Secret Life of Ted Kaczynski

by Chris Waits and Dave Shors

HELENA
INDEPENDENT RECORD

MONTANA
M A G A Z I N E

Dedication

To Americans who were literally held hostage by the notorious Unabomber for eighteen years; to the bombing victims and their families whose lives were shattered; and to those in Lincoln directly touched by the vengeful acts. All deserve and have the right to know the truth and the details.

Chris M. Waits

Acknowledgment

Our thanks to the Upper Blackfoot Valley Historical Society for their contributions about Lincoln history, from their book Gold Pans and Singletrees.

ISBN 1-56037-131-5 softbound; 1-56037-139-0 hardbound

© 1999 Helena Independent Record and Montana Magazine
Text © 1999 Chris Waits

Printed in Canada

Contents

The Discovery...12

Welcome to Florence Gulch 28

Lincoln, Ted's Haven 59

Changes in McClellan Gulch....................................69

The Lincoln Mysteries..77

The Arrest 110

The Investigation Begins...119

Tug of War 125

The Secret Cabin and the FBI 134

Secrets Revealed..152

Ted's Bed and Breakfast...164

Caught in His Own Trap 178

Interviews and Trial Strategies 213

The "Queer" Scale 228

A Closer Look 264

Introduction

Ted Kaczynski is a master illusionist, a sleight-of-mind artist who based his life on deception. He shrouded his violent acts beneath the gentle facade of a Montana hermit, pulling doves of innocence out of his scruffy beard, smelly clothes, and non-intrusive lifestyle while he injured and killed people with his deadly bombs.

Who would have thought on the morning of April 3, 1996, when the spring Chinook winds were thawing the small mountain community of Lincoln out of the grips of a long winter freeze, that Kaczynski's deadly bag of tricks would be exposed that very day.

By mid-day, Lincoln was abuzz. In the middle of the morning, Kaczynski had been tricked into coming out of his one-room cabin and was in the custody of federal agents. In the early evening dusk he was being transported along the same gravel Stemple Pass Road where he had often walked and ridden his bicycle, on his way to a small FBI office in Helena.

By midnight, when he was safely incarcerated in Lewis and Clark County Jail in Helena, the town of Lincoln had been jolted into the million-watt limelight of world attention, never to be the same again.

Chris Waits awoke that same April day in nearby McClellan Gulch, knowing dozens of federal agents were in Lincoln scrutinizing his friend and neighbor of nearly twenty-five years. At first Waits thought the investigation might be related to hunting violations, since Kaczynski lived off the land, and had shot deer and elk out of season for many years.

But there was too much attention, too many federal agents lurking in the Lincoln area for a mere poacher to warrant.

The Unabomber, though? Never. Waits was as shocked as the rest of the community when he learned Kaczynski was a suspect, and even

5

defended his innocence until the overwhelming physical evidence mounted.

Kaczynski's arrest shook Waits to the core and initially made him fear that he might even be a suspect in the case.

As the investigation unfolded and Waits was cleared of any possible involvement, the FBI's evidence search extended far beyond Kaczynski's small Lincoln cabin. Agents played a cat-and-mouse game with Waits while searching the rugged mountain terrain near his home.

What were they looking for? Waits determined it was something critical, something that would help prove the government's case against Kaczynski. And Waits was certain the evidence was hidden in the thousands of timbered acres behind his house in McClellan Gulch.

FBI agents were reluctant to involve outsiders, so Waits decided to start his own search, and spent all his free time combing the backcountry.

He hiked many back-country game trails looking for evidence that included Kaczynski's secret hunting camps.

Summer wound down, and Waits still hadn't discovered the key evidence everyone was after.

By late November a major arctic cold front threatened to turn the rugged mountain terrain into a no-man's land. Waits decided to take one last trip into the backcountry. As the day wore on, it seemed to be another futile search. Trudging through the snow in the late afternoon, Waits decided to drop off the mountain and return home. Yet a strange premonition pushed him farther into the mountains as darkness settled.

Something forced him to climb one last steep slope. He looked through the stands of lodgepole pine in the dimming light and saw the ghost image of a small log cabin. It was a secret shack and hideout Ted had built years earlier.

The discovery opened many doors with the FBI, as Waits later became a confidant and was tagged as a trial witness.

Who would have thought Lincoln could be the lair of one of the most threatening domestic terrorists in our history? The mere threat of his bombs could paralyze the nation or close down airports. He deceived two of the country's most prestigious and powerful newspapers into publishing his 35,000-word manifesto. In return, he wrote, he would stop killing people. But he continued to build more sophisticated devices and plot further acts of revenge.

As millions of Americans and the entire human community hungered for more information about Kaczynski after his arrest, sketchy details portrayed him as a mathematical genius and former Berkeley math instructor who had left academia to become a mountain hermit.

Stories focused on his early years in the Heartland, academic successes at Harvard, Michigan, and Berkeley, his reclusive childhood and failed forays into the world of lasting relationships.

But then in 1971, when Kaczynski built his cabin on a heavily timbered 1.4 acres in Florence Gulch within a mile of Stemple Pass Road, he literally dropped off the face of the earth.

During the next twenty-five years, almost half of his life, he survived as a primitive hunter-gatherer, much like the early miners and settlers who moved into this untamed part of the West in the mid-19th century.

But this was not Henry David Thoreau, living the peaceful life at Walden Pond. This was Theodore John Kaczynski, a criminal willing to kill at the slightest provocation of the technological arm—or tentacle of an octopus, as he would describe it—of our society.

He lusted for revenge. He wanted to rub his hands in the blood of modern technocrats. Only the death of a scientist, businessman or a Communist would ease the pain of his hatred.

How do we know this?

Not because Ted's secret twenty-five years were scrutinized during a public trial. The details of his twisted logic and hatred would have been aired before a shocked world-wide audience had he faced twelve jurors in Sacramento Federal Court. His thoughts, plans of revenge, and descriptions of his life would have amazed the people he threatened.

The FBI and the prosecution team had a detailed description of Kaczynski's life of crime, because he was a prodigious writer. His small cabin, heated only by a wood stove and with none of the conveniences of our time, was an archive of his written word. Organized in volumes of scratchpads, pocket notebooks and three-ring binders were some 22,000 pages of his life's script.

Most of his work was handwritten in English, some in Spanish.

The most incriminating descriptions of his crimes were disguised in numerical code. But it was all there, in conversations with himself, the thoughts of a would-be mass murderer, spelled out in detail.

When the FBI returned to Lincoln during the summer of 1997 to study the evidence found in the secret cabin and to search other areas of McClellan Gulch, Waits guided them through the terrain he knew so well. During the search Waits became the first outsider to see and study many of Kaczynski's documents, which included hundreds of pages from the Unabomber's personal journals.

As he worked with the FBI, Waits compiled notes daily and committed as much of the material to memory as possible.

Kaczynski's journals also described buried caches of ammunition, bomb parts, and food on Waits' land.

Waits was sure Kaczynski also had a cache hidden in McClellan Gulch containing copies of journal notes and his bomb experiments.

After FBI agents returned to Sacramento to prepare for the trial, Waits continued his search for the hidden caches and other evidence. Through his searches, and several unnamed sources, he finally obtained the motherlode—literally hundreds of pages of Kaczynski's personal journals and notes.

All the information would have become public record if the Unabomber had been tried. Instead, Kaczynski and federal prosecutors worked out a plea agreement in which he admitted his guilt in exchange for sentences of life in prison.

Ted's plea bargain was a disservice to the American people and his victims, because no one other than a few professionals had a chance to study the inner face of this modern-day terrorist.

The plea saved the country the great expense of a long public trial, one that promised to be a circus, but it also meant Kaczynski's written admission in his personal journals to dozens of crimes was locked away in some evidence room. Much of his self-analysis won't be seen for years, probably until after his death.

Some short excerpts have found their way into the mainstream press.

But only bits and pieces until this point.

Waits was probably the only outsider who had seen the Kaczynski journals. Certainly, he was the only person outside the select group of lawyers, agents, and psychiatrists who had actual copies of documents.

Waits also had an unusual perspective shared by no one. He had known Kaczynski for years, given him rides, fixed his bicycle, and watched the mountain hermit make regular excursions into McClellan Gulch.

Combining the knowledge of his friend, his experiences with the FBI and the material from Kaczynski's journals, Waits was able to compile a story that contains the first significant understanding of Kaczynski's secret years in Lincoln and his mental process as explained in his own words.

In the pages that follow, we glimpse, through Ted's own description, his anguish during a first attempt to kill a scientist in 1971. He backed out at the last minute, not because his plan was flawed, but because he lacked the final resolve. You'll study how he consciously broke down any moral fiber left in his dark soul so by the mid-1970s, he was ready to strike with a deadly venom. You'll read how the noise of helicopters and jet planes drove him to "tears of impotent rage," enough so that he hiked high into the mountains to shoot at passing helicopters with a high-powered rifle. His plan to cripple a helicopter wasn't successful because he found them difficult to hit.

He carried his hatred of aircraft and those who flew them to a much more dangerous plateau in late 1979 when he mailed a package bomb rigged to a barometer so it would explode at a certain altitude. The early device wasn't potent enough to blow up the aircraft carrying the package in its cargo hold, but the device did start a fire, forcing an emergency landing at Dulles International Airport.

The journal quotes you'll read for the first time here are but a small percentage of Kaczynski's massive writings. But they're revealing, and important in the process of our understanding and healing.

You'll read his own words describing why he pursued a life of violence.

You'll also come to understand that Kaczynski's is a multi-layered personality. His love of the wilderness lands of Western Montana was sincere and deep rooted.

The following quote from one of Kaczynski's journals supports that theory:

Saturday, July 14, 1979 in McClellan Gulch

Today I had the most wonderful morning I've had for a long time. At this beautiful dark, densely wooded spot, the Wisp began calling me, so I followed it to an oxen meadow. I slowly climbed to the top of the mountain through this strip of magic meadow. I gathered some mint along the way and felt as if it would bring me luck to drink tea from mint gathered in this enchanted landscape. (I didn't believe it, of course; it was just a feeling.) At the top of the mountain I looked down on the ridges below and contemplated the sight for some time. Then I climbed down through the Douglas Fir parks, over to the meadow strip again, and sat for awhile looking at the blue lupine and yellow flowers of some plant of the composite family, both of which dotted the meadow. Then I climbed back down to camp, looking at the plants. Only 2 jets passed, and those when my walk was nearly over, so that I was able to forget civilization and the threat it poses to these wonderful solitudes. Thus I was able to drink in the things that I saw with full appreciation. This gulch is a glorious place. It has special magic. I never get tired of seeing these fine old parks of Douglas firs around here.

What made Kaczynski different from you and me? He looked and lived like many others in the mountains of the West. He loved to read and reflect. He bought groceries, nurtured vegetables in his gardens, cross-pollinated wild and garden variety plants. He wasted little of the animals he hunted. He even boiled the head of a coyote over a campfire, opened the skull, and then ate the brains like pudding with a spoon. He loved the wilderness and wanted to live off the land, undisturbed by modern society.

His adopted lifestyle was acceptable in the Lincoln area, and would have been tolerated in many remote areas of this country.

Then there also was his abrupt inner face of a terrorist who wanted to taste revenge over and over. What made him into a serial killer?

At this point, only his journal entries can help us understand why he was so ordained, or why he ordained himself so. He readily admits his desire to kill was fueled by hatred. He recognized it early in life, but didn't retaliate because of his middle class mores and fear of social punishment.

That changed. During the mid-1970s, he conditioned himself to ignore fear of punishment, without regard for his own safety, recognizing early on he probably would be caught. Through a selected number of his own journal descriptions the reader will see this logic develop and understand how his attempts became more brazen as he realized he could outsmart the FBI and even escape detection.

Finally, we must ask, is Ted Kaczynski evil or is he insane? That would have been a key question had there been a trial.

The journal entries found in this book were chosen to help advance an understanding of his mind so you can make your own decision about his sanity.

Only his own words, mixed with an understanding of how he lived during the lost twenty-five years, will suffice as we try to explore the mysteries of the Unabomber's mind.

Dave Shors

The Discovery

Frigid northeast winds swept the spirit of winter through the heavily timbered Western Montana valley in the first bitter storm of the season. The jet stream was shifting south on cue, tracking right over the small mountain community of Lincoln, invigorating and adding energy to cold arctic air as it moved south out of Canada like a slow-moving mass of molasses. As dawn turned the mountain sky dismal on November 22, 1996, twenty-eight inches of snow already blanketed the ground. The freshness and fierceness of a mountain winter were in the air.

Breathtaking, the tallness of this place. First, the winding climb along 60-degree slopes. Then the soaring conifers, eighty- and hundred-foot lodgepole pine and Douglas-fir stretching into the gray mountain sky. A stranger here would be chilled by the shade, made dizzy by the altitude. But those who live and work in the mountain community feel sheltered and protected.

I had criss-crossed these mountains since early June, plotting methodical grids, searching for something important, very important. The FBI Unabom Task Force knew key evidence lay hidden in the mountains surrounding Ted Kaczynski's home, but they had packed up and left about the first of September, frustrated and confused by the sheer size and complexity of the country. Initially after Kaczynski's arrest as the suspected Unabomber on April 3, agents concentrated their evidence search on his one-room cabin and 1.4 acres just off the west end of the old logging road that led up into Florence Gulch near the graveled Stemple Pass Road. But soon the probe widened to thousands of undulating acres lying east of the crescent-shaped Upper Blackfoot River Valley.

During those summer months, rumors had spread like a searing forest fire driven by hot, dry August mountain winds. Did the mountain hermit leave behind explosives hidden in forest caves and old deserted hard-rock mine tunnels? Had he built an elaborate bunker system where he tested and stored the homemade devices responsible for killing three and injuring twenty-three others between 1978 and 1995? Had he hidden pipe bombs in the pristine forest, deadly booby traps ready to maim or kill unsuspecting humans or animals? Many mysteries were yet to be unraveled in the mountains near Lincoln, Montana.

When Ted bought his 1.4 acres four miles southeast of town in 1971, he also bought access to a million acres of mountainous terrain. That's part of the Montana culture, an allure reflected in the local newspaper, the *Blackfoot Valley Dispatch*, where, in the real estate section, you can almost always find an ad offering "Timbered acres, small stream, bordered by Forest Service land." When you buy 1.4 acres bordered by public land near Lincoln, you also buy access to the public lands that stretch all the way to the Canadian border almost 200 miles to the north. The FBI agents understood the "timbered acres" and "small stream" parts of the Montana culture. It's not much different in suburban Chicago or San Francisco. But the "bordered by Forest Service land" had given them fits.

Kaczynski lived that part of the local culture like a religion. His small acreage and one-room, 12-by-10-foot primitive cabin, with a wood stove but no electricity, was on a jumping off spot to an isolated primeval world of rippling streams, westslope cutthroat trout, mule deer and regal elk. Parts of this world haven't seen a human soul since the last of the gold miners deserted their sluice boxes in the late 1920s. Many segments of fragile earth here have never been scuffed by a Vibram sole. These days, the only trails are forged by deer or elk moving from their ridgetop beds past towering outcroppings of granite folds and Precambrian sedimentary argillite, reddish in color, to open parks for their moonlight browsing and to small streams for a drink of the earth's purest water. For a hermit-like man looking for total isolation, this was the spot.

It was back in mid-June when I first realized the FBI investigation had broadened from the intense search of Ted's cabin, root house and garden area to the surrounding mountains. A small plane, flying low on numerous occasions, an aircraft that I didn't recognize as being one from Lincoln, tipped me off. The continuing fly-overs were puzzling. Who was in the plane, and what were they looking for? The pilot was flying extremely low, even though he must have been well versed about the dangers of mountain thermals and downdrafts from the 7,000-foot ridgetops that could pluck the wings right off his small plane or slam it into a densely forested mountainside in an instant.

Suspicion turned to irritation when they moved up my gulch. One afternoon the plane circled four or five times over an area where I had some heavy equipment parked. What was going on?

> SATURDAY, JUNE 15, 1996 [CHRIS WAITS JOURNAL]
> I talk to Butch [Gehring, who lives and operates a sawmill near Ted's cabin] about planes flying low up my gulch. I wonder what they're doing. I ask Butch if it's him, he says no. He says that the agents are searching for something and that he thinks that there are firearms involved. He doesn't know. Mentions cliffs, water dries up in the fall, rockslide, diagonal rock, herbs in vegetation. I say I bet whatever it is, it's up here.

I talked to Butch and after he explained who it was and what they were doing, I was relieved. I had even started to wonder if I was being investigated as an accomplice.

The aircraft moved once again to another area, north and east of my gulch, and then the flying stopped altogether. Had they found what they were looking for? Most likely not. The terrain was far too rugged to yield secrets to agents in a plane that far overhead.

My theory that the search by air had been unsuccessful was confirmed during the next few days as I saw FBI vehicles parked in different areas along the Stemple Road and the surrounding gulches while agents searched on foot. I even saw a small boat sticking out of the back of one of their pickups—even though there are few waters for boating in the area.

> MONDAY, JUNE 17, 1996
> FBI is out. I see them out looking for some hidden

kind of cache, stash or something. I talk to [FBI Special Agent] Dave Weber and [U.S. Forest Service Officer] Jerry Burns. I see them around all over Stemple. I tell Dave how much Ted accessed the gulch and all the time he spent there. No reaction to reveal info. Jerry, Dave and a woman visit my house. Dave seems interested in returning. I wonder. I offer to help. They ask to go up the gulch. I say I would take them.

One afternoon while I was out working in the yard, Jerry Burns and Dave Weber drove up in Burns' white Ford Forest Service pickup. When they got out I noticed a woman I didn't recognize was with them; she stayed in the truck (I found out later she was Weber's wife, Sue).

Eager to find out what all the searching was about, I approached them, ready to offer my help. Dave asked me if they could go up the gulch. When I asked why, he said he wanted to talk to the person who owned the machinery. I replied, "You are talking to him." Jerry knows I own the whole gulch and everything in it. I then said they were welcome to go up and that I would take them. They seemed less interested after I said I'd go along.

Jerry asked several pointed questions about one drainage in particular. I said there wasn't any machinery there.

I had gotten to know Weber that year, and Burns and I go back many years. We had even worked together at the Forest Service in the mid-'70s. So I probed deeper, trying to dislodge a few more details about the object of the intense search. I dropped a few clues, but got little response. Our discussion seemed vague; nothing was confirmed.

I understood the integrity of the case couldn't be compromised, but I told Dave if we could trust each other I was sure I could help. I went on to say Ted spent a great deal of time in this gulch. It's all private but he had permission to be here. He used to cross Stemple Road, drop over a small ridge just below the house and then head up the gulch.

Dave appeared interested. He was polite and said he would return at a later date. I didn't know what to think. Dave thanked me for taking the time to talk to them, then they departed.

Now even more keenly curious about their interest in the gulch and the real object of their search, I was determined not to waste any more time, and planned to go out the following day and begin my own search. Maybe after I found something the agents would take me more seriously.

TUESDAY, JUNE 18, 1996
I am suspicious and go up the gulch alone and start looking for I don't even know what. Go up the main gulch. Meet Ted's lawyers at the center [Lincoln Center for the Performing Arts, in Lincoln] for an interview in afternoon. They say Ted would like me to visit him.

As June started to turn to July, I spent every spare moment in the woods. The first days were discouraging. Then I started to pick up subtle but definite signs of Ted's habits. Alongside a steep game trail I sighted chest-high blazes carefully cut with his hatchet into two lodgepole pines. From the appearance of the scarred cambium and the bark curled back into the cuts, the blazes looked about twenty years old.

Several days later, on June 25, I walked through a beautiful and secluded spot. A small spring—with water so clear each gray and reddish stone that made this natural mosaic was visible—flowed under my feet. Moss clung to every inch of the forest floor, light green and puffy proud about its existence. It was like an unspoiled section of coastal rain forest. The roots of Englemann spruce and Douglas-fir searched, exposed like heavy, muscular spider legs, for a firm hold in the boggy bottom; chest-high ostrich plume ferns carpeted the forest floor.

Just above the mossy spring I found a hidden, but well-used, campsite and a hollowed-out log Ted had used as a bed. The log cavity was a perfect fit for his lean 5'9", 140-pound frame. He didn't pack an ounce of fat; any city softness was worn away years ago on these mountain trails. Buried behind the log were a small plastic tarp, used as a cover when the thin mountain air chilled toward evening, and an aluminum cooking pot. A large, hard, red Douglas-fir stump just six paces from a spot where Ted would build his fire had been a great source of starter and kindling; hatchet marks showed where he had split hundreds of splinters from the stump. Dry and saturated with pitch, they would easily ignite with a match. There wasn't an obvious firepit. Ted had always been careful to cover any signs of his presence, especially in firemaking. To an untrained eye the many bleached-out deer bones scattered about would look like the remains of animal kills. But on close inspection the knife and hatchet marks of a hungry meat hunter were evident. I even found part of a broken arrow lying in the brush just down from this spot. The tip was broken off.

Below this campsite, near a game trail, I found a stash of firewood chopped into various lengths, piled together and covered with a large piece of fir bark; a nice supply of dry firewood for someone caught out in a storm. A red pine squirrel also had chosen this spot to hide his winter supply of pine cones. In preparing his larder, the squirrel had moved Ted's fir bark cover and exposed hatcheted ends of the limbs and poles that caught my eye as I walked along the trail. Ted had learned his back-country lessons well, and he obviously could live for extended periods in the woods.

This must have been a hunting camp; a most perfect and private place, the kind of place Ted loved.

Ted spent plenty of time in my gulch. I often saw him, even when he didn't see me, walking along a heavily wooded trail above the old mining tailings on the lower mile of my land. I hadn't cared, he'd been my friend and neighbor for twenty-five years. He had permission to be there, but he was the only one who had that permission.

SATURDAY, JULY 6, 1996
Went back up gulch to the end where it forks. I take Butch with me. I show him firewood cache and campsite. We hike up to some cliffs and caves. We find where some caves have been cleaned out and enlarged. Nothing major found. We talk about case all day.

In mid-July, I found two caves Ted had used, slender natural breaks in argillite outcroppings that opened into comfortable caverns big enough for a rough bed of pine boughs. Toward the back of one cave I found candles, canned food and empty cans with jagged, sharp, open lids. Whenever Ted ate fruit or vegetables from a can, he opened the top with a hunting knife he always carried, leaving a dangerous-looking lid, still hinged to the can. When finished, he would toss the can into his campfire, which often was started with the torn-off label. He would burn the cans until they were quite charred; a charred can will rust and decompose rapidly, especially when buried. Then he'd go to great extremes to bury the cans in the firepit and cover everything with soil and pine needles. Whenever I found one of these old firepits, I'd dig into it and find ragged, sharp topped, burned cans. They were one of his signatures, as personal as his fingerprint. I unearthed these cans wherever Ted stayed on my place, even under loose floorboards of an old miner's cabin I own about a mile above home. I searched the cabin because I had seen Ted there often and knew he had camped there overnight.

Even with these finds, there were many, many days of fruitless searching. I would sight an occasional blazed tree, but the haphazard trail markers were a mystery. None of the clues seemed to interlock, none seemed to develop into a pattern.

SATURDAY, JULY 20, 1996 [WAITS JOURNAL]
Dave Weber stops by to visit with a couple of agents. I show him some wild vegetables. Dave won't tell me even what they are searching for. I tell Dave that I have been doing my own search all summer and I wish I knew what I was looking for. I say if we have trust I can help. Dave asks for my notes. I refuse. I show him wild carrots. No response. Dave says he got the word. He can't talk about the case.

SATURDAY, AUG. 17, 1996
Continue search. I wish I knew what I was looking for. It must be really something good because the agents are still out searching. Haven't had any communication with agents for almost a month.

SUNDAY, AUG. 18, 1996
Whatever the agents are looking for I still think that

it's up here in the gulch. Continue on the east side of the main gulch. This is discouraging, but I know how much Ted was in this gulch. It has to be here. I won't give up no matter what.

In late August, I explored some of the rock outcroppings along the ridge. On August 31, I found two blazed trees one third of the way to the top. What did they mean? Maybe they marked a drop-off point or a place to turn off. In my journal I noted: "If the clues diagonal rock, rock cliff or rock slide mean anything, they all fit. Maybe I'm getting closer."

If I was getting closer, so was winter. In my journals, I noted several futile searches of caves and crevices during September.

SATURDAY, SEPT. 28, 1996 [WAITS JOUNRAL]
Take the ridge trail to the top and come out. Find some newer blazed trees about 15 years old. They have to be Ted's—no one has been up here for years. I remember following Ted's tracks this way.

On Tuesday, October 1, I was running a dragline three quarters of a mile above home. When I shut down about 5:00 P.M. there was a loud blast in the direction of the ridge that echoed down through the gulch. The explosion sent my mind racing in speculation and changed the tenor of any exploration. No one was in the gulch. I knew that. The only entrance into the five drainages is a narrow throat guarded by our home, and the only access is a rutted, ten-foot-wide mountain road some eighty feet east of the house. Anyone ignoring the no trespassing signs would have been seen. Or, my wife Betty's dogs would have sounded a hard-to-ignore alarm.

What if a deer, elk or small animal had triggered a booby trap? What if Ted had a secret cache or a cave, with a bomb set on a time-delay switch to implode the entrance after, say, six months of his absence? I knew booby traps and bombs were probably hidden in the woods. They could be anywhere. I had been searching with great caution. Now the stakes were higher, and I would be even more careful.

Oct. 5, 1996
Continue search on ridge. I have to find something.
Tell Butch about blast I heard. He thought maybe could
be seen from the air. I said I'm sure not. Mountains are too
steep and heavy tree cover.

The blast, and what caused it, ate away at me. But it also helped
me focus on the ridge. Even if the explosives covered the entrance
to a cache or a cave, there must be something visible—disturbed earth
or freshly broken stones or tree branches. I was determined to chart
my grid search of the ridge as long as the weather held, which would-
n't be long. Autumn and winter were in a teetering balance. Mornings
found hoar frost on the forest grass and leaves. Darkness and evening
came too quickly. Days and nights were almost of equal length.

In mid-November, that first winter storm hit like a blast out of
the north. Lincoln and its surrounding mountains were right on the
edge of slow-moving molasses, cold air. Higher in the middle than
along the edges, the bitter cold dome was centered over west central
Canada, but its nose poked into northwestern Montana where it was
gradually building up over the mountains. Warm, moist air was also
moving in from the Pacific, rising aloft above the cold mass and taking a ride to dizzying heights over the mountains where all the moisture was being milked away, falling back to earth as snow. Mountains
are especially good at producing moisture because of the way they lift
warm air. They certainly were showing their character on November
17. At the same time, the jet stream was slicing in from northwest
Washington, down over Missoula in western Montana, and then east-
erly toward Great Falls, right along the frontal boundary, where it was
energizing the storm. By the 19th, as the cold air stalled, much of western Montana was in its grip, almost paralyzed. Thousands were without power as high winds drove heavy snow and freezing rain, making
life miserable.

Around noon on November 22 near our home along the Stemple
Pass Road, there was a slight break in the storm. As I stared out the
back window of our house, I weighed whether or not to go out searching again. I didn't have any piano students scheduled for the afternoon, so I thought I might as well give it a try. What would it hurt?

I laced my high-top Wolverines, placed matches, a small flashlight, note pad and pencil in my fanny pack, grabbed my coat and headed out the door, realizing that darkness would cloak the mountain valleys by 5:30 P.M. here close to 46° north latitude. Wasting no more time I began my trip up the mountain. The outside thermometer registered just 18° Fahrenheit, but it was finally calm after five days of snow.

I hadn't been on the mountain an hour when slight movement ahead caught my attention. I paused, cautiously moved around a large Douglas-fir, and spotted a four-point whitetail forty feet away browsing on a clump of short mountain maple bushes. He lifted his head, ears alert and nose twitching, trying to pick up my scent, and gazed toward me. We watched each other nearly thirty minutes, both frozen in our thoughts. Finally, it was time to get back to my journey, and I moved off in earnest. The buck sprang off to the north, flashing its tail through the trees.

The day, which had started cold and overcast, stayed surprisingly calm. Barely a breeze blew through the mature lodgepole pine forest, with its scattering of fir, spruce, subalpine fir and junipers. The white snow cover and lack of bushy limbs close to the ground opened up the forest; I could see fifty yards or more in some spots. Huckleberry, wild rose, Oregon grape, red twinberry, and other low shrubs were put away for the winter, all covered by snow. Taller, scattered mountain maple, juniper shrub, alder, and serviceberry bushes stood above snow level, but their branches were arched heavily under the weight of the snow.

The afternoon wore on and the sky began to blacken as I neared a summit. A Clark's nutcracker and a Steller's jay chattered from nearby trees, as if to mock me. The wind started to gust and the temperature was dropping. I reached a small meadow just 200 yards below the ridgetop. I've always loved this spot, encircled by huge old gnarled Douglas-fir. Beargrass grows knee-high in large clumps. Deer and elk browse on the beargrass flowers when they bloom in the summer. But the animals won't touch the long, hollow straw-like stalks; that's been the bane of many a hunter on a sneak, to have the game startled by a loud snapping sound of the brittle stalks underfoot.

The weather turned even worse and I decided to move around

the mountain to the south instead of topping out and over. More sheltered, this route was protected from the strong wind and blowing snow on the ridgetop. Continuing south, I contoured the mountain at the top of a deep ravine that had to be crossed. Lodgepole grew thick on either side of the ravine, making it almost impossible to sneak through. The quarter-of-a-mile-wide thicket is the byproduct of a forest fire that swept through decades ago, pushed by strong, hot summer winds. Flames destroyed the old-growth trees, but at the same time the intense heat broke open the dormant lodgepole seeds, allowing them to grow as thick as hair on a dog's back. It's astounding how quickly these trees come back. They can regenerate in huge numbers, and, with no thinning, can completely cover large areas, growing only inches apart. These forests never mature; some eighty- to ninety-year-old trees are barely two inches in diameter.

The going was really tough. Fallen poles lay scattered every which way under the snow on the 70-degree slope, acting like deadly ski runners underfoot. The only saving grace of falling in such a thicket is you don't slide far before a tree catches you.

Tiring, but finally on the other side, I looked down toward a basin with a small creek running through the bottom some 1,500 feet below. A ridge ran to the southwest and I decided to follow it down, meandering back and forth in a continuing search, looking for tree blazes, markers, anything that would help direct my efforts.

Snow and cold winds were swirling through the trees like the honor guard of another major winter storm. This would be the last search of the year.

Exhausted, I wanted at least to explore a rock outcropping right below me. It was worth a final try. Formed by red argillite, a clay-based shale rock, the cliffs were cut and split by dozens of natural cracks and caves, much like those I had explored during the summer.

Working my way down the slope, I cut fresh elk tracks in the snow, probably a small herd of eight or ten. Minutes later, in the middle of a sheltered thicket, three mature bull elk jumped up from beds where they had planned to spend the night. In the dimming light I couldn't see how many points each had, but I saw a lot of ivory tips on their antlers as they crashed through the thicket. Their yellow rumps disappeared in a flash. I took a deep breath and paused. The overwhelming silence returned. I had dropped only about a third of the way down the ridge, and it was apparent this natural refrigerator was closing its door on another day. It was time to head home, so I picked up my pace down the mountainside.

Then a strange and spontaneous urge pulled at me to go around the ridge and look out. It didn't make any sense. It was getting too dark to see and what could I possibly gain by going the wrong way? Standing there, almost as an impartial referee, I weighed the arguments for returning home or to follow the force of some unseen hand to circle the ridge. Turning toward the ridge, I decided not to wait through a winter of wondering about what might be there.

As I sidehilled along the contour, my thoughts once again flashed back to all the incredible events since Ted's arrest. Who would have imagined, the Unabomber in my back yard all these years? I began to think about all the bizarre incidents reported in the Lincoln area during the last twenty-five years, incidents unsolved, with no conclusions or answers. I couldn't help but feel that when it was all over, the investigation, the trial, there would be answers.

The cold and darkness brought me back to reality. All at once I stopped as the ridge dropped off sharply; I could hardly make out the terrain. As strangely as I had been compelled to follow this path, I was now being pulled to walk back up the mountain.

I took a few steps up the steep incline, and was just able to see a small natural shelf cut into the 60 degree hillside. I decided to walk to the shelf and then turn back. My wife would begin to worry.

I took a few more steps. Something wasn't right. Even in the darkness I was seeing what appeared to be a right-angle corner that just didn't fit in this world of vertical trees. I ran upward, tripping in the snow. There was no doubt, there it was, like a pale gray ghost waiting for me in the darkness, Ted's secret hideout, a small log cabin.

It didn't seem possible. After all these days and months, the object of all my searches, and the FBI's as well, was inches away.

It took just seconds to catch my breath as I scanned the cabin. It was a complete one-room structure with a slanted roof, built from small logs. Cautiously peering through the open entrance I could see a home-made wood stove, built from a five gallon oil can. A bed fashioned from a board and covered with small poles for a mattress stretched the entire eight feet across the back. A pair of light blue denim pants hung, half through the roof corner, probably pulled there by a squirrel or rodent looking for warm nest-building material. Even though snow had blown through the doorway and covered the floor, I could still make out cooking utensils and a coffee cup inside near the stove. Coils of rope hung from the walls.

I didn't dare step inside. It felt like Ted might be there, even if it wasn't possible. Or there might be a booby trap, which was very possible. Plus, I didn't want to disturb any evidence.

With head spinning and thoughts racing I turned and headed home, knowing there would be one more trip very soon, no matter how cold and snowy, so I could photograph the secret cabin and visible items inside.

Would this discovery change the course of the investigation, and even the trial? Time would tell.

The path home was one quickly followed. I remember stumbling through deep snow, following ridges until I hit the old mining road at the bottom of the gulch. I didn't notice the cold, or mind the wet pant legs starched stiff with ice. My thoughts were in another dimension. I knew I couldn't fully explore the cabin until spring, maybe late March or early April, when the snows would melt off. How could I possibly wait? It would be a long winter, wondering what was inside.

Nearing home, I could see lights through the frost-covered windows, and smoke billowing from the stovepipe. What would my wife say? After all, she had told me more than once to give up the search until spring. Don't get me wrong, she had always encouraged me. She knew as well as I that Ted had spent long periods of time up the gulch. She had seen him or crossed his tracks on many occasions.

But how would I tell her? I'd take it slow. I reached the porch, took off my wet coat and opened the door to the smell of stew being kept warm on the stove.

"You're sure late," she said.

"Bingo!" I said. "I found it."

She paused, looked puzzled, stopped, and then everything clicked.

"Really? You're kidding?"

We stared at each other in disbelief.

"Ted built a secret cabin, you should see it. There's stuff inside, pants hanging out of the corner, a stove, things hanging on the wall, cooking pans on the floor..."

She interrupted me, telling me to slow down.

"Get your wet clothes off and tell me all about it," she said firmly, but she obviously was just as excited as I.

"We've got to go back and take some pictures," I said, knowing that it was starting to snow hard again, and I'd probably have to return alone.

"Where exactly is it?" she asked. "Why haven't we found it before now?"

I told her the cabin was built in a very carefully chosen, and secluded, shelf of land. I was sure Ted chose the spot based on the many conversations I had with him over the years, talks about the places I visit the most, hunting haunts, historical locations, and favorite hiking places.

Ted would always listen intently about these places without really letting me know which were of interest to him. It was a perfect situation. Ted knew he had permission to be in the gulch, he knew about all my favorite places, and he knew the areas I seldom or never visited. He came and went as he pleased. So he used all this information to help him pick a spot where he'd never be bothered.

As I described the exact location, my wife said: "I've never been up that high in that area of the gulch."

I also reminded her that this was one of the largest, roadless, trailless areas left around. Even the Lincoln backcountry, the Bob Marshall and the Scapegoat wilderness areas have much more traffic—hikers, backpackers, and hunters—than our gulch and surrounding area.

"Ted's secret cabin site," I said to her, "has none of the qualifications of a campsite, but all of the qualifications of a hideout."

I've repeated that observation to FBI agents, and others.

Located on a very steep mountainside away from water, in the thick lodgepole and fir forest, on a shelf, it's the kind of place you wouldn't ever hike to, but what a place to go hide and live undetected!

Ted knew if anyone might accidentally find him up there, it would be me. And what would I say to him? Nothing. He knew he was allowed.

My wife and I finally sat down and finished supper, and then she went to bed. It was getting late, but I decided to call Butch and tell him about the discovery also, because he still had open lines of communication with the FBI. He was excited and we talked about the next move.

"Butch," I said, "tell no one until I figure out what to do."

He agreed.

The house was uncommonly quiet as I sat by the fire, thinking, and I made my daily journal entry.

> FRIDAY, NOV. 22 [WAITS JOURNAL]
> Bingo! I found it! Finally while hunting in new area on my last search of the year. Ted's secret cabin! I can't believe it. Too dark to see much inside. Now I finally know what the FBI has been looking for. I call Butch and tell him, after calling Bobby D. I wonder how to go about telling the FBI. Butch says make the FBI earn it and don't give it to them too easy. He won't either. They are the ones who broke communication with me. I agree. Still snowing and cold.

I also called Bobby Didriksen, one of my closest and most trusted friends in Lincoln. He had been my confidant from the beginning, and the only one I shared information with other than Betty and those directly involved with the case. He was astonished.

I decided to think twice and act once. I had no concept how this single discovery might change not only our lives but also the potential course and outcome of the entire prosecution.

I finally dozed off in my chair, exhausted, at about 2:30 A.M.

I was awakened by my wife, calling from upstairs.

"Honey, come to bed. Tomorrow is another day."

I dragged myself up the stairs and fell into bed. Moving in and out of a restless sleep, I kept repeating to myself, "Is this a dream? How can it be real? What do I do next? Why me? Why me at this point of time, here in this place?"

> SATURDAY, NOV. 23
> I want to get pictures of Ted's secret cabin so bad, but

the weather is terrible and still snowing and cold. I will have to wait. Haven't heard from the FBI in months.

SUNDAY, NOV. 24

Still can't go back. When this storm gets over I will go back up, no matter how deep the snow is. I hope that Dave Weber calls. Got to get pictures.

Welcome
to Florence Gulch

When Ted Kaczynski had moved to Lincoln and purchased his small plot of land on June 19, 1971, with his younger brother, David, as a co-owner, the area surrounding his 1.4 acres was virtually uninhabited. Only two seasonal cabins, seldom used, and the remnants of one old miner's cabin upstream were located near small and narrow, secluded Florence Gulch, where he built his little one-room home cabin.

Ted's place, located on the very fringe of private land bordering Forest Service property, was the perfect spot for a man who wanted to live in solitary harmony with nature. With the hustle of the twentieth century buffered and filtered by thousands of acres of rugged mountainous terrain, Ted, as a vigorous young man in his late twenties, was determined to carve out a nineteenth century lifestyle.

A crystal clear spring, Canyon Creek, gurgled through the undergrowth less than 100 feet from the small, flat spot where he built his roughly framed cabin. That first summer, while leveling out an area and laying timbers for the wood floor, he broke ground on the west side for a garden. It was one of the few spots with an opening in the canopy of lodgepole pines, Douglas-fir, quaking aspens, and dense undergrowth where sunlight could penetrate.

It was perfect: With everything nature and the land provided, and more, there was total privacy. Little did Ted know just how drastically all that would change in the years ahead.

I first met Ted shortly after he moved to Lincoln, within the first year or two. At that time, besides me, only Ted, Kenny Lee, an older man who lived below Ted, and the Halls, an older couple who lived across from me, resided in this area along or near the Stemple Road.

My lifestyle at that time wasn't much different from Ted's, and in some ways, it was even more primitive. I lived in a tent and then a camper during those early years, until I moved a mobile home onto my land at the mouth of McClellan Gulch.

Our first encounter was brief and uneventful. I was driving my blue and white Chevy 4X4 pickup into town when I spotted Ted walking along Stemple Road. Dressed in dark blue denim pants, a green canvas army jacket and hiking boots, he was headed toward Lincoln, a little more than three miles to the north. He carried a small pack over his shoulders, but he didn't appear to be a vagrant. His dark brown hair was short, cut up over his ears. He wore no beard. Because he was walking and was unfamiliar to me, I thought he might need help. I stopped and offered him a ride. He cordially declined, so I went on my way.

Not long after that I saw him walking again, not far from the spot where I saw him the first time. I pulled over again and offered him a ride.

"No, thank you," he replied.

"Okay," I responded, and then went on to say, "I'm Chris. I live just up the road in McClellan Gulch."

He nodded, but turned from the truck and started to walk again, so I pulled away, heading down the washboard gravel road to Lincoln.

I had heard someone had moved into Florence Gulch and had built a cabin. After several other chance encounters, I assumed he was the one.

Each time I saw Ted along the road, I'd stop and offer him a ride. He always declined, but each time I'd tell him a little more about myself. I also was asking around and found out from a friend, Butch Gehring, that the Kaczynski brothers had purchased their land from Butch's father, Cliff. Butch didn't live near Ted at the time, so he didn't know much else about him.

Then one afternoon in mid-summer of 1972, ever persistent, I stopped one more time to offer him a ride.

Much to my surprise, he accepted.

Even though I was always the dominant talker, I learned my first details about Ted during that ten-minute ride to Lincoln. His voice was high pitched, slightly nasal, almost whiny. It didn't take me long to get used to it, though, and I didn't think anything more about it. But it was the kind of voice I could still pick out in a crowd of thousands.

He talked about the cabin he had built by himself, his garden, and some of the places where he liked to hike. I was amazed by the distance he covered on foot, even though he looked strong, lean and sinewy. He said he had even explored Copper Creek Basin, more than twenty miles away. He obviously was in excellent shape.

When Ted first moved to Lincoln he drove a Chevelle, which he sold or traded later for an early 1950s dark blue Chevy pickup. After that broke down, he didn't drive it anymore. I offered to fix it for free, but he said he liked to walk and would rather travel on foot. He later sold it for a pittance, $25, to a man who had moved into the area. Within a few years of arriving in the area, Ted had rid himself of motorized transportation.

Ted continued to walk everywhere he went until he got his first bicycle in the mid-'70s. Even after he started to travel on the bike, he still spent most of his time hiking. The scope of the areas he covered on foot was astounding. He thoroughly explored entire sections north and south of Stemple Road to the top of the 6,376-foot pass and far beyond, east and west, rugged and heavily timbered areas fifteen to twenty miles from his cabin.

He was methodical and calculating, plotting every trail he explored on topographical maps that were found after his arrest in his cabin hidden among thousands of pages of documents. As we got to know each other better, we often shared information about the areas around Lincoln. Whenever I talked to Ted about trails and special places I enjoyed that were unfamiliar to him, he would listen intently. He wouldn't usually tell me if he had been to a certain spot I described, but I knew if he had or not by his almost imperceptible signs of interest, usually a slight nodding of his head or his attentiveness.

Ted's most distinguishing trait was his demeanor. He was the most solemn and serious person I had ever met. Like the rest of the world I now study the famous "hooded sweatshirt" sketch and the photographs from his university days. Others may look for the madness or the brilliance. I look for the Ted I knew. I search for the somber lean face I grew accustomed to seeing on the passenger side of my truck, the high cheekbones and thin neck that held his head high, with chin jutting forward. His seriousness was much less noticeable in the early years; as time passed it became far stronger. He was always friendly and spoke cordially to me, but he was always deep in thought.

His reasons for walking everywhere or riding a bicycle instead of driving a vehicle became evident after he told me one day he could live on less than $200 a year after paying property taxes. I was amazed. Anybody who was able to exist, literally, on less than $20 a month in this era was to be commended. How could he do it? I admired him. It was then I realized that license plates, insurance and upkeep, even on an old pickup, would greatly exceed his annual budget, not even considering fuel and oil expense. Not only did he believe in his way of life, he lived it.

I had learned a lot about Lincoln and the surrounding country as a boy growing up in Helena, Montana's capital city some fifty miles up and over the Continental Divide to the southeast. My best friend's family owned a cabin in Lincoln, and we spent many summertime weeks and months together there fishing, hunting, and exploring. We even fished the ponds located on the north end of the property I now own. How could I have known as a boy I would end up living on the very property we had explored? All that time spent fishing and hiking as a child gave me a desire to live in the Lincoln area. After buying the lower end of the gulch before Ted arrived in Lincoln, I too spent countless hours hiking and exploring, especially in the Stemple Pass area southeast of town.

All the experiences in the woods, plus time spent working for the Forest Service in the mid-'70s as a slash crew foreman, gave me a great foundation of knowledge about the mountains around Lincoln, information I was happy to share with Ted.

I also had collected a large library on the history of the area and the early pioneers and miners, their ways of life and how they survived; these topics always captivated Ted. He'd listen intently, especially when I'd describe wild edible and medicinal plants and the places where they grew nearby.

We often talked about old mines in the Stemple area. I also shared a lot of information about "my" gulch, McClellan, spots and cabins scattered from the top of McClellan Gulch to its mouth near Stemple Road, an area nearly four miles long.

I told Ted more than once how much I loved my gulch and how it was blocked off to preserve it, to keep it pristine, private and unspoiled. And most of all, I made it clear I would never sell it. The gulch is its own wilderness area that spreads out from its mouth on Stemple Road like an outstretched hand into five drainages, each with a small stream that quenches its initial thirst in the shadows of the Continental Divide.

During the first few years, our conversations centered mainly on history, survival techniques, food gathering, hunting spots and food preservation. While Ted felt comfortable and would talk freely about the land and how to live off it, other topics were clearly off limits.

He was vague about his personal life, his past, places he'd lived, and his family. Ted always became tense when asked anything personal; his deep-set eyes, dark brown and penetrating, shut out such conversations immediately. The reaction was so obvious, I was careful not to probe too deeply, respecting his space. Ted never once, in twenty-five years, mentioned anything about his mother, which was unusual. Guys always end up talking about their moms. It's a natural thing. I never pried into his family life or questioned him about his mother. I thought perhaps she had died, maybe even in childbirth, and it was a painful event in his life.

I knew by his talk and mannerisms he had a college education, but he never shared any details, and he never mentioned he had been a math professor. His past and his family always seemed unimportant to him.

It's amazing what you can learn from people though, even if they don't want you to know. For instance, Ted often came into my Lincoln shop and I'd work on his bicycle. His chain was always squeaking, and after oiling it for him, I'd instruct him to keep it oiled because all the dust on the gravel roads would wear it out.

"I don't have any oil," he'd reply.

It was apparent from that comment he had no machines; no lawn mower, gas water pump, generator, etc. Every machine takes oil.

One time during the mid-'70s, an elderly couple who owned a summer cabin several hundred yards southwest of Ted's cabin brought their orange International 4X4 pickup into my garage in Lincoln for work. I repaired the carburetor and then delivered the truck to their cabin on a test drive. The day was beautiful, it was midsummer, so I decided to hike the short distance to Ted's and visit him. That first time I approached his cabin shadowed by the forest canopy, a compelling, uncomfortable, uneasy feeling came over me, one I had every other time I went there. It was like someone was watching, or that I was in a foreboding and secret place where I shouldn't be. Ted wasn't home and his door was padlocked, so I promptly left.

TUESDAY, MARCH 20, 1979 [CHRIS WAITS JOURNAL]
    Long, cold winter, lots of snow. I wonder what kind of runoff we'll have. Maybe flood this year. Haven't seen anyone on Stemple for months except for Roy. Come to think of it, haven't seen Ted for the longest time—maybe since last summer. Maybe he moved. Hope he's O.K....

Once during the late '70s I didn't see Ted for well over a year. I didn't know what to think. Had he moved away? Maybe he was hurt. Who would know? He could be lying up there somewhere in the mountains. By this time Butch had built a log home just northwest of Ted's cabin and while I was there looking at a spring, I thought I better check on Ted. I didn't make it over that day, but planned to go as soon as I could. Then, just two or three days later, I saw Ted out walking. I stopped and visited with him and said: "You've been gone a long time. I haven't seen you around."

He agreed, but that was the end of the conversation.

When Ted stopped at my Lincoln shop just to visit I felt almost honored, because I never saw him go anywhere except to conduct business, such as buying groceries.

But for him to stop, conditions had to be just right. The big garage doors at the front of my white, concrete block building along the Stemple Pass Road 100 feet south of Lincoln's main street had to be opened wide, and I had to be alone. It became quickly obvious our visits had to be one-on-one. If someone stopped while Ted was there, he'd be gone like a puff of smoke, disappearing even in the middle of a sentence. At first it seemed like odd behavior, until I gradually concluded that he was extremely shy and guarded around other people.

Ted would enter the garage, but never stray too far inside, usually staying close to the big, open doors, while I'd weld or repair equipment.

I remember one discussion we had about gardening when Ted started to talk about his vegetables. He liked to grow carrots, onions, parsnips, other root crops, and potatoes.

Knowing he had no power, plumbing or pump, and that his garden was uphill from his spring-fed stream, I asked him, "Ted, how do you water your potatoes?"

"I carry water up to my garden in buckets," was his reply.

"Doesn't that take a long time, and isn't it a lot of work?" I asked.

"I have plenty of time, and the work doesn't bother me," he said. By then he had grown a beard, which was full but didn't extend much above his mouth line or too far down his neck.

Ted raised an amazing garden, especially considering the climate the Lincoln area offers at almost 5,000 feet above sea level. Heavily timbered mountain gulches are not noted as garden spots. But Florence Gulch had a reputation among the old-timers as a place where they could grow things that wouldn't make it anywhere else in the Lincoln Valley. During the 1950s a man named Jack Parks lived in a cabin built in the late 1930s just above Ted's place. Parks was able to grow huge pumpkins in his garden. My wife, Betty, still remembers seeing them as a young girl when her family went to visit Mr. Parks.

There seems to be a natural inversion created in Florence Gulch, one of those mountain idiosyncrasies no one can really explain. My theory is the warm air that rises from the valley floor becomes trapped in the gulch by cool air above, at the foot of Baldy Mountain. The result is far fewer killer frosts than elsewhere and thus, a longer growing season.

But growing anything, anywhere around Lincoln, even in Florence Gulch, is still a challenge. The high mountain valleys can be nipped by frost any month of the year, plus there are plenty of animals to contend with. Ted had a tough time keeping rodents, rabbits, and other small animals away from his crops. Deer were a problem, too, but he had much better success in fencing them out. It required nearly a constant vigil to keep the small animals at bay. At night he often sat atop a pyramid-shaped stile that crossed his eight-foot-high fence, spotlighting and shooting small garden invaders with his .22 at his lower garden.

After Ted expanded his garden and started a second plot to the southwest of his cabin, he had enough extra vegetables to start drying them to keep and eat during the long Montana winter. Then he needed a place to store his dried food where it would keep, and wouldn't be eaten by animals.

One afternoon as I was driving him home from Lincoln, our conversation shifted to root cellars and how to construct them, a page out of the basic survival notes of the old-time Lincoln homesteaders. We discussed several designs, but the one I recommended was similar to a mine adit: an underground horizontal tunnel leading into a hillside, the tunnel reinforced with timbers, and with a wooden entrance and door. Such a tunnel would be labor intensive, but inexpensive to build, much easier and cheaper than building with rocks or concrete blocks. I suggested that with a proper door, and if the tunnel reached far enough into the hill, not only would food keep without freezing, but it would also be a good place to keep warm even during the most bitter cold weather. Even at -50° F., the temperature inside such a cellar wouldn't drop below +40°.

Ted didn't really give me much feedback about my suggestions, so I didn't know which method he would choose, or if he would even build a root cellar. But I did try to give him as much advice as possible, because I knew his construction techniques were crude at best.

When I finally saw the entrance to his root cellar, I was hiking on a nearby hill just to the southwest of Ted's cabin surveying some timber I had heard might be logged. After walking through the stand of trees, noting which might be worth harvesting, I dropped down to Ted's.

I couldn't believe my eyes. His new root cellar entrance was built from every type of scrap lumber imaginable. No care was taken to saw angles on any of the boards and slabs of wood, and the many holes and spaces between the boards were filled in and covered with tinfoil, plastic scraps, sections of corrugated roofing, and pieces of aluminum, anything he could find.

I had never seen construction like that in my life, but I didn't say anything about it to Ted, not wanting to hurt his feelings.

After looking at the root cellar entrance in the hillside, I crossed the creek and went to his door, which was located on the east side of the cabin. It was padlocked. Feeling that same overwhelming sensation of uneasiness again, I left.

Ted's cabin had its shortcomings, too, even though it was built much better than the root cellar and its entrance. His cabin, originally painted a brick red color, had no eaves on either gable end, and just inches of overhang on the sides. Green asphalt roofing, which covered the roof in horizontal rows, folded over the roof line onto the gable ends where it was attached with an almost solid row of roofing nails. The pitch of the roof was steep enough for the area's heavy snows, but with no eaves, the snow that slid off would pile up against the sides of the cabin and the moisture would eventually rot the wood; the only possible benefit being that the snow would act as insulation around the base of the cabin in extremely cold weather. Since the cabin wasn't connected to a foundation but was propped on Sakrete pillars, the space under it wasn't properly insulated so snow against the building probably served a useful purpose. The cabin had only two small windows, one on the south and one on the north; the north window was placed much higher than normal, just under the roof's edge. An aluminum pipe ran through the wall of his cabin to the garden on the west side, a convenient means of funneling his human waste to fertilize the garden.

Ted had trails everywhere around his cabin, well traveled paths leading off in all directions. A large, gnarled old Douglas-fir growing out of an outcropping of rocks at the northwest corner of his land was used as an observation tree. He climbed branches to reach a point twenty feet above the ground where the limbs were cut away, enabling him to see anyone approaching from the lower end of the gulch. Ted had numerous observation points in trees and rock outcroppings throughout the forest.

As much as Ted loved the woods and nature, the thing that always surprised me when I was around his place was all the junk lying around: bottles, cans, plastic jugs, a huge garbage heap of burned cans, and every other sort of thing.

The trash didn't make sense. It was out of place, not unlike the dark, almost sinister side of his character that I saw on rare occasions in later years, and only at times when he wasn't aware I was nearby. Ted was careful and calculating when he was around people. The few who knew him in town—the librarian, store clerks, the mailman—knew only the side of Ted he wanted them to see: quiet, but always friendly and cordial. For a long time, I was fooled, too.

I never told a soul other than Betty about this dark side, and she never told anyone other than me about things she noticed that didn't fit Ted's carefully managed persona.

I was in a unique position to learn things about Ted nobody else could know. He loved my gulch and the total privacy it offered him. Betty and I were the only ones who knew how much time he spent up there. Even when I didn't see him walking along the timbered trail above the old tailings piles on the west side of the gulch, I knew he was there because the dogs, who were penned up near the trail, would bark until we went outside to quiet them. Also, when we let them out to run every morning and afternoon, they'd race excitedly up the trail, barking and following his scent.

Our dogs could smell him, and they hated him. He hated them as well. It seemed like all animals reacted aggressively toward Ted.

There were a lot of times when Ted spent more days up my gulch than he did at his home cabin. I never mentioned this to anyone. I didn't want to get into a situation where people would say, "You let Ted up there, why won't you let us in?" There were a few people, like Butch, who knew they were welcome. But Butch never asked to go up my gulch.

Ted was always articulate, spoke intelligently, and had a good vocabulary, but it wasn't something he'd ever flaunt. I enjoyed visiting with him, always feeling like we had a lot in common.

He liked classical music as far as I could tell. I almost always had it playing in my pickup cassette deck, and he seemed to enjoy it when I gave him a ride. He never mentioned a favorite, but seemed to like the minor-key Beethoven sonatas. It was apparent he had a musical background, but he never told me he had played trombone in the school band. I also had played trombone in the school band.

Ted knew music was a huge part of my life, and even though he knew I was a classical pianist and piano tuner-technician, I never got to play for him; I would have enjoyed that. Another common denominator I learned about later was that we both spoke Spanish. As boys, we both had started coin collections.

We had a lot in common. We both used Latin names for plants and animals, we both liked history, exploring and searching the country, and we both were fascinated by the ways nature could provide for a person's every need. Propagation of wild plants and vegetables and cross-breeding them with domestic varieties to make them more palatable was a shared interest, as was the use of wild herbs, like yampa and chives, in our food.

I almost never saw Ted stray far from his measured and controlled demeanor. I never saw him euphoric, whimsical, elated; he never laughed uncontrollably, acted happy-go-lucky or anything even close. His occasional chuckle or light giggle always seemed to be more of a sneer, or sarcastic laugh, but it was always very controlled.

I've never seen a person—obviously so full of anger—who had so much control over his emotions. His mood would become even more solemn as the years went by, something that was very noticeable.

I'll never forget a conversation we had in 1982. I had just bought two books, *Electronic Nightmare* by John Wicklein, and *Puzzle Palace* by James Bamford. There also had been articles in *Scientific American* and other science publications I received monthly, that discussed in detail new surveillance techniques and street-to-satellite monitoring. All this material included discussions on how a person could be photographed in great detail from a satellite, and how a digital watch could be detected on a person, even if it was worn underground.

Ted's reaction to this technology wasn't passive. In fact, this was one of the few times in the early years where he was visibly disturbed. His knotted eyebrows and extremely serious look were clear indications he was diametrically opposed to this Orwellian *1984* invasive surveillance.

Later, I would learn that four years previously he had written*:

JAN 24, 1978 [KACZYNSKI JOURNAL]
   …There is a psychosurgical operation that relieves

Transcriptions of entries from Ted's journals and other writings have been edited to remove offensive language, which is found throughout the text, and have omitted the names of several Lincoln people, to protect their privacy, along with certain geographical locations. Ted's spelling, punctuation, and emphases have been maintained.

people who get angry too easily. They stick electrodes in your brain and burn out the gizmo that produces the emotion of anger. Of course, I would rather be miserable, or dead, than be relieved by that humiliating method. If I think I have a good reason to be angry at something, then I *want* to be angry, even though *it may make me miserable.*

He was such a deep thinker that even when he smiled I felt as though it was measured and not just because he was happy. It was as if the smile, its size and duration, had been planned. Ted became more withdrawn as the years went by, especially in the '90s. Yet he would always wave to me no matter what the weather or where he was. One time he waved so hard he lost track of where he was going, hit a pothole and crashed his bike. He picked himself and his bike off the dusty road and went on his way.

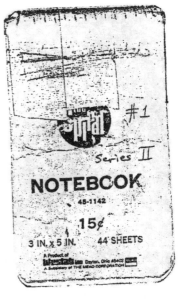

Ted's clothing varied little during his years in Lincoln. He usually wore shirts and denim jeans. More often than not his second-hand clothes, probably from the Salvation Army or some thrift store, were too big.

Frequently he wore a hooded sweatshirt, usually either dark blue or dark green, with a drawstring around the hood and pockets in front. When it was cold, he wore a green canvas army coat over the hooded sweatshirt. The sweatshirt hood would hang down over his back when it wasn't covering his head. He always carried a Mead pocket-sized notebook and pencil in his shirt or coat pocket. On rainy days he'd wear one of three ponchos, colored olive green, clear plastic or medium brown. The ever-practical Ted also used his poncho for dry temporary cover, stretching it over a pole or horizontal branch. He had a bright yellow plastic rain coat with a button front, but he seldom wore it, preferring more muted natural colors.

He also experimented with making useful items.

[FROM KACZINSKY'S SPANISH-LANGUAGE JOURNAL, TRANSLATED BY LANGUAGE SERVICES UNIT]
JAN. 14 [1982]

My gloves are fingers made from marmot skin they have suited me well last year and they have suited me well this winter until now. The skins are strong and resist survive [*sic*] to friction better than I thought; although they have been repaired a few times, generally at the seams. But I have observed that by tanning with smoke it does not turn out well that survives forever the wetting and drying. In the beginning, when the gloves were wetted, upon drying they would be almost as flexible as before they were wetted. But I would wet them almost every time that I used them, and little by little they would begin to turn stiff upon drying…

This may sound like a man living in harmony with nature, but later I learned the truth was quite different. Even though Ted was the intruder in the wild country, he demanded that the natives act as he wished them to.

KACZYNSKI JOURNAL

July 18: [1974, written at a camp away from home cabin]:…More woodrat trouble last night. A rat kept running over me, tugging at the blankets, etc., and so kept me awake half the night. Couldn't get a shot at it, because it disappeared every time I stuck my head out of the blankets to look. Worse, I found in the morning that it had chewed up my knife sheath so badly as to pretty well ruin it. I have set 2 deadfalls, with figure-4 triggers, baited with raisins, sugar, and oil, in the hope of catching that rat tonight. If I catch the [expletive] *alive* I will see that it dies a slow, painful death.…

July 19: Last night the rats chewed a piece out of the edge of my blanket and tarp, and ruined another piece of string. But I caught one in one of my deadfalls—worked like a charm. Most regrettably, this rat was spared the auto-da-fe, because the rock smashed its face so that it died soon. Bait was partly eaten on other deadfall, but I don't know whether rats or ants ate it. I have set up the deadfalls again. This time I have foxed the ants, I hope, by putting insect repellent on the stick they'd have to crawl over to get to the bait. In a short time I will learn what rat tastes like. Ha! Revenge is sweet! Later: According to Kaphart, it is the testimony of gourmets who survived the siege of Paris that cats, rats, and mice are the most misprized of all animals from a culinary point of view. If domestic rats are up to woodrat standards, I quite agree. That rat was [expletive] good eating. Provided about as much meat as a red squirrel.

July 31 (if it exists—otherwise August 1) [1974; written at different campsite from above entry]
...I hadn't previously been troubled by rats around here, but I just discovered that my pack has been chewed up so badly that it is nearly ruined, though I guess I can patch it up well enough to get my gear home....This means some deadfalls are going to be set. I hope I catch one of those [expletive] alive—I will torture it to death in the most fiendish manner I can devise.

Ted's shoes were of several different styles. He usually wore sneakers, work boots or hiking boots, but I often saw him wearing army-like laced dress shoes, black, short-topped, but usually without socks, especially when riding his bike. The low shoes always looked too large.

His hats were for all seasons, usually a pullover stocking cap or wool face mask for winter. My favorite, though, was a wide-brimmed summer straw hat. It was originally white, but most of the paint had worn off, allowing the natural straw color to show through the faded white. The hat brim was weakened from age and use and didn't have much of a curl, especially on the left side. Originally, the hat had a lanyard cord that could be pulled tightly under his chin to keep the hat from flying off when he was riding his bicycle in the wind. The original light, white cord gave way after a couple of summers to one that was darker, probably a shoelace cord.

Ted had several pairs of glasses; all protective in nature, needed to keep wind, rain, dust, sleet or snow—depending on the season—out of his eyes. Sometimes when riding his bike he wore a full, dark, rimmed pair that looked like reading glasses, or corrective lenses, but he didn't need glasses to see. Occasionally he wore a pair of dark green plastic sunglasses, the type designed to go over prescription glasses, or a pair of oval sunglasses.

One of his favorites, though, was a solid-plastic pair of sunglasses. They were dark-green, the one-piece wrap-around protective type that might come with a brazing or soldering kit purchased in a hardware store. There wasn't anything fancy about these glasses with their horizontal front and a small nose indentation. The bows, part of the same piece of plastic and bent off the frame at ninety degrees, tapered from lens height to about a half inch at the ear pieces.

He often wore those when he rode his bike, especially on hot days while his unruly nest of hair was capped by the straw hat. Then, to make this summer outfit complete, he'd wear a classic western red neckerchief tied around his neck. The neckerchief was tied just loosely enough so it could be pulled up over his face and nose when a vehicle approached on the dusty, gravel road. He looked like a kid on his broom horse playing cowboy, or a masked bandit, depending on whether the neckerchief was up or down.

Ted always tried to steer his bike to the upwind side of the road when a vehicle approached, to avoid the dust. When there was rain or snow, though, he couldn't escape the mud or ice.

His bicycle, which evolved over the course of time, was a dirt road machine, stripped down for efficiency and maneuverability on the primitive roads where it was always used. He removed all the unnecessary weight—fenders front and back, chain guard—allowing a very fit Ted to peddle this one-speed custom mountain bike all the way to the top of Stemple Pass and beyond, even in the mud. He tried several different handlebars over the years, the last ones extending up and back similar to the high handlebars of a Harley. Occasionally, the frame would need welding repairs because of the extremely rough places Ted rode. It was a far cry from the modern mountain bike, with ten speeds or more, knobby tires, and a comfortable seat.

The last winter before Ted was arrested, Betty and I were talking about Ted's bike and its poor condition. Betty said we should give Ted her old three-speed, which was just sitting in the shed anyway. We decided to surprise him with a reconditioned, cleaned-up three-speed. But Ted surprised us before we could surprise him.

Ted's one-speed favorite had its advantages, and its disadvantages.

Its major disadvantage was most apparent in rain, sleet or snow, when the lack of fenders, especially a rear fender, would mean Ted would be plastered across his back and his head with every drop of rain in a puddle and each glob of mud on the road. I saw Ted many times with a mud streak up his back, clear over his head; large mud balls would hang from his hair, swinging back and forth as he pedaled down the road. Often in bad weather he'd have to stop to clean the mud, rain or snow off his glasses. Ted rode his bike year around, in all types of weather, except on the foulest days.

I could always tell when he was out on his bike. Winter, summer, wet or dry, I could see his tracks along Stemple Road, weaving all over the place like a child who was just learning to ride. I knew he was an experienced rider and it was never clear to me why he rode that way; he must have gone to any extreme to miss a pothole or bump.

Ted nearly always wore a pack when he was on a ride, usually an army-green canvas one that he'd either carry frameless or attached to an altered aluminum tubing frame with white cord criss-crossing the bottom. He also carried a small pack when traveling out of Lincoln.

Ted always guarded his pack, as if it held something precious. There were a few times I saw the inside, almost exclusively at the store when he had emptied it so he could load his groceries. When I gave him a ride, he would sometimes put his pack in the back of the pickup, but usually he'd hold it on his lap; he'd never put it on the seat between us. It was usually loaded with something.

In the early years, he'd prepare for winter by laying in a large supply of groceries, mostly canned foods. After his gardens developed and he built his root cellar, Ted relied less on store-bought groceries and more on his own crops and game. When he went to town for groceries, he wouldn't ever buy junk food. He loved graham crackers, though. One time he bought six boxes of generic graham crackers, loaded them into his pack and rode home.

Among his favorite foods were canned fish, sardines, and kippered snacks, all high in protein. Ted enjoyed the tins of fish, plus they supplied much needed fat calories. As health conscious as he was, Ted had a real problem getting enough fat calories, just the opposite of most Americans. Wild game—rabbits, grouse, deer, elk, even porcupines—which Ted ate along with home-grown, wild or canned vegetables—has very little fat. Ted would eat canned fish or use cooking oil, which not only helped with his cooking, but boosted his fat intake as well. He also liked peanut butter, but only the natural types.

He'd buy only whole-wheat flour without preservatives. He also ate rice and took vitamins. He kept track of how much salt he used and kept his teeth as clean as possible.

Ted ran on the nearby inclined Humbug Counter Road on a regular basis just to stay in shape, as if he didn't get enough exercise in his daily routines of hiking and pedaling all over the country, cutting all of his wood by hand with either a bow saw or hatchet, and packing water uphill to his garden in buckets.

Ted and his bike are forever interwoven in the folklore of this small mountain community and the surrounding country. Some of his episodes of bike travel are almost epic in the mere distance covered, other incidents are just plain humorous.

I remember one midsummer afternoon in the '80s when I was driving up the road in my pickup. Ted was pulled off at a wide spot, crouched over his bike in a strange position. As I pulled up, I could see his dilemma: the right leg of his too-large jeans was caught in his chain. With no chain guard and pants too long and big, it was obvious what had happened. He was stuck. He couldn't go forward or back.

As funny as this scene appeared before I got out to help, I became serious because the predicament was no laughing matter to Ted. I helped him free his pant leg from the jaws of the sprocket teeth and chain. He thanked me and we both went our separate ways.

A few days later I saw Ted riding along, and wearing the same pair of pants. The right cuff was quite shredded, so I knew he had caught his pant leg several times since I last saw him. I passed him and waved, and the tattered pant leg whipped around in the wind as he pedaled toward Lincoln. He waved back.

Perhaps a week later, I spotted Ted riding toward Lincoln again, still wearing the same pair of pants. This time a red rubber band held the now extremely tattered right pant leg above his right calf just below the knee. He was wearing the black army dress shoes, partially laced, and no socks. The rest of his dress included a light-colored shirt under his dark blue hooded sweatshirt, his straw hat, wrap-around dark plastic sunglasses, and his red neckerchief pulled up over his face.

As he pedaled along, his squeaky chain sang a high-pitched rhythmic song. At times Ted's bike chain would squeak so loudly I don't know how he could stand it. Whenever he rode up Stemple past my home and I was out in the yard, I could hear him coming long before I'd see him. Since he was afraid of our dogs, his pedaling, speed and squeaking would pick up tempo as he neared my driveway, until it reached a frenzied pace.

Butch Gehring told me another funny bike story. Butch's sister had pastured her mule in his grass field near the sawmill. One day as Ted rode from his home cabin down along the fence line on the south end of the field, the mule trotted over and began to chase him. Ted tried to outrun the mule, but the critter was faster and started to catch up. While looking over his shoulder to see how fast the mule was gaining, Ted hit a hole in the road and piled up his bike. Butch and a couple of friends who were watching laughed, but Ted wasn't amused.

Ted's bike was serious transportation, and the distance he covered on it was amazing. Many times I saw him on his bike, or his bike tracks, straight up to the top of Stemple Pass and on both forest roads that led north and south along the Continental Divide, but never over the pass toward Helena. One day while Ted was parked just below the pass, an arduous eleven miles from his home, I stopped to visit him.

We started to talk about different forest roads and trails around Stemple and where they went. At one point I said a person could go all the way to Helena, some thirty miles away, without ever touching pavement. Ted was intrigued by the thought, so I described a route: From the top of Stemple Pass head south to Granite Butte and then down Marsh Creek to Little Prickley Pear Road. From there you can head southwest on Little Prickley Pear Road toward Ophir Creek, turn southeast on a back road that takes you to Marysville. From Marysville there are a couple of back ways to get to Helena, either through Birdseye or along the Mullan Pass Road where you can follow the rail line or a couple of other back roads. Either way, you end up on the west end of Helena and you probably won't see a soul along the way.

Our discussions about back roads, trails, and out-of-the-way places were always detailed, and intriguing.

I remember another conversation when we talked about old mines in the area and what was extracted during the glory days at the close of the nineteenth century. As I told Ted about one mining district in particular I asked if he had ever been up to the Seven-Up, Rover or Columbia mines.

He said he didn't think he had, so I explained about the discoveries of gold and other minerals and how easy it was to get to the abandoned old mines from the top of Stemple Pass. You just head north on the pass road that goes toward Crater Mountain, I explained. All the mines are close to each other at the top of a basin and drainage to the north of Crater, at the head of Seven-up Gulch.

What made this conversation so interesting to Ted, and something I of course didn't pick up on at the time, wasn't the description of the mines themselves and the riches, especially gold, taken from the area, but what was still lying around the deserted mine shafts and mills. I talked about an old assay house alongside one of the mill buildings, with roof timbers fallen and side walls of weathered lumber tilting in dangerous arrays, where sulphur sticks were still scattered in and around an old wooden box. Also, small ceramic crucibles used in the fire-assay of ore could still be found lying about the front of the building. We talked at length about these and some metal objects I had seen near the sites.

The next time I hiked into the old mines, several months later, everything was gone: no sulphur, no crucibles, no metal objects I had described.

I never mentioned it to Ted, nor did I ask if he was the one who went up there and took everything.

FROM FBI INVENTORY OF ITEMS SEIZED
    AT KACZYNSKI HOME CABIN
L59—Container of yellow crystals with plastic bags.
L60—Container of white powder.
L61—Six sealed bottles labeled sulphur.
MB26—One small white ceramic crucible.
MB27—Two off-white colored ceramic crucible lids.

One day when I was visiting with Ted, we got onto the subject of insect pests: ticks, mosquitoes, horse flies, deer flies that can make life in the mountains a pain. More than a nuisance, they can be truly dangerous at certain times of the year. Ticks are the first bloodsucking insects to appear in the spring. They prefer dry, brushy, warm areas instead of cool, damp, wet areas. I suggested it's better to always wear dark clothing; you'll get far fewer ticks on you.

The next pests to appear are the mosquitoes, which hatch out after the spring thaw and high runoff water. Their eggs can last for years without hatching while waiting for the high water to reach them. They're the opposite of the ticks in that they thrive in the cool, damp, wet and shaded areas, and really come out in the late afternoon and evening.

The very worst, by far, are horse flies and deer flies. They hatch out in midsummer and are most active during the hottest parts of the day, flying and sitting around the brush and trees. When you walk through the brush, they'll come at you and when bitten you'll swear they have taken a chunk right out of you, causing the bite to bleed.

During our discussion about insects and what could be done beyond the normal swatting and swearing, I related a story told to me by an old miner from Boulder, Montana, many years ago. The miner, who had spent his whole life in the woods, explained his remedy to prevent ticks and biting insects from attaching themselves or boring into the skin. Take a teaspoon of flowers of sulphur every day, he said. It can be swallowed dry and washed down, or mixed with water or another fluid as a drink. Flowers of sulphur comes in a jar or plastic bottle. It's ground sulphur with the look and consistency of pale yellow chalk.

FROM FBI INVENTORY
MB148—One white plastic jar, with white metal cap, label
    "Rexall Sublimed Sulfur, N.F. (Flowers of Sulfur [*sic*]),
    Parasiticide-Scabicide"
MB178—One white plastic bottle, with white plastic cap,
    label "Flowers of Sulfur USP, Whiteworth Inc.,
    Gardena, Ca. 90248, NDC 0923-3500-03," with masking
    tape around the base, with a small white square price
    tag "Bergums 217-6956 L5GJB $5.17"

I've tried the old miner's remedy in the past, and it works. When parasite infestations are particularly bad, I told Ted, the treatment of ingesting flowers of sulphur can be enhanced by bathing first and then applying a dissolved solution of sulphur and hot water to your skin, letting it dry and leaving it on. The downside is that you better be alone, because the odor emanating from your body is unpleasant, to say the least, causing you to smell like rotten eggs.

ON WALL OF KACZYNSKI SECRET SHACK
[Ted had penciled the old miner's instructions on a piece of plywood, which he then used to cover holes in the outside cabin wall. Part of the plywood had been ripped away, probably by an animal, so only a few words remained; they had been protected from the weather for years by an overlapping piece of wood.]

Then drink what...
keep that up,...
soap baths; let
on you...

To my knowledge Ted worked only two, short-lived jobs in all the years he lived in Lincoln.

When he first moved to Florence Gulch he cut

posts to sell at a local post-and-pole manufacturing operation. He didn't last long. I never knew if he quit because he was against tree cutting or if the work didn't suit him. I assumed it was the latter, because his second bit of employment was peeling logs for Butch Gehring during the mid-'80s, a pretty strenuous job of skinning the bark off with a drawknife, a double-handled, sharp-edged blade that's pulled toward the worker. I remember Butch saying at the time that Ted didn't last more than a couple of hours before he walked off the job, saying that peeling logs wasn't for him.

Ted made only two other inquiries about employment in the Lincoln area that I am aware of, one at Garland's Town & Country general store and one at the Blackfoot Market. Both contacts were in his later years in Lincoln, and I was surprised when I heard Ted had applied for work that could include time at a sales counter at either store. Stocking shelves, doing inventory, bookkeeping, or something like that might do, but I couldn't envision him working around people. At the time, I assumed he was desperate for money. It was so unlike his character to ask for employment in a public place.

Ted and I had many conversations about our remote, wild country southwest of Lincoln. We also talked about the seasonal extremes and how the mountains could be calm and benign one day, and then ravaging and deadly the next. Ted knew the full range of each season, because he lived outside much of the time. He was tolerant and tough about the weather, able to adapt to almost anything. Whether he was out walking at -30° F. with his beard and moustache completely covered with icicles, hiking up a steep mountain at a hot and steamy 95° with insects biting madly after a quick rain shower, fighting his way through a mosquito-infested swampy marsh with willows so thick he had to hack his way, or trying to negotiate his way down an ice-covered talus slope after a freezing rain, he not only survived and endured, but he did so without a complaint. Whatever nature dished out he would readily accept.

He never said to me: If I only had power and a furnace, it would be so much easier to stay warm and get through the winter. It just didn't seem to matter to him, the cold, the physical work, the inconvenience, anything.

If he were caught too far from his campsite or either cabin he would just roll up in his coat—no matter where he was, at the edge of a meadow or in the trees—lie down and spend the night.

Ted wasn't intimidated by being out in the deep, dark woods at night. He often traveled and hunted at night. When he spotlighted rabbits, for example, he followed a fresh set of tracks through the snow until the rabbit would stop. He'd shine a flashlight at the animal and then try to shoot it in the eye, which would show up in the faint light. If he hit his target, the rabbit died instantly. If he missed, the scared rabbit would bolt away, sometimes zigzagging through the snow for miles before it would stop again. Never giving up, Ted told me he would follow it, even through difficult terrain and deep snow, often crossing other tracks that would make the stalk even tougher. When the rabbit stopped again, Ted got a second chance to bag his prey. Sometimes it was a very difficult way to procure supper.

Ted was a good shot, and I later learned that he bragged to himself in his journals about how he seldom missed. He kept track of every round of ammunition he had, every round fired, including his misses, and how many rounds of each caliber he had remaining and buried in caches for reserve. He was secretive about his weapons. You never saw him carrying guns near a road or another place where he might be spotted. In addition to knives—G.I. survival and hunting types—and a bow and arrow, he owned six guns: a 30-06, 30-30, .25 caliber Raven automatic, .22 rifle, .22 pistol, and a homemade zip gun made from the barrel of an old air pistol with a crude trigger device and firing pin manufactured from scrap metal parts.

Ted and I never discussed the perilous circumstances one could confront in the forest, especially at night. Though we talked many times about grizzly and black bears, prowling mountain lions, and wolverines, Ted never once indicated he was afraid of wild animals. Most people couldn't be paid enough to spend a night alone in the wilderness, and yet it didn't seem to bother him in the least. If not harnessed by fear, a hunter or hiker could cover many miles on a moon-lit night.

As more people moved to Lincoln and the area around Stemple, they were always curious about Ted. They'd see him walking or riding his bike and then ask someone about him. People in town would say, "Ask Chris, he's been up there longer than anyone."

When people asked me about Ted they would say, "Who's that hermit friend of yours?" or "What do you know about your friend the hermit?" Hardly anyone who had seen Ted around or had heard about him understood him. Stigmatized by his appearance and lifestyle, he was blamed for every curious or puzzling act reported in the area. If someone's dog disappeared, people would tell me, "That hermit friend of yours probably ate him." If there was an act of vandalism, a theft or even a flat tire on a vehicle parked in the forest—anything—Ted was accused of doing it because he was different.

I always stuck up for him, saying "A book cannot be judged by its cover." My adamant support probably had an influence on the local public's understanding and tolerance of that "book cover," but my perception changed as time passed.

In the early years, Ted and I often talked about how lucky we were to have similar properties, lifestyles, locations, resources, and privacy. Both of us had land bordered by National Forest. No one lived above us. Clear, pure water sprang out of the ground and flowed through our properties. Each of us lived in a secluded gulch, where a variety of wild berries and game flourished.

Even with all the similarities, there were many differences, because the country around Stemple can vary dramatically with changes in elevation and orientation of the land.

Ted's home cabin was located in an east-west drainage, Florence Gulch. Canyon Creek appears and disappears quickly. It flows to the west less than a half mile from the spring's source to where it is absorbed into the ground at the mouth of the gulch, except during times of high water. The elevation at his cabin was 4,780 feet above sea level.

But my home at the mouth of McClellan Gulch, which runs north and south, sits at an elevation of 4,940, nearly 200 feet higher. My unpolluted year-round water supply comes from many springs that flow from more than five different drainages before they converge at different junctures starting about one mile above the mouth of the gulch. From an elevation of 4,940 feet at its mouth, my gulch ascends to almost 6,800 feet at the top, nearly four miles south, with the highest point being 7,428-foot Fields Mountain on the southwest side.

So despite the similarities, there are striking differences between our two gulches because of the contrast in elevation and the lay of the land. Both elements have a huge impact on variations of flora and fauna. The area north of Ted's home cabin, with its southern exposure, is more arid and the trees are more widely spaced than in my gulch. The area to the south of Ted's, a northern exposure, is more dense and moist and the predominant conifer species is Douglas-fir.

In contrast, there's no northern-southern exposure in my main gulch; even with five main drainages and additional smaller drainages, the predominant exposures of the mountains are east and west. The tree species are far more numerous and varied, plus there is a much wider range of plant species, including wild carrots, onions, and parsnips. The environment is more humid and the air temperature fluctuates more. These factors, together with the huge difference in roadless, trailless and uninhabited acres, mean my gulch has habitat for wildlife not normally seen around Ted's home cabin, nor in most other areas around Lincoln. My wife and I have seen not only whitetail and mule deer, elk, black bears and grizzly bears, but also moose, mountain lions, lynxes, and bobcats. Rough, Franklin, and blue grouse abound. Bird species vary from rufous and calliope hummingbirds, which nest in the willows each spring, to western tanagers, water dippers, pine siskins, and numerous other birds, all the way up the size scale to great blue herons, and eagles.

This greater variety of plant and animal species proved to be a great attraction to Ted at his secret cabin high up my gulch. The opportunity for him to cross-pollinate wild vegetables from my gulch—carrots, onions, and parsnips especially—with the domestic varieties he grew in his home garden was too exciting for him to ignore. He wrote in his journal pages about his goal of increasing the palatability of the hardy wild plants by crossing them with the more fragile, but much tastier domestic varieties. Such an improved plant would allow Ted to live in the woods indefinitely without suffering through a menu of only wild game.

Back in the early 1980s, I was placer mining for gold in Poorman Creek about two miles from home. I had dug a discovery hole down through the gravel about fifteen feet to bedrock close to the water at a wide spot just north of the creek. I worked this spot during the summers for several years in my spare time with my father-in-law, Leonard Orr.

Occasionally Ted rode by and watched us work. As usual, if I was alone he'd stop and visit. One afternoon as he pulled his bike to the edge of the road above me, I called up and asked him to climb down the road bank so he could watch and visit. He did. When he got down along the streambed he was very interested in what I was doing. I had moved my smallest dragline, a Northwest with a three-quarter-yard bucket, down to the site, along with a small trommel washer, a device used to separate gold from gravel through washing and tumbling.

As I continued my work, we discussed the advantages and efficiencies of modern placer mining techniques versus the old hand-methods of the early prospectors. Ted obviously favored the old method over the new, but at the time I didn't pick up on how serious his dislike of machinery was. I said I also favored slower hand methods if the more efficient modern methods weren't employed properly. I went on to explain digging, washing, and reclamation techniques, and how they could be used with minimal impact to the land.

The conversation shifted from mechanical mining to washing and extracting gold by hand with a gold pan. Not knowing whether Ted had a gold pan or not, I explained that placer mining and gold washing by hand didn't require a gold pan per se. Any frying pan, especially one without a handle, would do. I proceeded to grab one of my gold pans, shovel some placer gravel into it and demonstrate how to pan gold.

I trusted Ted unconditionally, so I pointed out a few likely spots and I wasn't the least bit worried he would pass along sensitive information about how and where you could find "color" in the area.

Ted didn't appear to be overly excited about panning, but he definitely showed interest. Plus, I could never be sure what was going on in his head. I explained that with patience and a little luck, and by spending enough time in the right place, a person could acquire a surprising quantity of gold flakes.

The old miners didn't get it all, I said, and even with the hard work involved, a teaspoon, just a level teaspoonful, is approximately one ounce of gold. Even with gold prices down, that teaspoonful was worth close to $300, far more than Ted's entire annual budget.

Once again, I told Ted he was free to pan in any of my spots. I didn't know if he would try it, even though it would be a perfect, private opportunity for him to acquire some money. Gold might not be legal tender these days as it was for the early miners, but no matter how small the amount, gold could easily be traded for currency at a variety of places—pawn shops, jewelry stores, coin stores—and gold could be sold anonymously, important to Ted, although I didn't realize it at the time.

Many times over the years Ted was carrying books as I picked him up to give him a ride. I usually didn't see the titles, because he carried them in his pack, with only the top corners visible under the flap, or wrapped in a sack. Early on I explained to him I had a huge library, thousands of books. I went on to explain that my collection was not a normal home library of novels and stories, but most of the titles dealt with science, history, mathematics, chemistry, botany, field identification. I had numerous "how to" books on topics ranging from making fishing nets to building a hydrogen generator. Ted knew where my books were kept and that he was welcome to borrow them at any time.

In addition to my books, he had ready access to more than two decades worth of at least six science-related publications I subscribed to, some since high school. These magazines included *Scientific American*, *Omni*, *Science*, *Mechanix Illustrated*, *Science Digest*, and *Popular Science*. Most of the back issues are stored in boxes, in chronological order. When Betty and I married she wanted to throw them all away. I resisted because of all the good articles and projects in the magazines.

I knew Ted had some of his own books, and I assumed most of the ones he carried were his own and didn't come from the Lincoln Library. The library was reluctant to let Ted take out certain new books because they weren't always returned in the same condition as when checked out.

Ted had complete access to my library, before Betty retired in 1986. I see how many of my books would have been useful to him, books like *The Charcoal Foundry, How to Build a Metal Working Shop from Scrap, The Blaster's Handbook, Metallurgy*, and *Metal Casting*.

Ted always was reluctant to accept any help. He would let me work on his bike, but if I said, "Ted, if you need any help with anything up at your cabin just let me know," he would respond with a nod, and never once asked me to help with any specific project. He never said, "Chris, can you come up and help me set up some beams across the creek?" I would have done that, and he knew it, but it was as though he didn't want to impose, or he didn't want me to see what he was doing.

There was only one way Ted would allow me to help him, and that was in the area of information. All he had to do was bring up any topic of discussion in my fields of interest and then leave the rest to me. I would openly and readily tell him everything I knew about the subject, from nature to welding. On the other side of the coin, if he stopped by and I was unloading something from the pickup or doing some other chore, he would pitch in.

I'll always remember an episode that took place about 1980. The mail had just arrived and I was on my way to my Lincoln shop. I usually picked up my mail in the evenings, but this day I had gone home to grab some parts I needed. It was just before 11 A.M. While I was there I saw the mailman pull away from my box, so I thought I might as well get the mail. As I headed toward Lincoln I saw Ted walking to town, so I stopped and gave him a ride. That day I had received an unusual amount of mail, most of it advertisements and solicitations. I brought up the subject that all the junk mail was a huge waste of resources, and a nuisance to boot. Ted said he never received any junk mail.

In fact, he seldom received any mail at all. There were many times I gave him a ride to his cabin from town; I'd usually let him off at his mailbox. Most of the time he wouldn't even open it. If I drove him farther up the side road to his cabin I'd offer to stop at his mailbox so he could check it. He always declined, saying he wouldn't have any mail.

The more I thought about it the more I began to realize just how invisible he was in Lincoln. He didn't receive any junk mail and he wasn't on any mailing list. Everyone who has a credit card or orders things from a mail-order catalogue ends up on a mailing list. Mailing lists are sold or shared with other firms. Few escape the cycle.

I don't know for sure, but I don't think Ted ever filed an income tax return while he lived in Lincoln, since he never worked and he basically lived off the land.

He first had a post office box in Lincoln and later a mailbox on Stemple Road below his home cabin. Knowing he picked up his mail only every few weeks, I always wondered why he even had his post office box, where he had to pay box rent as long as he did.

Ted's neighbor, Butch, didn't really like Ted after he walked off the log-peeling job and the two had several arguments about spraying weeds—Ted was adamantly opposed to spraying—but Butch still tried to help Ted. Being neighbors, they had their share of strange encounters. Butch told me about one involving logging work.

Butch had cut and moved some trees on the upper end of the gulch above Ted's cabin. Later in the summer Butch piled the brush and limbs quite a distance past Ted's and then later that fall walked up to burn the slash pile. Ted approached and asked Butch not to light the fire, saying he would clean up the brush. Butch replied that picking everything up by hand wouldn't be nearly as clean as burning it. Ted insisted, saying he would pick up every branch—to which Butch agreed.

Ted carried every scrap of branch and limb all the way down to his cabin, a huge task. Even though Butch told me Ted couldn't get all the small pieces and the pine needles, I marveled that he would want to take on a task of such magnitude, making countless trips carrying all that slash. Peeling logs wouldn't be nearly as hard.

The old saying "One man's junk is another man's treasure" certainly applied to Ted, who was the biggest pack rat I've ever seen. He saved everything he found in the woods. Whether it was a metal scrap from an old mine, a discarded piece of rope, a glass or plastic container found along the road, Ted would pick it up and take it to his cabin.

Ted's favorite water jugs were nothing more than discarded large plastic soda jugs, bottles with a fluted dark plastic base, a clear plastic container, and a screw-on top. He didn't drink pop but he didn't discriminate against any brand, using any jug he found, whether it was Coke, Pepsi, or Dr. Pepper. The last one I saw him toting around was a Dr. Pepper. These pop jugs are tough and make great water containers.

He even saved different types of wood. I saw many things up my gulch that were moved, as if they had been mentally catalogued and set aside, or just taken. What did he want with all that stuff? Was he just eccentric or did he have a use for pieces of wire, aluminum scraps, electrical components, and other things?

Ted's life was a complex array of puzzles and contradictions. He was so isolated at times he would lose track of all those things modern man has programmed into his life. If I picked him up after not seeing him for a while, he would promptly ask statistical questions like: "What time is it?" "What is the date?" "How cold is it?" He didn't wear a watch but I thought he probably had a battery powered or wind-up clock at his cabin.

I always kept a stick-on calendar, given each Christmas by a local fuel business, attached to the dash of my pickup. I also had built a digital clock and installed it into the dash panel. Whenever Ted rode with me he would check both and ask me to confirm the time and date. It didn't make much sense at the time why a man who lived off the land should be concerned with anything but the seasons of the year so he could be prepared for them.

Even though Ted lived his life almost entirely in the outdoors, he wasn't what you'd consider a sportsman. If he went fishing, which I rarely saw him do, it wasn't with a fly rod and a dry fly for sport and recreation. It was with a spool of line and a hook to catch fish for food.

FROM FBI INVENTORY
MF36—Plastic bag with two fish hooks, string, and two
boxes of matches.

When he hunted he wasn't interested in stalking the biggest buck deer or bull elk. A trophy meant nothing to him unless the horns could be made into a useful item like a tool, or be sold. When he hunted or fished it was solely for the meat he needed, and not for the outdoor experience. I realized that early on, and it was always a mystery to me.

Most people move to a place like Lincoln for the scenery, outdoor sports, and recreational opportunities. It was clear from our conversations those weren't the reasons Ted was here.

Why did he live here? Even people like myself who are attracted to a lifestyle like Ted's eventually grow tired of the struggle to survive in the wild, and then they either get a job or move on. Ted did neither. His lifestyle changed very little during the twenty-five years he lived in Lincoln. In fact, in many ways living off the land became much tougher as the world began to move in around him.

Lincoln, Ted's Haven

The mountains surrounding Lincoln, Montana, form a natural geo-logical observatory where the work of the ancient forces of nature lies close to the surface. Much of the Upper Blackfoot Valley was carved by glaciers slowly grinding off the mountains to the north during the Ice Age, glaciers that left behind expanses of sand, gravel, and boul-der plains of glacial till. To the northwest the majestic Swan Range with its snow-covered peaks was uplifted skyward as huge jagged blocks along the Swan fault. To the east are the Rocky Mountains and the Continental Divide, composed of Precambrian Belt sedimentary rock layers that crushed together, uplifting giant slabs to form the overthrust of the Rocky Mountains.

One of the area's anomalies is the Boulder Batholith, a large and out-of-place mass of granite, the earth's ancient magma, that gurgled molten through the basement rock of our planet's crust about 70 mil-lion years ago and then solidified. Most of the Boulder Batholith reach-es south and east between Helena and Butte, but pockets intrude through the sedimentary slabs in the Lincoln area, especially around Stemple Pass. The batholith and other igneous intrusions that pushed through the sedimentary rock some 40 million years later carried rich-es for modern man in their veins.

During the early 1860s, prospectors were attracted to strikes throughout a vast area of the gold frontier that was to become Montana Territory in 1864—Bannack, Virginia City, Grasshopper Creek, Gold Creek, Blackfoot City, and Diamond City. Placer riches were discov-ered on July 14, 1864, along Last Chance Gulch, launching Helena, Montana's capital city. Prospectors quickly spread out and explored drainages north, south, east and west, searching for granite and tell-tale signs of ancient stream beds—rounded stones washed by centuries of water, and white rims showing old water levels around the hills—including those in the Upper Blackfoot Valley just fifty miles to the northwest.

Jib Longhandle McClellan, an old-time prospector whom many called one of the best of his era, came into the Blackfoot Valley in the late summer of 1864. He and his two companions decided to spend the winter, but stories of rich strikes in Last Chance Gulch were more than his friends could stand.

McClellan, who wasn't impressed by the news of riches, remained and explored the riffle bars on Poorman Creek as he awaited the first winter snows. With a pick and shovel, he sank a hole to bedrock. It was a fruitless effort. Then farther upstream in the mouth of the gulch that bears his name he found a giant ponderosa pine blown over by the wind, with its root ball high in the air. The hollow left by the uprooted pine had been filled with gravel carried by centuries of rushing water. McClellan worked the cavity and found gold all the way to bedrock. But rather than develop the paystreak, he decided to spend the last days before winter prospecting for the mother lode and setting up a cold-weather camp.

By spring others had joined McClellan. They removed the overburden and followed streaks of placer gold deep under the stream and against the hillsides. The McClellan strike became one of the richest in Montana. McClellan Gulch was cleaned out quickly, giving up almost $4 million a mile by the end of 1866. It was reworked with a brief flurry of success in 1873. Some areas were worked a third and fourth time. During one of those more recent excavations through old tailings, two miners discovered a 57-ounce lump of gold in 1924.

Many of the miners who moved into the valley were attracted by the rich McClellan Gulch strike. These prospectors, carrying little more than picks, shovels, gold pans, and small grubstakes, discovered more gold northwest of McClellan along the Blackfoot River in 1865.

As they staked their claims, food came from the nearby forests— venison and other wild game—complementing staples carried in their packs.

We know these early miners were patriotic because they chose to call the place Abe Lincoln Gulch, a popular namesake throughout the country during the first years following the president's assassination.

The camp that boomed with the discovery was called Springfield City, honoring the president's hometown. That name soon gave way to Lincoln City, which actually was located about five miles northwest of present-day Lincoln.

These early prospectors were accustomed to the most difficult labor, hours of digging, shoveling, and moving heavy boulders in the cold stream waters. We know that only a few of them really struck it rich. We also know they seasoned their hard work and usual bad luck with a healthy dose of good humor, calling the Blackfoot Valley streams where they set up their rocker boxes names like Poorman, Sauerkraut, Beaver, Humbug, Sucker, and Keep Cool.

"Keep cool" was appropriate advice for the early miners if they wanted to keep their scalps because they had struck gold and built their mining camp right in the middle of a popular seasonal travel route for several Native American tribes, including the Salish and Kootenai, the Crows, and the great warriors of the plains, the Blackfeet.

Skirmishes between the settlers and Native Americans were common. Early Upper Blackfoot Valley miners often were caught off-guard, until they set up a lookout tree south of Keep Cool Creek near the river, and manned it day and night. When the guard sounded the alarm from a perch high aloft in the towering yellow pine, miners and their families escaped into the surrounding forests.

Long before gold miners arrived, the valley was a favorite among nomadic Native American tribes who hunted and gathered roots, wild vegetables, and berries, except during the season of heavy snow. Those early travelers followed the Cokalanishlot (River Road to the Buffalo) through the valley and then crossed the Continental Divide to the game-rich plains of present-day eastern Montana. Along the way they found important staples for their survival. Camas roots were abundant in the Alice Creek area. The roots, which were cooked for several days in a shallow hole filled with coals, had a sweet taste and could be kept for long periods of time in loaves.

Those early travelers also cut bark shields off ponderosa pine trees in the spring when the sap was flowing, exposing the cambium layer, which was then removed with scrapers for food and medicinal purposes. Several of these so-called shield trees can still be seen in the Lincoln area. Plus there was plenty of game: deer, elk, and even buffalo that had wandered over the mountains and into the valley. Nearby, stone quarries on Willow and Nevada creeks were known for their chert, a stone resembling flint that could be chipped into weapon points.

Meriwether Lewis was the first to map the area when he and his small group of explorers crossed this valley on July 6 and 7, 1806. Lewis and William Clark had split their forces on their return trip after wintering at their Fort Clatsop in today's Oregon, enabling the Corps of Discovery to explore more of this wilderness territory that was part of Jefferson's Louisiana Purchase of 1803. Clark took his larger group down the Beaverhead River to the Three Forks of the Missouri, where they split. Sergeant John Ordway would lead nine men down the Missouri to eventually meet Lewis's men at the Great Falls of the Missouri. Clark would take the remaining ten members of the party overland to the Yellowstone River, then explore downstream to its mouth on the Missouri, where the whole Corps was to eventually reunite.

Lewis's group, with seventeen horses and some Nez Perce guides, departed from Traveler's Rest near present-day Lolo, Montana, on July 3. The five Native American guides left the Corps the next day. On July 6, they "passed the north fork of the Cokalahishkit [*sic*], a deep and rapid stream, forty-five yards in width, and like the main branch itself somewhat turbid, though the other streams of this country are clear."

From there Captain Lewis noted a "multitude of knobs," and he called this country the Prairie of the Knobs. "They abound in game, as we saw goats, deer, great numbers of burrowing squirrels, some curlews, bee martins, woodpeckers, plover, robins, doves, ravens, hawks, ducks, a variety of sparrows, and yesterday observed swans on Werner's Creek.

"In the course of the day the track of the Indians, whom we supposed to be the Pahkees [Blackfeet], continued to grow fresher, and we passed a number of old lodges and encampments," his journal notes.

That night Lewis and his group camped just west of present-day Lincoln.

"At seven o'clock the next morning, we proceeded through a beautiful plain on the north side of the river, which seems here to abound in beaver," Lewis wrote.

After following Alice Creek and crossing the Continental Divide at later-named Lewis and Clark Pass (elevation 6,421 feet), Lewis noted the group was "delighted at discovering that this was the dividing ridge between the waters of the Columbia and those of the Missouri.

"We procured some beaver, and this morning saw some signs and tracks of buffalo, from which it seems those animals do sometimes penetrate to a short distance within the mountains," he wrote.

After Lewis crossed the Blackfoot Valley, there was no other recorded visit by white explorers until Major Isaac Stevens led an expedition on a quest for a transcontinental rail route in the mid-1850s. Stevens actually recommended the Blackfoot Valley in his report, but his suggestion was ignored.

Another decade passed before word spread about the rich discoveries in Montana's gold fields. The mere prospect of finding a mother lode brought settlers into western Montana valleys quicker than any railroad could.

The population of Lincoln rose and fell with the success of the mines. In those early years as miners and their symbiotic comrades jumped from one strike to another, the population of the valley might have reached 3,000. More than likely the numbers were less, especially when the area was locked in the grips of a frigid mountain winter. But as for most Montana gold boom towns, the bust wasn't far behind. By the 1880s, mining was already on the decline and, by the 1920s, most of the miners had left the valley. But during their heyday, Lincoln Gulch mines produced more than $7 million in gold at $12 an ounce.

In the fall of 1916, town folks decided they needed a community gathering place where they could socialize, and hold picnics and dances. That winter, workers took advantage of deep snow to sled 120 logs out of the surrounding forests and started to craft the Community Hall. The logs and a false ceiling were in place after the first winter of work. Built with care and with a long life in mind, each log was mortised and then pegged to the one below with a piece of wheel spoke. It took almost two years to finish the center, and the dedication was held the night of February 22, 1918. The dance literally lasted all night, because a blizzard had blown in from the northeast as Lincoln celebrated, and few wanted to risk a trek home through the darkness during a storm. The octagonal building, with a more recent frame addition, is still a community sentinel on the west end of Main Street.

As the miners pulled out searching for new claims, they left behind a legacy of placer scars, huge heaps of gravel and mine tailings from their placer operations along the stream bottoms, and hard-rock adits, mine shafts, assay buildings, and mills along several mountain ridges. But Lincoln wasn't about to become a ghost town like many other Montana gold camps, even though it came close.

By 1928, Lincoln's year-round population dropped to twenty-five. The downtown area consisted of a hotel, a grocery store owned by Paul and Elsie Didriksen, a blacksmith shop, a corner bar, and post office. Lincoln then witnessed several growth spurts, first as an attractive place for summer vacationers who built their seasonal homes at Lincoln Estates, and then again as the result of mining activities. The town grew rapidly during the early 1940s with new ventures near the headwaters of the Blackfoot River at the Mike Horse Mine and several smaller operations. But this time, along with the miners, the valley was being settled by ranchers, loggers, and merchants who created livings from what the land would give them. By the time the Anaconda Company closed the Mike Horse in 1952 and many of the miners pulled out, the community had achieved the balance it needed to survive and prosper.

Since prehistoric times, the Upper Blackfoot has been one of those mountain valleys where its people and nature, by necessity, live in harmony. The valley is flanked to the north, east and south by imposing mountain ranges with the only access over one of six mountain passes: Dalton, 6,450 feet; Lewis and Clark, 6,421; Cadotte, 6,080; Rogers, 6,376; Flesher, 6,131; and Stemple, 6,376. Today, only foot trails traverse the divide at Cadotte and Lewis and Clark passes; Dalton has a seasonal gravel road; and Stemple has a year-round gravel road. Only Flesher and Rogers have paved or blacktopped roads into the valley. Conifer forests paint the mountainsides a thick, dark green as far as the eye can see, broken only by the lighter splotches of deciduous aspen and cottonwoods along river and stream bottoms. Outcroppings of granite and sedimentary stone burst through the forest tops, nature's towers scraping at the sky with their jagged tops.

Only to the west is there an escape route for spring and mountain waters, which pour together into the legendary Blackfoot River. The Blackfoot was the favorite fishing haunt of Norman and Paul Maclean and was the setting for Norman's *A River Runs Through It*.

"Paul and I fished a good many rivers," Maclean writes in his popular novella. "But when one of us referred to 'the big river' the other knew it was the Big Blackfoot. It isn't the biggest river we fished, but it is the most powerful and, per pound, so are its fish. It runs straight and hard—on a map or from an airplane it is almost a straight line running due west from its headwaters at Rogers Pass on the Continental Divide to Bonner, Montana, where it empties into the South Fork of the Clark Fork of the Columbia. It runs hard all the way.

"From its headwaters to its mouth it was manufactured by glaciers. The first sixty-five miles of it are smashed against the southern wall of its valley by glaciers that moved in from the north, scarifying the earth; its lower twenty-five miles were made overnight when the great glacial lake covering northwestern Montana and northern Idaho broke its ice dam and spread the remains of Montana and Idaho mountains over hundreds of miles of the plains of eastern Washington. It was the biggest flood in the world for which there is geological evidence; it was so vast a geological event that the mind of man could only conceive of it but could not prove it until photographs could be taken from earth satellites."

Running parallel, and always negotiating for space with the Blackfoot, modern man traverses the state on U.S. Highway 200. Power and phone lines also share the sometimes narrow mountain corridor. There's no rail line, unusual for major mountain valleys. But early rail entrepreneurs found little potential here, and James Hill's Northern Pacific drove the golden spike of its transcontinental railroad some thirty miles southwest of Lincoln, as the crow flies, at Gold Creek in 1883.

Even though it wasn't a natural for a rail town, Lincoln was a good town site, a high mountain valley at 4,540 feet above sea level, with enough room to grow if settlers were willing to carve a homestead and a lifestyle out of mature stands of lodgepole and ponderosa pine.

Today, U.S. Highway 200 stretches taut as a mason's string through

Lincoln, acting as an adopted-by-necessity main street. Roadside traffic signs warn truckers and travelers anxious to negotiate the eighty-nine miles east to Great Falls or seventy-eight miles west to Missoula that they better slow to 30 mph. The only sign of a traffic signal is a single yellow flashing light, gently swaying in the mountain breezes above the Stemple Pass Road intersection.

If you walk through Lincoln east to west, it's 1,742 paces from Sucker Creek Road, where a Ponderosa Snow Warriors Club sign welcomes snowmobilers, to Leepers Ponderosa Motel with its small cabins scattered in the pines. Slowing from the east, weary travelers looking for a shaded campsite on a hot summer night find Hooper Park with its softball fields, horseshoe pits, and picnic and camping spots. Hooper also is one of the places people gather to watch Montana's premier sled dog race, the 300-mile Race to the Sky held each February. Just west of Hooper, and shaded by the same cover of stately pines, is the Lincoln Community Library, a brown lap-sided rectangular building with a green metal roof that often catches rafts of pine needles in its valleys.

Across the street, a yellow sign in front of the Lincoln Public School salutes student activities, especially those of high schoolers. Lincoln people are especially proud of their school, built after a devastating fire destroyed the town's seven-room elementary school in 1978. Out of the ashes of the disaster came a reward for the community. Before the fire, Lincoln's group of twenty or so teens was bused daily some forty miles northeast along often slick two-lane highways to attend Augusta High School or even southeast to Helena. The new Lincoln School included high school classrooms.

From the school, Lincoln's business district stretches west, without any of the congestion of a big city strip, to Garland's Town & Country Store, a false-fronted mecca for hunters and fishers; Lambkin's of Lincoln, a popular bar and grill; the Community Hall, where a sign promises bingo every Friday at 7:30 P.M.; The Lost Woodsman Coffee House Cafe and Gallery, with its espresso bar and carved totem pole out front; the chalet-styled United States Post Office; the Three Bears Motel; the Lincoln-log Masonic Lodge; and the Wheel Inn Bar. Also along the way there's a scattering of bars, restaurants, offices, and a hardware store. Lincoln folks can find almost every staple they need in town, but most do their serious shopping in nearby (by Montana standards) Great Falls, Missoula or Helena.

Lincoln's population varies. It's about 1,200 most times of the year, yet in the fall, deer, elk and bear hunters can add significantly to that tally. The same is true in the depth of winter when the Ponderosa Snow Warriors attract visiting snowmobilers to town for weekend poker runs at the Sucker Creek Clubhouse. Snowfall that can exceed two hundred annual inches helps snowmobilers and cross-country skiers forget the frequent, double-digit-below-zero temperatures. Nearby at Rogers Pass, the lowest temperature ever recorded in the continental United States—69.7° below zero Fahrenheit—was posted.

In the surrounding mountain gulches can be found several hundred independent folks who call Lincoln home. They mushroom the registered voting base to 730, but they rarely come to town, unless supplies are needed from Garland's or the Blackfoot Market, or if they want to check out a book at the library.

While he wasn't a registered voter, Ted Kaczynski was one of those loosely connected Lincolnites. His independent lifestyle and his dreams of living off the land certainly melded here better than they would in most places in the United States. Lincoln was a place where he actually could follow a nineteenth-century lifestyle. It was a place where people left him alone.

Most were friendly, but respected his need for privacy and kept their distance. Some avoided him as they would a tramp—and he gladly avoided them—occasionally crossing the street so they wouldn't have to say hello to the bearded, often unkempt and sometimes smelly recluse. He adapted, almost like a crooked Douglas-fir along a high-country stream bottom. A little different, but there's no reason to cut it down, no reason to damage it, because it never really takes too much water or gets in the way. Then again, you can't really look under the bark to see what vital juices flow and pulse through the cambium layer.

People ask how Ted could live in Lincoln almost twenty-five years and never be suspected of being one of the most cunning and notorious criminals in this country's history.

The answer is quite simple: The Upper Blackfoot Valley was a perfect place for Ted to blend into the landscape. Then it became a perfect hideout. He'd probably still be here today plotting his acts of terrorism, constructing and testing his deadly bombs if his brother, David, hadn't linked notes from a 1971 essay written in Lincoln to sections of the Unabomber Manifesto.

Changes
in McClellan Gulch

When Betty and I were married in a simple ceremony on November 19, 1981, in Coeur d'Alene, Idaho, it put a subtle damper on my membership in Ted's fraternal order of single mountain men.

I wasn't aware at the time it would strain our friendship, at least from his perspective. Who would think the sincere bonding of two human spirits would be threatening to one of their friends?

During the first decade Ted and I knew each other, we had a steady and somewhat predictable relationship.

I dated several different women during the 1970s, but still maintained a single lifestyle much like Ted's.

We talked and saw each other more before Betty and I were married and she moved into our McClellan Gulch home. In the old days, Ted and I were the only ones hiking, hunting, and exploring in my gulch. Then suddenly here was Betty, petite, but an athletic Lincoln native who also loved outdoor activities, and maybe more importantly, here was her dog, Jigger.

Jigger was a once-intimidating 120-pound male black Labrador retriever who soon became protective of his new home. While we were away working Jigger would lie on the lawn or the porch and guard his domain.

Betty was usually the first one home each day, around 3 P.M., since her work day started at 7 A.M. Jigger would be waiting patiently and then he'd jump up and run out to greet her. He took his watchdog job seriously, and even though he was good natured and loved to chase sticks, he was on guard for intruders and quickly sounded the alarm.

Jigger's and Ted's first encounter while Betty and I were away working must have startled them equally, because they immediately established a mutual dislike. Jigger had no way of knowing Ted had permission to be in the gulch, and Ted didn't realize this was now Jigger's home. The dog loved everyone except Ted, who provoked an immediate growl and a flash of sharp yellowish teeth. Jigger didn't pretend to hide his feelings; neither did Ted.

Ted had made it apparent the first time we talked about Betty and her dog that something had changed. The mention of the two mustered little comment. Instead of warm congratulations, there seemed to be resentment toward us and animosity for my new wife, later confirmed in the way Ted treated her.

He continued to catch rides and I'd weld his bike as needed in my Lincoln shop, but it gradually became apparent Ted didn't want to talk to me or accept a ride when Betty was along.

At first the strange behavior was discounted as just another manifestation of a "Teddism": If I met him when I was alone he felt comfortable, and if anyone else was around he wouldn't speak other than to exchange his usual succinct on-the-street greeting.

But Betty never even got a simple "hello," other than during one unavoidable encounter with her in the gulch when he was forced to act friendly and talk to her. She thought his reticent behavior was curious in the beginning, but when it continued she was offended. She saw Ted often, but he always ignored her, even when they were standing together in the check-out line at the grocery store. Betty said it hurt her feelings that a friend of mine wouldn't extend the simplest effort to be nice to her.

His reaction was amazing because she was neither an outsider nor a city girl. She was right at home in the mountains, having spent her entire life in Lincoln.

After everything we've read since Ted's arrest about his reaction to his brother David's marriage, we now can see parallels with our own union. Ted's reactions seem strikingly similar, except for one important difference: Ted couldn't cut me off completely as he did his brother. He was forced to maintain a relationship so he wouldn't jeopardize his unlimited access to the safe haven and home away from home, McClellan Gulch. Whatever anger, disdain, or animosity he felt about my logging, road construction, and mining—or even my marriage—he kept hidden away. He needed to.

His reaction to Betty, though, caught me off guard. Not so much with Betty's dog, as plenty of people don't like dogs.

That first summer Betty and I were together, I was welding on a neighbor's truck in my Lincoln shop when Betty called crying, in great distress. She had driven up into the yard after work and Jigger hadn't run out to welcome her. She found him lying hurt on the grass, unable to get up.

I quickly locked up and headed for home. Ten minutes later I found Betty in tears, cradling Jigger's head and comforting her companion of fourteen years. Jigger was crying and groaning, tearing at our souls as only an animal in misery can do.

After a careful examination, I found someone had repeatedly stabbed and gouged the entire area under his tail, shredding his colon, hips, and rectal area. Whoever attacked Jigger may have tried to make the wounds look like he had been in a fight with a bear or coyote, but unmistakably the cuts were made with a very sharp knife or spear-like instrument. There were no other marks or wounds anywhere else on the dog.

Aging and suffering from hip dysplasia, Jigger wasn't very agile anymore. He must have been stalked, pursued, and stabbed many times while he tried to run feebly back to the safety of his porch.

The poor dog wouldn't live long enough to make it to the veterinarian's office in Helena, an hour away, so I went into the house and got my pistol. After we said our good-byes and shed plenty of tears, Betty went into the house and I put Jigger out of his misery. We took him up the gulch and buried him in a beautiful spot near some maple bushes. The household was especially quiet the rest of that evening.

Jigger had been successfully removed from the gulch by someone. But other dogs would take his place and he would not be the last canine of ours to meet a mysterious fate.

Several weeks later we bought a purebred female Alaskan malamute pup to raise, not only to fill the void left by Jigger's absence, but also to be our watch dog. We named the new arrival Tasha, and she soon felt right at home.

I told Ted about Tasha and the sad mystery of losing Jigger. Ted showed little compassion and didn't indicate he knew anything about the events.

After Tasha turned two, Betty still missed her Lab, so we adopted two, year-old male Labs from the Lewis and Clark Humane Society in Helena. Soon after, we purchased a purebred golden retriever pup and named him Boomer.

Our stable of dogs was growing, but why not? We both loved animals and they had plenty of room to roam. Tasha had a great time with the new retriever pup, and with Buddy and Lucky, the pound mates.

Not only did the dogs play outside every day, but it soon became impossible for anyone to enter the gulch without their giving ample notice, whether it was us arriving home from work, the UPS truck or the Montana Power Company meter reader driving up to the house, or Ted hiking through. Although Ted traveled a discreet route when entering the gulch, he was unable to enter from the west and walk along the steep hillside above the tailings, his usual path, without the dogs howling.

Four dogs just didn't seem like enough, so we bred Tasha with another malamute. After we sold all the litter except for a male and female, the McClellan Gulch canine forces reached six. So, by 1986, a dozen alert dog eyes were constantly watching every area of the lower gulch. Sneaking in would prove to be an exercise in futility.

When I explained to Ted the dogs wouldn't bother him and he was always welcome, he passed it off as no big deal. But it wasn't hard to imagine his frustration as the pack berated him for fifteen or twenty minutes every time he walked along the mountain trail above our home. We could sense the intense animosity he felt for our dogs, knowing they infringed on his privacy and anonymity.

It seemed like the dogs had a special bark for Ted, and they'd sound it often. Ted's movement through our area was apparent and became a usual topic of conversation. The dogs would run, barking madly, over to the west side of the stream and follow his scent along the trail.

I'd say to Betty, "Oh, that's just Ted going on up," and I'd walk out the door and whistle, calling them back—at least when we were home.

Betty and I didn't have any problems with our pets again until 1987, when strange incidents increased both in frequency and in evil.

After Betty's retirement in August 1986, she and all the dogs had fallen into a routine of walking up the gulch together. The daily pattern was fairly predictable. They'd either move up along the bottom and the small streamed for the first mile and then backtrack down on our road along the east bank, or switch and hike the routes in reverse.

As our Stemple Road neighborhood continued to become more populous—new cabins, more people—the dogs informed us of Ted's increased presence in our gulch. It was easy to understand why he wanted to avoid the noisy weekend gatherings at the cabins scattered in the small pockets of private land across from our gulch. No longer was he able to hike the area near his cabin without seeing four-wheelers and motorcyclists scooting across every trail and open spot that could be found.

In McClellan, only the dogs were an infringement on Ted's privacy.

One July day during 1987, when I arrived home from working in the woods Betty disgustedly told me the dogs had crossed the gulch and later returned covered with human excrement, smeared into their coats more deeply than if the animals had merely rolled in a find. She had just given them all a bath, and said there was little doubt it was from a human rather than a wild animal. It's easy to tell the difference.

Betty thought out-of-town campers were responsible for this mysterious event. That didn't make sense to me, especially when it happened again and again. Our dogs were irritating someone who had an incredible mean streak, and it was about to get worse.

In 1988, we took a short trip to Helena to shop. We arrived home to find one of our two-year-old malamutes lying in the yard, paralyzed. He died before we could do anything for him, a victim of poisoning.

During 1988, we acquired a breeding pair of Shar-Peis, the wrinkly dogs from China bred as guard or fighting dogs. The first litter of puppies arrived the following summer. By this time all our dogs, including the more aggressive Chinese breed, were well aware of Ted's habits and the places nearby he frequented, especially the trail above the old miners' ditch where he crossed into the gulch.

It wasn't long before the dogs had worn a trail resembling a cow-path on that hillside just from running back and forth between our house and the old ditch and then along the ditch sniffing for Ted.

We were forced to build kennels for the stud dogs because they were too aggressive, especially when a female would come into heat. But even when the males were locked up all day, the first thing they'd do when released would be to run up to the ditch to see if Ted had passed by that day. The young dogs learned from the older dogs and were quick to follow suit. If they caught his scent and followed it up the gulch, we knew he was around. If they ran up and right back we knew he hadn't passed that day or he was staying up in the mountains for a while.

I felt bad the dogs interrupted Ted's solitude, but there was little that could be done. He knew why we had them. The dogs weren't only for Betty's protection, but also to help keep us from being vandalized or robbed, as many of our neighbors had been. At the time, I didn't know my pity was ironic.

The dogs continued to be the targets of mean-spirited acts. Quite often, one or more of them would limp home with cuts or deep rock bruises.

And on occasion we'd have to scrub them thoroughly. Betty's theory of who was plastering them with feces still didn't make sense to me. I said to her: "Honey, I don't have an answer for you, but I have a hard time believing people would drive all the way to Lincoln just to make our lives miserable by smearing our dogs in that way."

The next two dogs to meet their demise were both Shar-Peis, a male and a female. The two incidents occurred within the same year. After refusing to eat, they both died the same day they became sick, also victims of poisoning.

One of the hardest losses for me to deal with was the death of our aging malamute, Tasha. Betty told me one summer afternoon Tasha had stopped eating and was lethargic. After going to the porch and checking her over, I told Betty there wasn't anything wrong with her and attributed her lack of movement to the heat.

Tasha's condition deteriorated rapidly. I tried to hand-feed her roast beef, but she refused even that and just lay on her side with lungs working heavily in the summer heat. I stayed with her and comforted her. She tried to twist her head back and lick herself, so I checked the area and found a small string of loose hide where she was trying to clean.

What I then saw made me extremely furious. There was a small-caliber bullet wound in the rectal area. It seemed someone had carefully shot Tasha with a .22 caliber sized bullet there, perhaps thinking the wound wouldn't be noticed. She was bleeding internally, intestines pierced by the slug, and she was dying a slow and agonizing death.

It was late that night before the wound was discovered, and I planned to take her to the vet first thing in the morning. But she didn't make it through the night.

Who was responsible? There were similarities between the ways Tasha and Jigger died. I blamed everyone possible except Ted. But I couldn't find motive or proof that any neighbor or weekender had committed these acts. Everybody loved Tasha, and after quizzing each person who either lived close or visited on weekends I didn't have an answer.

Our dog population held steady for a time after we lost Tasha. We didn't want to add any new pets until we could find out what was happening. A couple of years passed without any more losses. Everybody in the area, including Ted, knew how upset I was over Tasha and that I was keeping a close watch on our remaining pets. But with them running daily up to the ditch and along the trail they'd still have occasional run-ins with whoever was smearing them with human feces.

Then during the early 1990s we lost four more dogs, all poisoned.

In the spring of 1996 all the gruesome dog incidents stopped. Since that time we've never had any of our dogs plastered with human waste nor have we had any injured and die from strange wounds or poison.

The heavily used dog trail that was so prominent leading up to the old miners' ditch has now begun to grow over, barely noticeable. Our dogs have lost interest in running up there anymore.

One summer day a few months after Ted's arrest in 1996, neighbor Butch Gehring and I talked about our dogs while out hiking together. He said one of his dogs got violently ill, but he managed to get it to the vet for treatment in time. The vet examined the dog, took blood samples, and discovered it had been poisoned with strychnine. Even though the dog's life was saved, its immune system was destroyed and up until its death it was never the same.

As we talked about symptoms and how many of our dogs had died, I realized their deaths must have been caused by the same poison.

Then something clicked in my mind, jarring loose a detail I hadn't thought of for at least fifteen years. There was a small bag of strychnine-laced oats I brought home from a farm where I had done a lot of welding years ago. Strychnine wasn't illegal at the time and there were many pack rats nesting in my equipment and chewing up and destroying fan belts, wiring, and hoses, so I placed a small dish of poisoned oats in each machine that fall.

Other things took priority and I didn't plant more of the poison. But a year or two later I went to the old van where the oats were stored, away from the house, and they were gone.

I had removed the oats from their canvas bag because it was rotting, and then poured them into a plastic bottle and capped it securely. I didn't want to spill any for fear squirrels or birds might eat them and be killed.

I remember writing in bold letters on a piece of paper, "Poison— Strychnine Oats," and taping it to the outside of the container.

FROM FBI INVENTORY
L-9—Black pepper can containing several metal pieces
and a plastic bottle labelled "Strychnine Oats"

It had been so long since I had even thought of those oats. As Butch listened to the story, I shuddered to think how easy it would have been for someone to prepare a lethal cocktail or a deadly snack of meat and oats to feed to an unsuspecting dog.

Things were starting to make sense. Some answers were surfacing in the wake of Ted's arrest. I still wondered how anyone could be so totally and remorselessly cruel.

The Lincoln Mysteries

Eighteen thousand pounds of Cat diesel power pulled a half-dozen eighty-foot lodgepole pine logs with a winch across the forest floor. It was early afternoon in a heavily timbered area just west of 6,376-foot Stemple Pass, and one of Montana's major environmental controversies was being played out under the watchful eyes of Ted Kaczynski. Ted, perched across the way on Windy Point, seemed extremely interested in what was going on, watching the equipment and my crew hard at work.

He had arrived about 10 A.M. and sat quietly in the trees as the 475-horsepower diesel came to life with a deep-throated roar and a cloud of black smoke. At full throttle it generated enough power to move a small house off its foundation and then crush it under its twenty-inch-wide steel tracks.

It's not a gentle machine, but this wasn't gentle work.

Montanans have struggled for decades over how best to manage their public land and its resources. Should the mature trees be harvested, milled, and cut into lumber, and then used to build homes in Helena, Billings, and all points east and west? Should this huge storehouse of natural resources provide wood to the rest of the world? To some, the price of harvesting is too great. To them logging crews can disrupt the natural scheme of things—everything from habitat to watershed—cutting roads and entire forests, leaving mountainside scars that last a generation while the trees regenerate. To them, wilderness and protected areas managed for recreation preserve this land for future generations. To others, the future is now and the forest is a renewable resource. Logging provides important jobs and materials needed by people throughout the country. They say logging isn't nearly as damaging as the natural cycles of fires, winds, and floods.

That's an oversimplification of an often passionate conflict. But on this particular day any dissatisfaction about my logging job had long ago been settled during public hearings conducted by the Forest Service, which had solicited and approved bids on the work at hand.

It was 1985 and I had successfully bid on the very large Forest Service contract to log 4 million board feet of timber and build more than six miles of specified roads into a virtually roadless area near Stemple Pass just a few miles from my house.

It was just one of the major changes taking place in the Stemple area around Ted and me at the time.

I was excited to secure a contract for work so close to home, a job that would last at least four years. Meanwhile, my friend, and Ted's neighbor, Butch Gehring, had purchased a sawmill and set it up just a few hundred yards from Ted's cabin. I bought a sawmill a year earlier and had been cutting lumber for an addition at my home. My mill was a small one-man outfit; Butch's was more of a production-size mill he planned to operate full time.

One day not long after Butch had his mill up and running, he heard a different sound coming from the Allis-Chalmers diesel engine, which had been in excellent running order. He immediately shut down and tried to figure out what was causing the strange noise.

He was startled and angry to find that a white, heavy, sandy material had been poured into the fuel system. He could feel the sharp grit in the diesel fuel as he rubbed it between his finger and thumb.

Later, as we had a long talk about what had happened, he described the material and said he was thankful the engine hadn't been destroyed. He asked what I thought it might be; he was sure it wasn't sugar.

I told him that I'd bet anything it was white crystalline barite. I immediately thought of barite when Butch described the sand as being very dense and heavy and that it resembled sugar, but was coarser.

Barite is uncommon around Lincoln and I told him I know of only one place where it can be found—in my gulch.

White barite sand has settled to bedrock along with black sand and garnet sand we usually see when looking for gold. Barite is easily mistaken for quartz except for the obvious weight difference. With a high specific gravity, its heft feels more like lead than quartz. Its density and heaviness allow low-grade barite to be used as drilling mud for oil rigs, because it will travel downward easily. Higher grades are used in manufacturing paint and glass. If ground up and introduced into an engine, the results would be disastrous.

Butch was furious, and we talked about who might have done it. Right away he suspected Ted. Butch said he and Ted didn't always see eye to eye, and he felt Ted had a motive, and he didn't trust Ted.

I agreed there was motive—Ted surely didn't like having the sawmill and its noise so close to home he could hear it all day—but I still didn't think he would sabotage the mill. As a neighbor he wouldn't want to draw attention to himself.

I reminded Butch that if the substance was ground barite, it would greatly limit the number of potential suspects because the person would have to know where to find it and also have a good knowledge of minerals. Unfortunately, Butch had thrown the gritty fuel away, so nothing more could be done.

As the summer passed, I completed the first two miles of road on my job and started logging. I added several new pieces of equipment to my fleet: a Kenworth truck with a lowboy trailer, another crawler dozer to skid logs, and a motor grader to blade roads.

I started to see Ted frequently while I was working. I'd see him sitting on an opposite hill scrutinizing our work, but I didn't think much of it, assuming he was curious about the various kinds of equipment and how it was used in logging.

I even gave him a ride home from the job site one afternoon and he didn't say anything derogatory. At one time I had considered offering Ted a job, but I remembered Butch telling me how Ted had walked off the job after just a few hours. Since I was working on a tight contract schedule I decided not to risk it, not wanting to break in a new man who might quit right away. Also, I didn't want to chance a potential work conflict with Ted that might even strain our friendship.

The changing of the seasons is subtle in a lodgepole forest without deciduous reminders. As summer turns to fall, first you'll notice the shorter days, then how quickly the high mountain air chills as the sun sets. I planned to log all winter, so when I heard the first bull elk bugling in search of mates, I knew it was about time to prepare my line skidding machine with the large drums spooled with hundreds of feet of steel cable. I'd attach the cable to logs and skid them uphill across the snow to a landing where they could be loaded and hauled to the sawmill.

I saw Ted much less during the winter months that year, but he'd still show up once in a while to watch our work. That winter I completed the first three logging units within the first mile of road built the previous summer. Each logging unit contained about 200,000 board feet of lumber, enough raw material to build a small subdivision.

Spring was especially welcome since my crew and I had worked many days in the -10° F. and -20° range; other days were so much colder we weren't able to work at all. It was a winter of heavy snow, making it difficult to keep the roads open. After the spring thaw in 1986 I went back to road building and completed the first three- to four-mile stretch. Then I moved my equipment to the next site to begin building the last road required by the agreement, a three-mile jaunt into a roadless area virtually next to the Continental Divide Trail.

That summer another local Forest Service contract was awarded and it included a short, one-mile road to be built between my road and the top of Stemple Pass. I had declined to bid on this much smaller job, knowing I already had my hands full with nearly 3 million board feet yet to log on both roads.

After that contract was awarded, the successful bidders asked me to help with their road construction. Since things were moving pretty smoothly on my job, I consented and did all of the road grading for them.

Gates were installed on all of these roads, per contract requirement, and I was glad, considering all the recent acts of vandalism in the Stemple area. So far I had been lucky, with only one incident where people cut firewood out of my log decks, ruining the lengths and costing me about $1,000. It could have been much worse.

I was thankful none of my machines had been hit, especially after learning that a state-owned motor grader parked near Lincoln had been badly damaged. Its hydraulic hoses had been chopped up and its windows and gauges had been broken, along with other damage.

As lucky as I felt, I began to wonder who would be next and hoped it wouldn't be me. I didn't have to wait long to find out.

Actually, I had been feeling much safer since we were working more than a mile from the main Stemple Road. Far behind my locked gate, we were totally out of sight.

Then one morning while I was working on the upper road, a crew member who had been skidding below with one of my Cats drove up in his pickup. He stepped out and approached with a stern look on his face. As he neared, a large lump stuck in the pit of my stomach and a sick feeling came over me.

He said I needed to come down to the Cat to check it out. It had lost engine oil pressure and he was lucky to get the machine back to the road.

The first thing I noticed at the Cat was some equipment was missing, including shovels, a fire extinguisher, and other fire suppression tools required on every machine. My operator said the items had been gone when he came to work.

Surely, whoever took the equipment had tampered with the engine. My apprehension turned to extreme anger and I swore I would break every bone in the body of whoever was responsible. All I had to do was catch him.

The engine had been nearly destroyed; the rods, crankshaft, and most other moving parts were ruined. When I finished repairing the Cat, the parts bill exceeded $13,000, and if that wasn't enough, the down time cost me even more.

This was the work of someone who knew the Cat was back there. My confidence in having my equipment parked out of sight, far off the main road and behind a locked gate, had been misplaced. The site had made it more private for the criminal to accomplish his dirty work.

What was sobering and frightening was that the person was becoming even craftier. My operator informed me he had checked his machine carefully as always. I knew he had; he'd been working for me for some time and we had a routine we followed before start-up.

While overhauling the engine, I examined it carefully and discovered the perpetrator had cleverly poured an abrasive down the dipstick hole, thus bypassing all protective filters. The abrasive, upon close scrutiny, appeared to be a fine, heavy, white sand.

I remembered Butch's episode the year before. Instead of answers, this only prompted more questions. I still couldn't put things together since I was thinking the material used had to be coming from somewhere else, somewhere far away.

But was it? Or was I just too blind to see what was becoming more and more obvious? It couldn't be Ted, the friend I totally trusted?

Lincoln, usually a peaceful mountain community, first started to develop a much darker edge during the second half of the 1970s. No one could really explain the curious and often dangerous events, but some strange new force was in the air.

My first brush with the unexplained had occurred in 1975. My younger sister, Anne, and I planned a camping trip for just the two of us prior to her marriage that year. I took her to one of my favorite camping spots about a mile up McClellan Gulch to spend her last weekend as a single young woman. We felt it would be a perfect opportunity to talk about her life, and for me, as her older brother, to give her the best advice I could about her future.

We took along my dog Jo-Jo, a four-year-old black Lab cross. I set up our tent late Friday afternoon on a flat spot just above a firepit surrounded by a circle of rocks. I had built it several years earlier and used it frequently.

As the early-summer afternoon turned to evening, I gathered wood for our campfire. After cooking a supper of steak, fried potatoes, and camp beans, I stoked the fire and banked it to last well into the evening.

The bed of coals, now deepening, glowed a dark ruby red and flickered in the night air. Nights in the mountains can be quite cool even during the summer. We moved closer to the fire as we talked. Jo-Jo lay nearby with his head resting on his paws.

Suddenly without warning a rifle shell exploded in the coals. First one, then another and another.

At the first loud report I screamed to my sister to lie flat on the ground so she wouldn't be hit by any shrapnel. I too hit the ground and both of us were protected by the rim of rocks around the firepit. Jo-Jo ran to the tent and hid inside.

When the shells stopped exploding I carefully scattered the coals and doused the remains of the fire. Miraculously neither of us was injured.

It would be many years before I would understand why this incident occurred. The one thing I did know at the time was someone had deliberately placed live ammunition deep within the campfire bed, so that the rounds would explode the next time a hot fire was built.

But why? Was this an early warning to stay out of the upper areas of my gulch?

Aug. 7 (8?) [Kaczynski journal]
...I had tacked up the hide of the first deer I killed on this trip. I found the hide was gone. I don't know whether a bear or a coyote took it to eat, or whether a human found it. But I don't know what a human would be doing in such a steep, overgrown place, or what they would want with the hide. The possibility of a human going through there outside hunting season is disturbing. If that place is not secluded enough, what is?...

In summer of 1975, a small trailer sat near an old mine in Fields Gulch, a large area that lies just west of McClellan. Talk around Lincoln was that miners intended to reopen the adit of the Black Widow Mine and begin a new venture from the old workings. They successfully re-opened the portal, entered old drifts that hadn't caved in and then began to clear the caved-in portions of the tunnels.

The trailer that served as quarters for the men was parked a short distance away. After taking a few days off the men returned to find their portable dwelling completely trashed. Everything inside was broken and scattered about, and many items were missing. No one was ever caught.

Another mine was vandalized the following summer. The Gold Dollar only a quarter mile from my home had been worked off and on over the years, and I knew the men currently operating it and a small placer site nearby. When I stopped by to visit one day, one of the men asked if any of my machines had been tampered with recently. I replied that they were all okay. He said their compressor truck had been vandalized, and that someone had poured a lot of sugar into the tanks, and had done other damage. I promised to keep a sharp eye out from now on, and check their machines when they were away.

Not too long after that, another acquaintance told me that his truck, parked in the woods a couple miles from my house, had been sugared while the owner was away from the site. Later that fall, there was similar news from a few miles to the east, at Rochester Gulch.

Late one afternoon in 1975, I decided to walk along an old trail east of Rochester Gulch to the top of the mountain, circle around and then come out at an old mine on the other side. I had followed this trail plenty of times in the past, either on foot or on my motorcycle. I had seen other motorcycles in the area from time to time, but with the old access over Poorman Creek washed out, I hadn't ridden the trail since at least 1972.

More motorcycles had been in the area recently; you could hear the high-pitched buzz of their tightly wound engines echoing for miles in the mountain gulches. I was curious how they were getting up to the trail. After spotting what appeared to be a new trail next to the timber that cut from Stemple Road straight up the mountain to the edge of a grassy hill, I decided to check it out.

I crossed Poorman Creek near the old access road and hiked up to find where it seemed the new trail would intersect with the old one. I found the spot and could see there had been a lot of use; the trail was deeply rutted and eroded into the mountain. Once grass is killed by motorcycles going straight up a fifty- to sixty-degree slope, erosion is not far behind. Runoff from rain and snow washes out the straight and steep trail quickly and easily. The old access trail had never had that much traffic—very few people knew about it—and it followed a more contoured route.

Looking up the mountain, I was surprised to see that the new trail not only joined and crossed the old one, but then it cut a new path straight up the ridge. This new breed of mountain motorcyclist obviously wasn't going to waste any time following switchbacks or contours. Their method was quick and straight toward the top. Now I knew where all the cycles roaring past my house were headed. I decided to follow the new trail to its end.

I had always known that if a few trees were removed, a motorcyclist would be able to ride to the top of the mountain. Once on top he could ride miles across the ridges, east and west. Was this where the new trail would lead?

I climbed about a quarter of a mile to a very steep, almost vertical slope where the trail went through the trees just before it broke out into a large, grassy meadow on the mountainside.

Walking through the trees I pulled up short. A half-pace away was a small but strong wire stretched across the trail at neck height in a most dangerous place. The wire was oxidized, not shiny, and was nearly invisible. Pulled taut, it was firmly wrapped around a tree on each side of the trail in a location where the path narrowed amid numerous trees. The deadly trap was strategically placed where it would be impossible to steer a bike quickly clear, even if the rider saw the wire. The steep section of trail added to the danger. Powering uphill, a rider would build speed to make it to the grassy meadow; going down would be disastrous as well, since it would be almost impossible to stop the quickening pace of a cycle. The wire was capable of lopping a rider's head cleanly off.

I promptly removed the wire from across the path, twisting it together and wrapping it around one of the trees. Still amazed, I cut my hike short and headed back, shaking my head at yet one more mystery in the woods. What would happen next?

The next strange event unfolded in the spring of 1977 or '78 about two miles up McClellan, where there was a small piece of property that was one of the last private holdings in the gulch I hadn't been able to buy. Since I owned the rest of the land, I kept the gulch blocked off to prevent theft or vandalism to some of the old structures left from the early mining days.

One afternoon, when I returned from town, I saw that my cable across the road had been removed and fresh vehicle tracks led up through the timber. I followed them and found a man who had hauled a small crawler tractor with a dozer to excavate and mine along the streambed.

He said he was working with a Missoula man who had purchased the property, which puzzled me because the owner was from Helena and I had been trying for several years to work out a purchase agreement with him.

I didn't argue, deciding to let him stay while I found out what was happening.

Soon he erected a small, twelve-foot-square tin-covered cabin, and started to build a road above and beyond a historic section of the gulch. I visited the site one day while he was gone and felt sick about the damage I saw. Trees were pushed over with root balls sticking into the air, and the logs were covered with dirt. No drainage dips were constructed in the road so the runoff was cutting a channel into the road bed causing severe erosion and siltation of the stream. I felt especially bad because I had tried to be friendly and the man had promised he would treat the fragile mountain terrain with due respect. I had even ridden up earlier with him to help unload a small chest freezer to use as a cooler for his food.

I called the Helena man who owned the property. He was furious, and the whole property dispute headed for court.

Several days later the miner arrived, went up the gulch where he had been working, and promptly returned.

He was angry. Someone had trashed his cabin, vandalized his small bulldozer and stolen its magneto so the dozer wouldn't run. He wanted to know why I would let people go through my locked gate and up the gulch.

I assured him I hadn't and I was unaware of the vandalism. I went on to say that whoever damaged his cabin and dozer must have hiked in over the ridge from the south.

He reported the incident to the Lincoln deputy sheriff and I promised I would keep a closer watch and would check his things from time to time when he was away. I didn't want any of my things vandalized either, and hoped the culprit would be caught.

It was a real mystery. But the mining activity and the man's careless damage to the environment were obviously bothering someone other than me.

The property dispute was settled quickly in court. The original owner, the Helena man I knew, prevailed. Soon after the court decision the miner obtained a replacement magneto, repaired his tractor and hauled it home.

He was gone, but his mess remained. A few years later I was able to buy the piece of property, but the mystery still was unsolved.

After that incident had come more and more acts of vandalism and theft. These weren't the acts of teen pranksters in the woods for a weekend kegger. For example, an area rancher found one of his cows shot dead, but neither hide nor flesh taken. A few years after that, area electric power went off one late summer day. That in itself isn't unusual in the Lincoln area, but a few days later I happened to have coffee with a Montana Power Company employee. He mentioned that someone had chopped down a power pole, as if felling a tree, and that caused the outage.

The only common denominator: everything was happening in the Stemple Pass area. The only lull in the activity lasted from summer 1978 into 1979, which at the time I didn't relate to Ted's absence from the area.

One late summer afternoon around 1979 the local deputy pulled up into my yard, got out of his pickup, and began to question me about who might have been involved in an incident he was investigating.

Somebody had demolished an almost new and very nice cabin less than a half mile from Ted's home place.

The deputy, whom I knew well, mentioned a couple of possible suspects. Then he brought up Ted Kaczynski's name.

"I don't know who would have done this, but I know it wouldn't be Ted," was my immediate response.

At that time I really believed that statement. I hadn't yet seen the side of Ted that was capable of such a crime.

We discussed other possibilities. Then I asked him, "Why would Ted be considered a suspect anyway?"

The cabin owner said he and his kids had ridden their snowmobiles up around Ted's cabin and it had made him extremely upset, the deputy replied. I explained the family had done the same thing to me and I was upset at the time. I caught them and told them to leave.

I argued that if I had the same motive and didn't do it, that fact alone wasn't enough to pin it on Ted. The deputy agreed.

We then talked about the cabin and the destruction. I was shocked. The person responsible had devastated the cabin and machines parked there and most everything was beyond salvaging. An ax had been used to hack a hole in the cabin to gain access. After entering, he then had chopped up the kitchen cabinets and emptied the contents of the refrigerator and thrown them across the floor. Mustard, glue, bleach, and other substances were squirted and poured all over the carpet, furnishings, and bedding. Even the phones were smashed and phone lines were pulled out of the walls.

Virtually no spot inside the cabin was left unscathed. All this anger was then directed outside where, after growing tired of unscrewing fasteners around the window of the small mobile home used as a camper, he finally smashed the glass to get inside, and ravaged the camper.

The snowmobiles and motorcycles were next. After chopping and slashing the machines, he pounded and broke their engines with an ax. Some things, like a chain saw, just disappeared without a trace.

It was a scene of destruction. Whoever was responsible was a very angry and vengeful person. At the time, I heard the damage was estimated to be from $20,000 to $25,000.

I couldn't believe it. Who could have committed this terrible act? I had successfully helped get Ted off the hook, and even if there was a question of his guilt or innocence at the time, nothing could be proven. Whoever was responsible would get away with the crime for the time being.

Every area around my home was hit. It seemed as though nobody was safe.

During the late summer of 1980, a family moved onto some property that had just been logged. They set up a camp and had a couple of motorcycles for mountain transportation. The family left for several days. When they returned they found the motorcycles a sorry sight. All the tires were slashed, the bikes were smashed up and sugar had been poured into the gas tanks. The motorcycles were nearly destroyed.

Earlier that same summer a potentially deadly episode occurred in my gulch. I had just moved a 16-by-26-foot cabin to a spot near the trailer where I was living.

I had started a low-scale logging operation, selectively removing some large Douglas-firs that were beginning to die or fall over undercut banks heavily eroded by a recent spring flood. I skidded the logs down to a landing near the Stemple Road where I decked and prepared them for hauling to the Champion International peeler mill west at Bonner, Montana.

I left for the weekend on a welding job near Toston, some ninety miles to the southeast. I had hooked up power to the new cabin since I planned to fix it up and build an addition at some point. I accidentally left a light on when I left, and I never locked the doors since the building was tucked away in brush and trees, and was barely visible from the main road.

When I returned I was alarmed to find a bullet hole through the wall just below a window near the light that had been left on. The bullet had ripped through the wall at an angle about chest high and then hit a protruding corner next to a mirror. If it had pierced the corner it would have shattered the mirror.

I followed the path of the bullet by line of sight and determined this was no accident. The trajectory led to a cluster of trees and brush on the hill behind the cabin far from the road where someone could have discharged a gun.

Ted was the last one I ever would have suspected. Looking back I now realize how easy it would have been for him to think it was a person other than me in the new cabin. I never had explained to anyone what I was doing. Logs piled along the road, a new cabin moved in, the circumstances could be interpreted as signs that some loggers had moved into the gulch and were beginning operations. Ted knew the cabin and tractor I later found out he vandalized a couple of years earlier didn't belong to me so it would be easy for him to think this situation was similar.

What topped everything else about the shooting was that whoever fired the gun then entered the cabin to see if he'd hit anyone. When he found the building empty he dug the slug out of the wall, removing any possibility of identifying it. Later I explained to Ted about the logging activity and that I was trying to save the timber before it toppled into the stream, and told him about my new cabin. He looked surprised and concerned. Although I said I was finished logging here and never wanted to take more trees out of McClellan Gulch other than ones I was losing, I never mentioned anything to him about the bullet hole in the wall.

After a short lull, a period of relative calm, Lincoln area residents were surprised to learn of a cowardly shooting.

Two men had started a small placer mining operation in a streambed that flowed into a drainage some fifteen miles southeast of where we live on Stemple. After clearing the timber and brush from the site they set up a gold washing plant and equipment used for excavation and moving placer material.

Things went smoothly for a while. Then one afternoon one of the men was perched atop the washing plant. He bent over to inspect the machine while it was operating.

A shot rang out. The man fell over, hit in the back. Miraculously he survived, but after a long, slow, and painful recovery, he remains partially crippled to this day.

The gun used in the shooting was a 30-30, determined by ballistic tests on the slug that was recovered. Once again, there was plenty of speculation, but nobody was ever charged; the shooter remained at large. Now the stakes were even higher; a man's life and health entered into the equation.

From the early 1980s on, rumors surfaced from time to time that someone was shooting at aircraft: helicopters, planes, even passenger jets far overhead. Nobody knew where the shots were coming from. At the time I questioned the validity of the reports because I didn't believe anyone around Lincoln could do such a thing. There was much I hadn't learned yet.

With the summer of 1981 came another bid for a logging job. During the 1970s and 1980s, logging and road construction contracts on National Forest land were on the upswing. The emphasis on increased timber production directed from the federal officials in Washington, D.C., trickled all the way down to the Lincoln District. It was a period of high productivity, with local foresters' jobs graded critically by the board foot—the amount of lumber the public forests were yielding.

This dictum ended in 1990, when the Forest Service philosophy swung in favor of multiple use and the recreational value of public land.

During the period of high timber productivity many millions of board feet were logged around Lincoln, and dozens of forest roads built, with one new local road system alone stretching into twenty miles of otherwise inaccessible mountain terrain.

One of the logging jobs contracted during the summer of 1981 was located east of Dalton Mountain Road, less than ten miles by road and five by air from where Ted and I lived. Rubber-tired skidders were being used on the job. There also was new road construction into a mountain area some wanted to remain roadless. The contractor had crawler tractors for building roads, a log loader and other equipment at the site. The job had run smoothly for a year, until the late summer of 1982.

Leaving the site one day after work, the crew felt all the equipment was secure behind a locked Forest Service gate, ready to go when they returned.

Since it was the end of August, fire season was in full swing, with fire lookouts constantly scanning the forests for any early sign of trouble.

When a call came in that smoke was sighted near the timber sale area, a fire crew was immediately dispatched. A short time later they pulled their fire trucks into the area and found the log loader had been set on fire, and that flames then spread to one of the rubber-tired skidders, leaving charred smoking hulks of steel. Flames also had spread to nearby trees and several acres were burned. Fire fighters were able to extinguish the blaze quickly before it built into a dangerous forest fire.

Investigators determined damage to the machinery alone was $75,000. The stakes were escalating. Whoever was responsible had turned from vandalism to total destruction of local cabins and expensive equipment.

How could this criminal be caught with no one knowing where or when he would strike next? He was clever; no clues were left behind.

In late May 1985, a little thing happened that meant nothing at the time but would take on great significance a dozen years later, when I learned of Ted's travels as the Unabomber. I drove my 1975 light blue Blazer out of my shop after overhauling its automatic transmission. The vehicle was new to me. I had purchased it in Butte, making a good deal because of the transmission problems. It would be a fine vehicle for my wife to drive during the winter, since she was still working at the time and usually left home before the snowplows got out to clear the road.

After locking my shop doors, I headed for home, eager to let Betty try out the vehicle. I crossed the Stemple Bridge over the Blackfoot River, passed the square concrete-block sheriff's office just outside of Lincoln, and headed south along the gravel road. About a quarter of

August 25, 1982:

Top: Incinerated rubber-tired log skidder.

Center: In addition to destroying logging equipment, the vandal nearly caused a major forest fire.

Bottom: The log loader was a total loss.

92

a mile ahead I spotted someone holding his thumb out, walking backward and trying to hitchhike. As I got closer it looked like Ted. I was taken aback as I had never seen him hitchhike, before or since.

He had no way of knowing I was driving the Blazer, since neither he nor anyone else in Lincoln had yet seen it. I pulled up alongside and he promptly hopped in, appearing relieved it was me and not some stranger.

I knew he had just arrived in Lincoln from town, probably Missoula, because of his dress and the time of day. He was wearing his "going to town clothes," a little nicer than his everyday garb, and he carried his small nylon travel pack, not the larger green canvas army pack he always carried while hiking around Lincoln. Also, it was just a few minutes after the bus arrives daily from Missoula, a little after 3:15 P.M.

Ted barely acknowledged what I was saying, even with me talking non-stop about my new vehicle. He seemed even deeper in thought than usual, anxious and nervous, and he was in a hurry. As I pulled up to his mailbox where I often dropped him off, he barely uttered his usual thanks or good-bye as he promptly got out, and immediately headed toward his cabin. Even though it puzzled me at the time, I passed it off, eager to get to home to present the Blazer to Betty.

In the fall of 1986 I started to spend all my spare time cutting lumber at my sawmill so I could expand our home. I was building an atrium where I could install a large spa, raise exotic birds and grow tropical plants. One day after milling lumber all morning I walked toward the house to get something for lunch, leaving my pickup over by the sawmill, where it was invisible from Stemple Road.

As I approached the door I heard Ted coming up the road, his bike chain squeaking as usual, the pace quickening as he neared my driveway. Betty was at work and with my pickup out of sight, it appeared nobody was home.

All at once our dogs, which were loose and lying on the lawn, ran out toward Ted barking wildly. The sight, sound or smell of him still drove the dogs mad. What happened next stunned me.

Ted let fly with a string of extreme profanities that floored me. I had never even heard him cuss before.

Was Ted so controlled he could display total calm on the outside while he was seething with anger inside? I was learning new things about my friend. Looking back, even when considering such odd behavior, there was nothing concrete so I remained in a state of denial, refusing to consider him guilty of anything.

After that incident, though, I knew Ted had a great deal of hidden anger. What I didn't know was how he had handled it and would in the future. How well did I really know Ted? I talked to Betty about the incident and I was surprised to find out she had heard the same vicious profanities several times.

When I asked why she hadn't told me, she replied, "Why? I don't know Ted and whether it's out of character for him or not." I saw her point. Ted never waved to her or took a ride with me when she was present, so why would she recognize his "usual" behavior?

Early in the fall of 1986, my wife came home from her job permanently. She was having great difficulty with her back, lifting sixty-pound tubs of meat all day long on a cement floor at the High Country Beef Jerky plant, where she had been employed for more than seven years.

Her constant presence at home would change things in the gulch for Ted, giving him less privacy around the access area near Stemple Road. I continued to use every spare moment away from my logging activities to work on my new building addition, finishing the roof, and buttoning things up for winter.

The first heavy winter storms came relatively late even though there were periods of -30° temperatures and some light snowfall during January.

One cold, -20° morning Betty took the dogs for their daily walk. I remained home from the logging job to do some paperwork. I knew the job site, 1,500 feet higher in elevation, would be at least 10° colder, too frigid even to start the machines, so I called the crew and told them to stay home. It was the end of February 1987.

Before I ever got a good start on my work, Betty unexpectedly returned home, very startled, and said Ted was up the gulch about a mile, camping at the old miner's cabin. The dogs smelled him first, barked and ran at him. It frightened her. She held the dogs as well as she could while Ted talked to her, asking what day it was, what time it was, and how cold it was, his usual line of questions when he had been out for a while. He then told her he had been hiking on the ridge above, got caught in a storm, looked down into the gulch and spotted

94

the cabin. He moved down off the ridge into the bottom of the gulch and took shelter in the cabin, spending the night. He had a campfire burning right outside the cabin door.

Betty and I were amazed. It was the first time Ted had ever spoken to her. He obviously had been caught in a compromising position. Even though Ted knew he was always welcome in the gulch, he had reacted strangely. I really began to wonder what he was doing up there in such cold weather.

But it wasn't even the weather that made me the most suspicious. It was what he had said to her that alarmed me. He had lied. You can't see the cabin from the ridge. In fact, it can't be seen until you get within a hundred yards of it. And he had known for years the cabin was there; he'd hiked by it hundreds of times.

Troubled, I decided to hike up the gulch and talk to Ted. I promptly left the house, but by the time I got to the cabin Ted was gone. He had doused his fire with snow and left, following his usual trail along the other side of the gulch. I followed his tracks until they crossed Stemple Road. He had been walking down as I was going up. He must have seen me.

Still not satisfied I decided to trace his trail back up the mountain and find which ridge above the cabin he had come down. Returning to the cabin, I then followed his tracks upward through the trees. It was like he was returning from somewhere and he had been working his way back to his home cabin.

I knew he wasn't out hunting. Betty had said he wasn't dressed warm enough for the cold weather. Also, he hadn't cooked any meat on his campfire, only canned food.

I continued backtracking his trail for more than three quarters of a mile, then the wind started to kick up and snow drifted into his tracks. I could have picked my way farther but it would be a lot of work and I wasn't really dressed for a long trek through cold snow. I dismissed the encounter, turned and headed back. I decided to ask Ted about it the next time I saw him, but I wondered if I would get a straight answer.

Little did I know how close I had come to finding his secret cabin that day; I had followed his tracks to within a quarter of a mile of its location on the mountainside before I turned back.

Just as other strange events had entered and then left my mind, this one was destined to follow the same path. No single event by itself meant too much. I still did not connect Ted to anything related to crime.

The spring of 1987 arrived; late snows and early rains kept the roads muddy, halting my logging work.

One afternoon while Betty and I were returning over Stemple Pass from a Helena shopping trip, we came upon Ted across from my logging operation at Windy Point, his bike parked at a wide spot on the road. We were surprised he had ridden all the way up there in the mud; he was about ten miles from home.

He was sitting on a grassy knob not far from his bicycle—the same spot where he had sat many times before—looking across to my logging units. I pulled over to visit with him. He was friendly, but seemed preoccupied. I mentioned he was a long way from home in very difficult riding conditions with the mud in places extremely soft and slippery. He agreed, but didn't elaborate.

The conversation didn't last long. After commenting to Ted about the beautiful day and that maybe spring was here to stay, we headed for home to put the groceries away.

I remarked to Betty that if Ted was just out for an early spring ride, why didn't he head west where it was lower and drier instead of up around my logging operation? I wondered why he was still so interested in that site after I'd worked there for two years already.

Summer arrived and with the addition of several more contracts my logging and road construction company was expanding and spreading out. This meant more employees, more responsibility and less time away from work.

I cherished my free time and I hiked as much as possible, by myself or with my wife, when I wasn't working on equipment. The leisure trips were mostly in and around my gulch, but I'd also hike into some of my favorite old mines in other gulches near home.

During that summer and fall, a placer mining operation opened in Sauerkraut Gulch, just a few miles west of Ted's place. I was hired to clear trees around the portion of creek to be mined. I didn't think of it at the time, but this mine meant that each direction but one from Ted's home cabin now was the site of major logging or mining work.

North, east, and west were no longer untouched wilderness. But to the south, McClellan Gulch still was.

Fall came, and along with it a curious pre–hunting-season invasion. It seems, at least to Lincoln people, National Guard helicopter pilots out of Helena log a lot of training exercises and flying time at the start of hunting season. The helicopters create a great deal of noise while flying low over the mountains, with the valleys acting as echo chambers, amplifying the "whop, whop, whop" of the rotors.

That fall was no exception. The helicopter activity seemed to increase with the late-October opening of deer and elk season. Locals knew the pilots weren't out just to spot game because it's illegal in Montana to fly and hunt on the same day, but it made for good conversation over morning coffee at Lambkin's. Even if the guardsmen were trying to take advantage of their time in the air, the extreme noise would surely scatter the game.

The noise was apparently seriously irritating a person around Lincoln. Rumors again circulated about somebody randomly shooting at the helicopters overhead. Was it true? I wasn't sure at the time. Others swore the guilty party was out there and remained at large.

As the 1980s wound down, acts of vandalism and occasional cabin break-ins continued. Some cabins were hit and nothing of value was taken; these acts of destruction seemed to be related more to the noise level of the receational forest activities of the people who used the cabins.

Another Forest Service contract was in the works, but to the southwest of us. I didn't bid on the sale because I had my hands full with three or four other contracts. Loggers from outside Lincoln were awarded the job. After they started up I heard their equipment was hit; skidding cables were cut and dirt was put into their machines' oil and diesel fuel. Luckily, one crew member noticed a machine had been tampered with, so all were checked quickly.

It's a time-consuming and costly job to repair cut cables, drain and clean oil and fuel systems, and replace all filters, but not nearly as expensive as major repairs or the downtime that follows.

The criminal acts were so scattered, times varied and methods were diverse enough that it seemed there had to be different people involved. But were there? Could one very crafty individual be responsible? Nobody ever listed all the events together and compared them for time, frequency, severity, and most of all motive.

The Stemple area is just one that has grown in recent years as a popular seasonal recreation spot. Rochester Gulch, just a few miles from my house, runs north and south just off the Stemple Pass Road. Straight south across the road is Prickly Gulch, also a north-south gulch.

Both are popular spots for cabins, mostly older and scattered, but there are a few newer ones as well, and some trailers and trailer spots where people park their rigs for the summer. There are probably a dozen or so places in Prickly Gulch and half that many in Rochester, nearly all close to Stemple Road. Nobody lives in any of these cabins year-round, but at times during the summer the area is very active as people enjoy outdoor activities. Some of them stay around until the winter snows fall.

These summer dwellings had become frequent targets for break-ins and vandalism because of the number of buildings and scarcity of people.

The last cabin to be hit was also the biggest and newest cabin in Prickly Gulch. One summer in the early '90s the people had a small gold-panning operation north of their cabin. They returned home after a time in the woods to find someone had destroyed the set-up. Things were missing, tools and equipment smashed, shovel, pick and ax handles broken, and the most remarkable of all, a large pick head was broken. Someone had pounded and beat on the head until it literally broke in two. As they searched the area trying to find clues, they discovered some of the missing items partially buried or hidden under old logs. Hatchets were broken or thrown away, but not until they had been used to destroy a wheelbarrow and other mining-related equipment. If all that wasn't enough, they went on to find that their cabin, too, hadn't escaped the vandal's wrath.

The method and potential motive were becoming clearer. Somewhere out there, an extremely angry person was set off, apparently by their mining activities.

About this same time, I started to think in earnest about not only all the destructive and potentially lethal activities, but also how drastically the country, especially the area around Ted and me, had changed.

Nearly a dozen new places had been built near Ted's cabin where only two or three existed when he arrived in Lincoln. Likewise, near me, almost twenty dwellings now exist where only four had stood prior to 1971.

Additional cabins mean more people, more dogs and pets, more motorcycles, snowmobiles, and four-wheelers, more cars, trucks, and machines of all types, and most of all, more noise. A flurry of Forest Service logging jobs during the '80s brought in more heavy equipment and workers. Cloistered privacy was a thing of the past.

Even though Ted had always spent most of his time out in the surrounding mountains, his time away from his home cabin increased as the years went by. He spent more and more of his time up my gulch, sometimes not coming down for days or even weeks.

I knew Ted had camping spots up McClellan, and I found a few I was certain were his. He had others outside McClellan that he also used in the earlier years. In about 1980, for example, while hiking a few miles northwest of the South Fork of Poorman Road, I came upon a small lean-to. It was in a thicket that consisted predominantly of wind-thrown lodgepole pine trees. The lean-to was constructed from a fallen pole with an olive drab green plastic rain poncho draped over it. Evidence of past fires could be seen near the front. The shelter was barely visible, and I found it by accident. The green plastic rain poncho looked familiar. But the camp looked like it had been deserted after some use; it probably wasn't nearly remote enough for Ted. Even though it wasn't far from Rochester Gulch, another of Ted's favorites, I believe he abandoned this camp because it was far too accessible by the hunter traffic that increased every fall.

Another spot Ted had used for shelter when caught out in a storm or late at night was a cave high at the head of Fields Gulch.

In the early '70s, while out hunting elk in that area, I had crossed mountain lion tracks of a mother and two kittens in the snow. I followed the tracks until they entered one of several natural caves in the area. I left the animals alone, and on the way down found another cave. It was a nice spot and would be a good location to take shelter during a blizzard.

Years passed and, while hiking again close to the area, heading for the top of the ridge to walk a portion of the old pack trail, I neared that second cave. Curious, I entered it and found some candles and canned food stashed inside.

Later that year a friend of mine discovered the cave and described what was inside. I had never told anyone it was there.

Even though the spot was remote I knew it was only a matter of time before word about the nice shelter would get around and it would be used by others.

To Ted, privacy was more than something to enjoy; he had to have it. Privacy was essential and even his outdoor hidden camping spots were being discovered one by one.

He still had one sure bet: my gulch. With me as the gatekeeper to thousands of solitary acres, my gulch was his one private haven—and he knew I would keep it so. He had permission to be there and could come and go, day or night, anytime he pleased. It seemed as though he couldn't find privacy enough anywhere else, including at his home cabin.

Another incident during the early 1990s was related to me by a friend who had ridden his motorcycle past Butch's sawmill and up an old logging skid trail near Ted's cabin.

Ted heard him ride by and raced out cursing and screaming at him. Ted's hair was long and wild; with no shirt on, he was covered with dirt, waving his arms wildly, severely admonishing my friend to leave and never return. Needless to say he made quite an impression on my friend, who said he would never ride up that way again.

A puzzling chain of events occurred at the first old cabin in my gulch, a mile south of home, where Betty had found Ted that cold February day in 1987. The cabin, built in the 1930s, was constructed of planed lumber and covered with heavy, black tar paper. Other than its slightly larger size of 13 by 15 feet, this cabin was nearly a carbon copy of Ted's home place, with a similar pitch to the roof, no eaves, the door on the same side, and three high windows. Even the stovepipe came through the roof in almost the exact location.

Like Ted's, this cabin never had electricity, running water or plumbing. Inside were a wood stove, low bedspring, table, and a food cabinet made from wood reinforced with angle iron and covered with sheet lead to prevent hungry mountain rodents from devouring its contents. Even though this cabin was close to my access trail up the gulch, the site is still very private.

The cabin, unoccupied since the early mining years, is even located in a spot similar to Ted's home cabin, close to a creek, and is set among conifers and deciduous trees in a small opening.

I knew Ted not only passed by it frequently while hiking around but also he used the cabin once in a while. I didn't care.

But something strange was going on that I couldn't quite pin down. Something was different. In retrospect, I believe the changes started during the late 1970s or early '80s when I first observed boards beginning to disappear from around the windows. Soon pieces of tar paper were vanishing from the outside of the cabin, exposing the lighter colored, unfaded wood beneath.

I dismissed the matter, blaming the wind and weather. Even though I wasn't in the habit of inspecting this old cabin, I did pay attention as things continued to disappear.

The interior of the walls had been sheeted with plywood and the glue holding the plies together had long since decomposed, leaving sheets of single plies still attached to the walls. These plies started to disappear too.

Again I thought the wind was to blame, but I wasn't sure; I really didn't have any other reason that made sense. The mystery deepened when I later noticed part of the food box missing; more than half of its angle iron and sheet lead were gone, and more tarpaper was missing from the back, which you wouldn't see unless you walked behind.

The next thing that disappeared was the bottom of one truss, a twelve-foot two-by-four that strapped the roof truss together. The two-by-four had been removed from one of the trusses near the back and wasn't readily noticeable.

My eyes had been drawn upward inside because I had at different times used this cabin to hang game while it aged before butchering. The blue-and-white nylon ropes I had always kept tied to one of these trusses to secure the game were gone as well.

Then rows of nails were missing from along the outside cabin base on the side away from the door and the back.

With my work heavy schedule, I once again was distracted and didn't try to satisfy my curiosity. "Out of sight, out of mind."

The cabin materials wouldn't be the only things to mysteriously disappear out of my gulch.

I finally completed my big Forest Service contract up near the top of Stemple Pass in 1990 after two extensions. I hated to see it end, a job that good so close to home. I had taken other contracts in between to prolong that job as long as possible. It is a real rarity to find logging and road construction jobs of that size just a few miles away from where you live. I had logged many millions of feet of timber all over the countryside, as far as sixty-five or seventy miles away.

As the job wound down and the machinery was hauled home, I left one line machine down near Poorman Creek to do some more mining. I removed the logging rigging, replaced it with a bucket and used it as a dragline to dig placer gravel.

I didn't get much mining done that fall since I had to haul equipment to another logging job about ten miles west of Lincoln. After spending the winter there I was pleased to find out that severe winds had toppled trees on my old contract area near the top of Stemple Pass. After being awarded a new contract for a small salvage logging sale, I gladly returned to the old work site for a couple of months.

Logging was starting to get tougher with the jobs not only fewer, but much farther away as well. I had decided years before I wouldn't take any jobs that were too distant. I didn't want to have to live in my camper. That situation might be okay, or it might even appeal to a single person, but not me. I was married and if I couldn't eat at my own table and sleep in my own bed every night, I didn't want the job. There was other work I could do.

My father-in-law and I were very close and had been friends even before I was married to his daughter. Having spent a great deal of time mining during his seventy-six years, Leonard was my partner on every mining venture until his death in 1992.

He enjoyed it as much as I did and even when we weren't mining together he was nearly always with me, going together to the woods almost on a daily basis. He is still, to this day, greatly missed.

When the high water dropped in the spring of 1991, we went down to the Northwest dragline that I had left near the creekside spot where we had worked some years before. We planned to do some more mining. This was one of my more secure machines, with all the cab's doors and windows equipped with locks.

As we approached the dragline I noticed that the door and window on the blind side, away from the road, had been severely cracked from being pried open. After unlocking the doors and entering the cab, I spotted a large rock lying on the floorboard.

A sick feeling came over me, much like the one I experienced a few years earlier. What would I find? It appeared as though someone had started to pound on the engine parts with the rock when apparently he quit and ran off, unable to finish the destruction. Perhaps a vehicle coming along the road startled him.

After a very close inspection I was grateful to find only broken windows, bent doors, and other minor damage.

We decided to haul the dragline home. It wasn't worth risking a whole machine just to do a little placer mining. The culprit had succeeded in shutting down our operation, as small as it was. It goes against my grain to give in, but I couldn't sit up there every day and night just to catch someone, especially since I didn't have a clue if or when he might return.

The winter of '92 passed slowly. Without my late father-in-law, working in the woods seemed hollow. The magic was gone without him to share the labor. For years I had dreamed of the day when I'd be able to quit logging and road construction and take only smaller jobs I could handle alone, allowing more time for the mining Leonard and I both enjoyed so much.

That spring I bought a screening plant and an additional conveyor to add gravel production to my businesses, since I would complete all the year's construction and logging contracts within a thirty-day period. The time was right to cut back on the heavy and intense mountain work. It had been good to me, but it was a hard life and had taken a toll on my health.

Betty and I spent many nights talking about our future before we decided I shouldn't take any more large logging and road construction contracts.

After I wrapped up my last logging job, I hauled the heavy equipment home for the last time, excited about starting a scaled-down life. I screened gravel for driveways, septic systems, erosion-control rip-rap, and other uses. Once again, I was able to do a little placer mining.

Ted continued to hike into my gulch on a regular basis but we spent less time talking, except for occasional greetings. I felt sorry for him because the peace and solitude he craved was almost impossible to find near his home cabin, where noise and development were escalating.

You could sense that frustration in his appearance alone, reflected in a slow but sure decline from the early '90s on. He started to look thin and unhealthy, and I could tell he spent little if any time cleaning himself. He presented an eerie figure, appearing more and more like the forest animals, except they spend considerable energy preening and grooming themselves.

In the summer of 1991, Robert Orr, manager of the Lincoln Telephone Company, and Betty's brother, told me about Ted's bitter complaints that the pay phones in town often "stole" his money. These pay phones were among the rare models that required you to dial the number before depositing the money, which was still only a dime. The instructions were clearly posted, but for some reason Ted just didn't get it, and continually had problems making calls. Finally he wrote a formal letter of grievance to the Montana State Commerce Department's Consumer Affairs Division.

Ted became even more withdrawn, quieter, almost lethargic, as if his life was winding down. This continued right up until I last spoke to him about a month before his arrest.

The longest conversations I had with Ted during 1993 took place at a couple of local yard sales, those small community melting pots where just about everyone digs through their neighbor's junk to discover some little treasure.

The first sale was held in late spring, May or June. My long-time neighbor, Roy Hall, had died. He had lived almost directly across from me along the Stemple Road since 1969. His widow, Leora, was preparing to sell the house and move closer to one of their sons in Oregon.

Betty and I were there talking to Leora and other neighbors when Ted walked across the lawn and into the garage, and started to study almost every item on the sale tables.

I tried to talk to him, but as usual he wouldn't say much with other people around. A few minutes later I saw him walk outside to look at

Theodore J. Kaczynski
HCR 30 Box 27
Lincoln MT 59639
July 9, 1991

Montana State Commerce Department
Consumer Affairs Unit
1424 9th Avenue
Helena MT 59601

RECEIVED
JUL 09 1991
CONSUMER AFFAIRS DIV.

Dear Sirs:

I have a complaint about the Lincoln Telephone Company of Lincoln, Montana. I do not know whether this is the right government agency to which to direct a complaint about a telephone company; if it is not, I would appreciate it very much if you would inform me what state or federal agency oversees the operation of telephone companies and receives complaints about such companies.

The problem is that some of the Lincoln Telephone Company's pay phones malfunction in such a way as to steal the caller's quarters. You put a quarter in and it gets jammed, or it doesn't register, and the coin release doesn't work, so that either you can't put the call through and your quarters are lost, or else the call does go through and you've put into the phone 25¢ or 50¢ more than the price of the call. This problem has persisted for several years.

Over the past few years I have repeatedly complained to the Lincoln Telephone Company about the condition of their pay phones; once in person at the company's office and several times over the phone to their operators. But the malfunctioning phones are still in place and are still robbing the public of quarters.

The worst offender is the phone at the corner of Highway 200 and Stemple Pass Road (phone number 362-9281). This phone has malfunctioned and stolen quarters from me more than 50% of the times I have tried to use it. (I still try to use it sometimes because it is the only pay phone I know of in Lincoln from which one can make a call with reasonable privacy.) The phone company knows that this phone consistently malfunctions and steals quarters, yet they neither repair it nor replace it. Thus they are consciously defrauding the public.

I have also had trouble, though only occasionally, with the phone on the outside wall of the Blackfoot Market in Lincoln (phone number 362-9291).

Clearly the phone company has an obligation either to replace defective pay phones, or to repair them effectively and permanently, or to remove them altogether.

Thank you very much for your attention to this problem.

Sincerely yours,

Theodore J. Kaczynski

Theodore J. Kaczynski

---

items in the yard so I followed and told him about some of the good buys I noticed.

Ted showed me a cast iron fry pan he found for two dollars, which made him quite proud. I agreed it was a steal for the price. He moved to a table where the family's old silverware lay in bundles, each containing about ten pieces for fifty cents.

As he looked through the silverplate I showed him some nice and much newer stainless steel flatware for the same money. He said he really preferred the old silverplate and bought several bundles.

I never would have thought of the silver again except for another yard sale encounter several weeks later in Lincoln. My wife, sister-in-law, and I stopped, and there was Ted again. Just the fact he was there didn't intrigue me, but what he bought—another big bundle of old silverplate—was mystifying. He must have carried off at least thirty spoons and other utensils. Why did he need it?

I wasn't able to come up with an answer from Ted. I just scratched my head, knowing there must be a logical reason for his purchases. One thing I did know, Ted wasn't entertaining large groups at dinner parties. Years later, I would learn that the Unabomber had a use for silverplate.

FROM FBI INVENTORY

MB157—One white plastic bag, containing one small, round, cardboard "Quaker Old Fashioned Oats" cannister, containing one aluminum foil envelope/pouch, containing "Flash Powder"; handwritten notations on top of cannister "Spoons" and "Ekp. [*sic;* experiment?] 220" (crossed through)

That summer it rained almost daily, making work difficult. Fall brought the nicest weather we had experienced for months, and I was finally able to start placer mining, working gravel with my large washing plant to separate the gold from the loose material. The water washes away lighter gravel and smaller stones, leaving behind concentrates of heavier materials and the gold.

I became involved in other projects so I left some of the concentrates in the plant until a later date when I could separate the finer gold, a time-consuming process, from the remaining gravel.

An early winter cold spell froze the material containing the gold in the sluice box of the washing plant. I'd have to wait until spring. That didn't really bother me because everything seemed secure behind my house and almost a mile from public access.

A long hard Montana winter followed, the first where I wasn't out plowing roads, logging, and trying to juggle contract work during the nicer days. Spring brought high water, which in turn slowed my return to gravel production as I waited for the swollen streams to flow back within their banks.

One morning as I checked my gravel equipment, getting it ready for spring work, Betty walked up the gulch and returned with surprising news. She said someone had managed to sneak up the gulch and steal the concentrates from our washing plant, taking gravel, gold, everything, leaving the box swept clean.

It was apparent my gulch wasn't invulnerable anymore, and after a close inspection I found many other items missing; I had no idea how long some of them had been gone.

From various storage sites, a mysterious combination of things had been stolen, including many with little value: yellow nylon ropes once used to tie up dogs; the top pipe of a collapsible plant-stand; four-inch aluminum vent pipe, two or three two-foot sections; an 8-by-12-foot blue tarp, various science magazines, including *Scientific American* and *Omni*; waterproof matches; a number of books, including a copy of *The Blaster's Handbook*; maps that had been stored in a pickup; food items from our camper; a length of aluminum irrigation pipe; ammunition cans; and many other smaller things.

I had been lax for many years. I didn't even lock my house doors when I was gone. It was time to change my habits.

Then I started to think about other missing objects and acts of vandalism that I had dismissed during the last twenty years. I remembered a pickup parked up Fields Gulch during the mid-'70s that was found with sugar in the gas tank; several snowmobiles and other vehicles that had suffered the same fate; hunting camps that had been torn up, the food stolen; and many other missing items that were reported to local deputies.

Lincoln always has seemed like a proving ground for sheriff's deputies, highway patrolmen, and other law enforcement officers. The turnover is high, with people transferring in and out quickly. This had to affect any continuing investigation into the Lincoln-area crimes. One officer would get a possible lead and then be transferred out, with his replacement left to start from the beginning.

In looking back, the same dilemma plagued the Unabom Task Force. Investigations that cover a long time-span, whether they are cases of vandalism or bombings, can be the toughest ones to crack because of personnel turnover, especially when the criminal proves to be exceptionally sly and, most of all, private.

Even though Ted and I didn't visit as much, he was always around in the gulch and I noticed changes in his habits. In the mid-1990s, he became careless in leaving obvious tracks in the gulch, crossing wherever convenient instead of walking off main trails and jumping the creeks in hidden spots. In the past, I knew he tried to hide the amount of time he spent there, but I always knew when he was there and I didn't care. Knowing how private he was I felt he was more comfortable that way, so I left it alone.

I saw and spoke to Ted for the last time during the winter of 1996, near the end of February, not much more than a month before his arrest. It wasn't far from where I had met him for the very first time.

He was out on his bike for a quick afternoon ride to get groceries during a short break in a long siege of bitter, snowy weather. I was on my way to Lincoln and saw his tracks heading toward town.

I picked up what I needed and on my way back spotted him about two and a half miles south of town. I pulled up alongside and asked if he wanted a ride.

Ted was friendly, but said he didn't have far to go and it would be too much trouble to unload his pack, put his bike into the truck and then reverse the process at his mailbox.

I said okay, and asked him how he had been. After he replied "okay," and "thanks," I drove away.

He was very thin and haggard. He was having a hard winter.

As I look back at our last meeting in the shadows of the mountains so important to both of us, even knowing his crimes, I can't help but have a sense of melancholy. His burdens must have been immense to be manifested with such violence.

Our first and last meetings weren't much different, even though almost twenty-five years separated them.

The Arrest

The winter of '96 was proving to be one of the toughest we'd seen in years. By early March, when the calendar promised spring wasn't far away, more than 200 inches of snow had fallen in McClellan Gulch. Seven miles to the northwest, downtown Lincoln looked like a Siberian village with nearly three feet on the level and head-high snowbanks beside many roads and sidewalks.

During a twenty-one-day stretch in January and February, the mercury in our thermometer, hanging just outside the front door on an aspen tree, never found the energy to climb above zero.

The only short break, when the sun momentarily poked through the gray, soupy cloud-cover that clung to the sides of the mountains surrounding the Upper Blackfoot Valley, came that late-February afternoon when I had seen Ted for the final time.

No wonder he looked so weary, considering he had spent such a severe winter in his primitive cabin with only a small wood-burning stove for heat. On many bitter nights that winter, when our wood stoves were burning red hot, I had wondered if Ted might be huddled in his root cellar to keep warm; at least there the temperature would be a constant 40°.

March wasn't providing us much of a break, and many days greeted me with snow, cold and wind as I traveled the Stemple Road to teach a full roster of piano students at my building in Lincoln, my repair shop for the prior twenty years.

During the fall of 1995, I had been inspired to clean out the 45-by-75-foot building and turn it into a music center. Using lumber cut at my one-man sawmill at home, I framed in a stage across the back of the building, then sheeted it with finish flooring. After remodeling some of the side rooms, there was still floor space for about 200 seats for recitals and performances. The seats were donated by Helena's Grandstreet Theatre after I helped reprogram the theatre's Roland keyboard and remove old carpet and the seats during a remodeling project.

I had been teaching a few students at home for many years and the remodeled building enabled me to handle additional students, much more conveniently and efficiently. Since I'm also a piano and organ tuner-technician, the center provided ample space to work on, rebuild, or refurbish several instruments at a time.

The building now was called "Lincoln Center for the Performing Arts"; I often joked this modest building was the "real" Lincoln Center because it was in the very center of Lincoln.

Teaching piano students has always been a labor of love, since the piano and music have been important in my life since my earliest recollections. I played trombone in the school band, and drums for a small musical group during my teens and twenties. I also sang, and one year was named best male vocalist in the Helena junior high school.

During a trip to Lincoln to teach a day of lessons, in late March, I saw a couple of shiny new vehicles pass by, heading up Stemple Road. They looked out of place. It wasn't that new vehicles were so strange, but they didn't belong to anyone living up there. It was the wrong time of year for hunting, and winter recreation was winding down. After hunting season, Stemple Pass road receives very little traffic, except during the times of peak winter activities, usually weekends and holidays, when snowmobilers and cross-country skiers love to traverse the wide trails and open parks along the Continental Divide. Many winter days we'll see only the snowplow, which keeps the pass open, the mailman, and maybe one or two other vehicles go by our home.

I just figured these outsiders were sightseers on a ride through the mountains.

I was somewhat anxious when I arrived at the center, since a snowstorm was moving in, so I got right to the task of teaching the five grade school children scheduled for that afternoon. When the last student of the day finished his lessons, I immediately locked up and headed home, trying to beat the storm.

After supper, while I was sitting in my favorite chair going over music for the next day's lessons, the phone rang. It was my good friend, Bobby Didriksen, with some intriguing news.

He said a stranger stopped at the library while he was there and asked the library worker questions about some of the old mines in the mountains around Lincoln.

Bobby was across the small room looking at a book when the librarian pointed at him, saying he could help since he was the president of the Upper Blackfoot Valley Historical Society, and he also had lived in Lincoln his entire life, more than seventy years.

The man introduced himself to Bobby as John Grayson, a mining enthusiast eager to learn about and photograph some of the old mines in the area. That in itself wasn't so unusual, but what piqued Bobby's interest was Grayson's claim that he was particularly curious about mines in the Stemple Pass area near Baldy Mountain and McClellan Gulch.

Bobby told him about a couple of old mines near Baldy, but said he might as well forget McClellan, going on to say he knew the man who owned McClellan Gulch well, that he was protective and didn't let anyone into the gulch. But Bobby promised to pass the message along and then I could decide whether to let Grayson look at my old mine sites.

John Grayson told Bobby he was staying at the Sportsman's Motel in Lincoln and could be reached there.

The whole story seemed plausible, and since I also sat on the historical society board of directors and was a mining enthusiast, it seemed appropriate to help him.

But one thing started to make me doubt his entire story. The man had told Bobby the company he worked for wasn't in a hurry so he had no time limit. Yet, why was a mining enthusiast running around Stemple this time of the year, and better yet, how could he photograph old mines with two to three feet of snow still on the ground?

Something wasn't right, and the more Bobby and I discussed the situation, the more perplexed we became. We agreed to keep our eyes and ears open and stay in close contact.

My suspicion deepened every day as more new vehicles kept showing up on Stemple Pass Road between my house and Lincoln. There were white Broncos, Blazers, and pickups, blue and green, some with Wyoming license plates, others with snowmobiles on trailers towed behind.

All the vehicles were brand new, shiny, and the more you saw them the more they stuck out like a sore thumb, quite a contrast to the older, muddy vehicles owned by the few people living up on Stemple. With no local car wash, Lincoln people couldn't drive a clean vehicle during the winter months even if they wanted to.

As the days passed, these vehicles were seen most often traveling along the two gravel roads that led toward Baldy.

Something was going on, and it definitely wasn't related to photographing old mines. Heading toward the Center to start piano lessons one afternoon, I bumped into a friend who owned the Sportsman's Motel and asked if he knew anything about the out-of-towners who were staying with him.

He said he wasn't supposed to say anything, but they were undercover FBI agents, posing as a man and a woman on their honeymoon, employed to document and photograph old mines.

I asked if he knew what they really were doing in Lincoln and told him of their interest in my gulch. He said he didn't know, and then asked me not to repeat a word. I agreed, but it was hard to concentrate as the first piano lesson started.

Another friend, who was bookkeeper for my logging and road construction company and also for the Lincoln Telephone Company, told me something strange was happening along an old driveway that led to a cabin near his house.

His son was the first to notice a couple of vehicles parked there that didn't belong, back in the trees below the seldom-used cabin less than 200 yards from Ted's place.

My friend said a federal agent familiar with the area, known to both of us, had stopped him just the day before and asked where Ted lived.

"You know where Ted lives," my friend replied. He thought it was a strange question, since the agent already knew where Ted's cabin was located.

So they were watching Ted. But why?

My first thought was game violations. Ted had poached deer, elk, grouse, and plenty of other wild birds and animals during the twenty-five years he had lived here.

A long-time Lincoln game warden who knew that Ted lived off the land had been determined to catch him in the act. One winter he thought he had Ted, with evidence in hand. The warden had been watching his movements and crossed fresh tracks, with a red blood trail alongside, leading through the snow down from Baldy toward Ted's home cabin. Hunting season wasn't open, so the warden followed the tracks to Ted's, ready to make the arrest. When he arrived at the cabin he was dismayed to find Ted had killed nothing more than a porcupine for supper and it was nailed to a tree near his door.

But surely it must be something more than poaching. So many federal and FBI agents wouldn't be called in simply to catch Ted for shooting a grouse or a deer out of season.

The next clue came from a good friend involved with the investigation. He wasn't at liberty to talk, but he said it had something to do with Ted sending threatening letters through the mail. that's what he'd been told. He could say no more and admonished me to keep everything to myself.

I was getting a little nervous. If the FBI was observing Ted, they might be watching me as well. After all, they had showed an early interest in McClellan Gulch. I was worried about how they might interpret my efforts to keep people out of the gulch. They might think there was something to hide. Maybe I was being investigated as an accomplice, but I had no clue what the crime might be.

Then on the morning of April 3, 1996, all hell broke loose.

As I drove into town there was lots of early traffic, all new vehicles that were either moving slowly along the Stemple Road or were pulled off on the double-tracked side roads that lead off into the mountains.

I had barely unlocked the door to my building to continue the remodeling work when the telephone started to ring off the wall. The first caller stunned me. A reporter asking questions about the infamous Unabomber wanted to know if he had been arrested near Lincoln.

It couldn't be possible, but it had to be Ted he was asking about. They must have the wrong man. My friend and neighbor, the man I had helped and who had virtually lived in my backyard all these years, could not be the Unabomber. When asked who the suspect was, I wouldn't give them Ted's name. They said they would find out anyway, but I still refused.

The day of Ted's arrest is still a blur in my mind as I, along with the rest of the nation, tried to sort out the details. It was amazing how quickly the media arrived, droves of reporters from all over the country. All flights into Helena and Missoula were booked solid. All of the motels were full within the first few hours after the news broke.

BULLETIN COMPILED FROM FIRST-DAY NEWS REPORTS
UNABOMBER SUSPECT ARRESTED
IN MONTANA MOUNTAIN SHACK

HELENA, MT. (April 3, 1996)—A bearded and unkempt mountain hermit in tattered clothing, believed to be the notorious Unabomber, was led into an FBI office in downtown Helena early Wednesday night with little ceremony.

Handcuffed and escorted by two FBI agents, 53-year-old Theodore Kaczynski was questioned for several hours in a third floor FBI office in the Arcade Building before he was taken to nearby Lewis and Clark County Jail at 10:30 P.M. and locked away. About 50 reporters and onlookers, who had been poised there for hours, watched as he was brought to the jail in a white Ford Bronco.

Kaczynski, a former Berkeley math professor and brilliant student who graduated from Harvard University at 20, purchased land south of Lincoln with his brother, David as co-signer, in 1971. It was his brother who found a 1971 essay at the family home in the Chicago suburb of Lombard written by Kaczynski. His brother became suspicious after comparing it to the 35,000-word manifesto, unnamed federal officials said. The work was jointly published last September by *The New York Times* and the *Washington Post*, and distributed in the *Post*.

Kaczynski's neighbors in the mountain community of Lincoln, located about 50 miles northeast of Helena, said Kaczynski was reclusive and didn't seem to bother anyone. "He was a quiet little guy," said Butch Gehring, who runs a sawmill near Kaczynski's one-room cabin.

The Unabomber has been responsible for a deadly 18-year bombing spree in which three were killed and 23 others were injured. Many of his homemade bombs were mailed, others were left for unsuspecting victims in parking lots. His manifesto was published after he promised he would stop planting deadly bombs. His last victim was a timber industry executive who was killed in Sacramento, Calif. when he opened a mail bomb on April 24, 1995.

FBI agents with a search warrant surrounded Kaczynski's one-room mountain cabin earlier in the day. They lured Kaczynski outside where he was detained after a short scuffle.

Kaczynski was not placed under formal arrest Wednesday. Officials said he will make an initial appearance in Helena Federal Court Thursday or Friday.

Word traveled quickly. Reporters discovered almost immediately Ted and I had been neighbors and friends since he built his cabin.

I spent the better part of the morning after Ted's arrest talking to Bobby Didriksen, but I was pursued everywhere I went.

By afternoon, when it was time to start teaching piano lessons, reporters, cameramen, and technicians were lined up across the Lincoln Center's stage. At times, more than twenty patiently waited for a comment. Eventually they were all told the same thing: I couldn't and wouldn't talk until the investigation was complete.

Getting through the piano lessons was almost impossible, with the telephone perpetually ringing and more reporters showing up by the minute. Most were friendly, but some were rude and they were promptly sent away. The answering machines at the Center and at home filled to capacity and, by nightfall of the second day, April 4, five satellite up-link trucks were parked in Lincoln—a sight never seen before here and probably never to be seen again.

News people called from all over the world—England, Japan, France, Australia, Canada.

Most people in Lincoln were overwhelmed. Some chased cameras, wanting to be interviewed. Others made fools of themselves talking about someone they didn't know, confusing Ted with other people who lived out in the hills.

I'll never forget an interview on television the first day, when a prominent Lincoln man stood on camera and said, "You are saying Ted is about 5'9" or 5'10"? Ted is nowhere near that tall." He quickly proved he didn't know Ted or what Ted looked like. Many townspeople lost their credibility early on, victims of the press, caught up in all the hype. It was like a feeding frenzy of sharks in shallow water loaded with prey.

Some reporters used various ploys to get people to talk, everything from flattery about on-camera appearance to putting a conclusion into their mouths and then waiting for a nod of affirmation so they could broadcast the supposed response.

There also were many professional journalists who showed restraint and patience, knowing that when all the hype subsided there would be an important story to tell. I made many friends among that group, promising to talk when the time was right. Some tried to convince me now was the perfect time to tell my story. I even received phone calls from higher-profile newspeople, like Tom Brokaw, attempting to get an immediate interview.

I was more anxious to spend time with the federal agents to make sure they didn't implicate me in any way with the Unabom events. It was easy to see why agents would be looking for an accomplice. Not only did the manifesto speak in the plural when it mentioned responsibility for the acts of terrorism, but it also seemed improbable Ted could plot and carry out the complex acts without money and a car.

The more you dwell on the unknown, the easier it is to become more paranoid. I started to think about my two manual typewriters, which had been stored for years in an old camper up the gulch. What would the agents think if they knew? I didn't know if Ted had used them or not, but he certainly had the opportunity. Would agents want to check my typewriters to see if they were used to type the manifesto?

Since I also worked in water-well installation, I had literally truck loads of different-sized pipes that could have been employed in the pipebombs, sitting close to the campers where things were stored. It wasn't long before I started to worry about the dynamite that had been so essential for many years in road construction and mining, knowing it was stored near the other things.

Sleep was impossible. Even though I wasn't guilty of anything, what did the agents think?

My paranoia increased as I considered the implications. It was important to talk to the federal investigation team soon. It became imperative to arrange a meeting, but I still hoped they would come to me first. I didn't want to appear guilty.

Later, as I worked with FBI agents searching the gulch for Ted's camps and caches, they confirmed that early on I had been a suspect and was thoroughly investigated.

But at the time, I explained my concerns to Butch Gehring, knowing he had spent time with the FBI. He recommended I keep tight-lipped about the typewriters and other materials that might appear incriminating, at least for a while longer until they were sure Ted had acted alone. Even though Butch knew I wasn't guilty of any crime, this was a high profile case. The agents were out for blood.

My meeting with the agents would come soon enough, but even knowing I would eventually be cleared, it was impossible not to be obsessed with the fact that I had unwittingly helped provide not only sanctuary, knowledge and instruction, but also the materials needed to wage an eighteen-year reign of terror. The scrap piles, not only at my Lincoln shop, but also the larger ones behind the house up the gulch, included every type of metal, electrical wiring, switch, and any other part needed to construct a bomb; plus the construction and testing of bombs could have been carried out in the complete privacy of my gulch. Ted knew these items in my salvage piles couldn't be traced. He even had easy access to arc and acetylene welders, drill presses, files, grinders, and every other tool. He could borrow anything and I likely wouldn't miss it because of the sheer volume of materials and tools located there.

I also felt great sympathy for the unsuspecting victims and their families, picked at random, who had met their fate at the hand of the mad bomber.

My wife comforted me often, saying, "There's no way you could have known."

What she said was true, but the haunting feeling will never leave me completely.

The Investigation Begins

Three days had passed since Ted's arrest with absolutely no peace to be found at home or at the Lincoln Center when I taught piano. I finally cancelled lessons for a while, at least until things quieted down. The way it was going, that wouldn't be anytime soon.

Reporters dogged me everywhere I went. It didn't take any of them long to figure out what my pickup looked like, so even if they saw me traveling up or down Stemple Road they would whip a U-turn and follow me to my destination. I tried to be courteous and talk to each one, but I still stood firm and didn't divulge any information.

In Helena, Ted was being held in the Lewis and Clark County jail's 8-by-10-foot protective custody cell with a bulletproof window through which the jailers could watch him twenty-four hours a day. The constant observation, even in his most private moments, was a far cry from the solitude of his mountain cabin.

As the Easter weekend neared and temperatures reached into the upper sixties, the long bitter winter was finally coming to a close. Ted was finally warm, but in a hard jail cell where he certainly wouldn't enjoy the many spring smells of the forest.

As he was escorted across the asphalt lot and led into Helena's Federal Building and U.S. District Court on April 4, television cameras followed his every move. In homes across the country, his face filled television screens; the world got its first chance to study the Unabomber suspect. As I watched him on television, surrounded by federal agents and a crushing throng of media people, I could see the same look of confidence on his face that I had grown to know so well. His hair and beard had been slightly cropped and cleaned, surely a concession for his first court appearance, but his head was held high and his eyes were calm, showing neither fear nor intimidation. On a couple of occasions he even seemed to flash an arrogant sneer. It reminded me of times when I had seen Ted convey a disdain for everyday people in Lincoln.

Meanwhile, defense and prosecuting attorneys around the country were discussing what a difficult case this would be to prove in court, and information about the first bits of solid evidence linking Ted to the mail bombings and the manifesto was being leaked to the media.

On April 5, various news agencies reported two manual typewriters were taken from Kaczynski's cabin and that one of them was probably used to type his letters and the manifesto. An unnamed federal agent in Washington, D.C., told the Associated Press, "It looks like the manifesto and the letters from the Unabomber were typed on" one of the machines.

In Helena's federal court an affidavit was filed with information about other items found in the cabin: three-ring binders containing writings and sketches; hand-written notes describing chemical compounds that could be used in explosives; pipes of various types and sizes; containers of chemicals; papers and logs of experiments; a cylindrical package that appeared to be a partially completed pipe bomb; books on electrical circuitry; and tools. Much more from the cabin would be logged and then entered into evidence, but the search was slow and methodical because of the fear of booby traps, another unnamed agent said.

Members of the local and national press were relentless, talking to anyone who seemed to have a shred of information about Kaczynski. A drop of knowledge soon attracted a torrent of media attention. For many people in Lincoln, merely remembering a chance meeting with the now infamous suspect was worth a front page story or an interview on the nightly news. Just listening to media questions and carefully going over and logging each name and telephone number left on my answering machines at home and the Center seemed to be taking all my time.

By the afternoon of April 6, I was still very nervous about my potential involvement and that I hadn't yet been contacted by any of the investigators. Lincoln residents knew that besides FBI agents, postal inspectors, and Bureau of Alcohol, Tobacco and Firearms agents were in town. I was anxious to meet with authorities, and still hoped they would come to me before I had to make the arrangements to meet them. But the tension and stress were becoming almost unbearable.

Then about 1 P.M. a good friend called, local postmaster Don Pearson, whom I had known since he moved to Lincoln in March of 1990. Even though it was Saturday, everyone involved in the case was working extra hours.

Don asked me if it was a good time to visit, and wondered if he and two postal investigators could stop by.

I was at the Center trying to catch up on some work neglected and set aside during those first chaotic days, but I eagerly said yes and told him to bring the agents.

I hung up with a sense of relief: finally, a chance to talk with investigators on the case. Maybe I could find out if they felt I was involved.

While waiting for Don and the postal investigators, it was natural to mull things over and grow more nervous by the minute, wondering how the interview would go and what questions they might ask. I was sure of one thing: I wanted to be conservative in any responses and not volunteer too much information until I felt in the clear. The motive wasn't to withhold information or impede the investigation, but to keep things as simple as possible and not offer too many details until a level of trust was established.

It wasn't long before a vehicle pulled up out front. My pickup was hidden behind the telephone company office across the street so I wouldn't be disturbed. Don knew that, so it had to be them.

As the men showed their credentials, Don introduced them as Paul Wilhelmus and Tom Berthiawme.

We shook hands and sat down at a large table located just a few feet from where Ted and I had visited in the past. The whole scene struck me as surreal, sitting there where I often had talked with Ted, now getting ready to talk with federal agents about Ted and the past twenty-five years.

Both men were not only pleasant, but even friendly, putting me more at ease. As they prepared to begin the questioning, Paul, the senior of the two, asked if Don's presence during the interview might make me uncomfortable.

I replied that Don didn't make me nervous, and he certainly could stay; we often sat next to each other in church and I trusted him to hear anything that was said.

Don stayed and as the interview started he appeared to be more nervous than me. His hands and head shook continuously. His face was red. It looked like he might have a heart attack. I had never seen him like that before or since. I emphathized with Don's reaction, having such a high-profile, mail-related case unfolding in his postal jurisdiction.

As Tom and Paul took out tablets and pens for note taking, Paul talked about the purpose of the interview. It seemed odd that with all the high-tech recording and taping equipment available they would take notes by hand.

The small talk seemed to ease the tension, but not on Don's part. He appeared nervous throughout the entire three- to four-hour discussion. It was hard on him, but it was nice he stayed. I kept telling myself everything would be okay, and I was sure Don had already put in a good word for me.

With my mind focused on taking it slowly until we developed a trust, they proceeded with the questioning. I didn't feel pressed to tell them everything because there would be time later to provide more details.

Their areas of interest soon became clear. First they asked about Ted's clothing and packs he carried, specifically hooded sweatshirts and any eyewear, as in the Unabomber composite sketch. They wanted to know, too, whether Ted discussed his feelings about technology and the environment—"Did he have radical environmental views?"

They probed my connection with Ted and what kinds of favors I might have done for him, from giving rides locally or to Helena or Missoula, and asked whether I'd ever mailed a package for him. Had I lent him any tools? Had he borrowed a drill press or a welder? They wanted to know whether I watched Ted all the time when he visited the shop, or whether he could have taken anything from the workbenches. What kinds of materials were in the shop scrap piles?

A few questions focused on Ted's travels, whether he told me about them or whether I had noticed his absence at any time. Finally, they pursued what Ted had said about his background: home, education, previous employment, the topics he never had raised.

After the questioning, both Tom and Paul thanked me. So did Don, who finally looked more relaxed as he said he'd like to come up and visit sometime soon. I suggested to Paul that they should return at a later date because there was more to share, including dates, times, and other information that could be relevant.

As they collected their notebooks, Tom and Paul acted satisfied, like they understood Ted a little better. I felt relieved and fairly confident a major hurdle had been cleared and we had opened up a line of communication.

During the first week of the investigation misleading and false stories about Ted abounded in newspapers and on television. It seemed everybody, even people who had just moved to Lincoln, had a Ted story. We also got a good taste of the competitive nature of the news media and it had left many of us with sour feelings. It seemed reporters and producers tried to promise each of us more than anyone else could, all for the sake of the most sensational story possible.

I started to think that if anything accurate was going to come out, it would have to come from me or one of the few other people who knew Ted.

I had been approached by many media people. Among them was Rhonda Schwartz, a producer for ABC who worked on shows like *20/20* and *Turning Point*. She asked me to do an interview for *20/20* and I finally agreed, wanting to talk about Ted and the case on a credible news program instead of a tabloid type show.

On Tuesday, April 16, we taped at the Center and at home for the *20/20* show to be aired on Friday, April 19. The title of the show, which caught me by surprise when it aired, was "The Man Who Knew Him Best."

Even though a few liberties were taken in the editing process to make the information a little more sensational, overall ABC deserved high marks and I felt fortunate with the results, especially after seeing some of the tabloid show pieces.

But it still made me happy I had shared only less relevant facts, holding back the most sensitive and important information until the case developed.

In the early weeks after Ted's arrest, leaks from unnamed law enforcement sources were still priming the media pump almost daily.

Among other things, it was reported investigators had discovered and defused a live bomb at the cabin. It also was widely reported the original copy of the manifesto was found in Ted's cabin, along with the letter about publishing the manifesto that was sent to *The New York Times.*

On April 15 in Helena, defense attorney Michael Donahoe went before U.S. District Court Judge Charles Lovell to argue the "lethal media blitz" had "poisoned" the pool of potential grand jurors nationwide and asked that the charge be dismissed. In his motion, Donahoe argued most of the evidence reported about the case had come from anonymous federal sources. Later that week Kaczynski, sporting a new haircut and trimmed beard, appeared before Lovell, who called the leaks regrettable. But the judge denied the motion to dismiss the charge Ted was being held on—possessing bomb components found in his cabin. He still hadn't been charged with any of the Unabom crimes.

The legal tugging and maneuvering was in full swing and as the case developed, it would almost require a contortionist to track it during the two years before the final plea bargaining in Sacramento.

In Lincoln, as April matured, members of the media were still everywhere. The opportunities for interviews and trips for shows abounded. My original intent was to do only the one interview with *20/20.* But that ended up backfiring because soon I was confronted with statements like, "You talked to ABC, why not us?"

Respected journalists from NBC, CBS, CNN, and many other news gathering groups continued to contact me. They were all told the same thing: there was much more to tell when the time was right.

"When might that be?" they'd ask.

"I don't have any idea," I'd respond.

That was true. There was no way of knowing what might unfold during the weeks and months leading up to Ted's trial.

Tug of War

The complexities of Ted Kaczynski's mind will never be fully understood. The calm and polite outward image of a mountain hermit, shattered occasionally by outbursts of uncontrolled anger, hid the calculating energy of a master gamesman, capable of plotting the most intricate moves and schemes. His mind was as sophisticated as his appearance was unkempt.

Kaczynski must have been thinking non-stop during that first month in Lewis and Clark County Jail. What he was plotting was unknown, even to his court-appointed defense team. They, too, were pawns to move and sacrifice in his plan. All could and would be surrendered to save him from the death penalty.

On the outside world, members of the media were still puzzled. How could anyone live in a small community for almost half his life, some twenty-five years, in total secrecy? It didn't make sense; someone in Lincoln had to know more than he or she was saying.

Yet all the probing questions led reporters to the same shallow mine shafts where others had dug for stories before them. Journalists know those interviews too well: As they unfold, the information sounds interesting and there's a confident feeling that finally a good story has been told. But with the actual notes and a deadline at hand, the words ring hollow. Nothing new has really been said.

But the media weren't ready to give up. There was still a huge gap in Ted's story—missing details from half a lifetime in Lincoln. The number of local people who might help fill in the details could be counted on one hand. The journalists who were still dogging the story had cut them away from the herd, but they weren't talking.

At the end of April a producer from Toronto, Canada called and wanted me to do a program called *Sunday Morning Live*. I liked the show's format as she described it, and also the fact it aired outside the United States.

I told her some areas would be off limits and she said that was okay. She said she had seen the *20/20* piece, which was "very moving," and she was more interested in focusing on Ted and me, our relationship and how we lived, instead of things relating to the bombings.

I'm never that eager to travel but the trip provided a welcome break. Tickets were sent and at 7:05 A.M. on Saturday, May 4, I boarded a Delta 727 headed to Salt Lake City, where I'd catch a flight to Toronto.

Sunday morning the interview went well. The correspondent seemed to ask questions I felt comfortable answering. The weekend passed quickly. By 10:35 A.M. Monday, I was headed back to Lincoln.

A few days later the producer called and said the show had a huge and positive response from viewers all across Canada. We discussed doing another interview at a later date.

By May the media were finally starting to disperse. Phone calls were still frequent, but now mostly from out-of-state journalists and producers of documentaries interested in more detailed broadcasts and magazine articles.

Any relief, however slight, was welcome. The town had been in the grips of the Unabomber obsession for more than a month.

But then on Thursday, May 9, a prankster called in a bomb threat at Lincoln School. Classes were dismissed at mid-day while authorities searched the school. Nothing was found, but people in Lincoln were reminded that Ted's negative legacy had a slow fuse and could go off anytime.

I tried to get back to some sort of routine, but it just wasn't possible. There were too many questions in my mind. The investigation, I was soon to find out, was really just beginning.

FBI agents were still camped out near Ted's cabin, and it was during this period the area of their search broadened considerably, extending into the rugged mountainous terrain in the Stemple area surrounding my home and Ted's cabin.

And it was about this time a perplexing string of events started.

Monday, June 17, arrived and with it came a phone call from Betsy Anderson, Mike Donahoe's partner on Ted's Helena defense team.

She said she wanted to set up an interview for the following day. We agreed to meet at the Lincoln Center right after the lunch hour.

She said she was working from a very short list of names Ted had given her of the people who knew him best, and that my name was at the top of the list.

The way the evidence was rapidly stacking up against him, I knew his defense would be a long, uphill battle, and thought the outcome looked dim. I disliked being in the position of having to say things that might incriminate him further.

With everything I knew, coupled with the physical evidence obtained from Ted's cabin by the FBI, I began to realize he must be guilty.

At one point, I had told investigators they must have the wrong man, but when they replied they had the original manifesto, the typewriter it was written on, and not only triggering switches for bombs but a completed device, I became convinced. Such physical evidence is hard to refute.

How would Ted defend himself? The interview with the defense team might satisfy my curiosity.

Betsy Anderson and paralegal Charlotte Hoffman arrived right after lunch on June 18 as scheduled, and we sat down at the same table and chairs where I had been interviewed by the postal inspectors.

Betsy once again explained she was working from a short list of names Ted had given the defense team. She said Ted always liked me and wanted to know what I thought of him.

It didn't take long to figure out Ted had compiled the line of questioning for his lawyers. It was a fishing expedition in the middle of legendary trout country; a few questions, and almost all of them directed us into open-ended discussions about Ted, the area, the people he knew, and the places he frequented. Ted obviously was curious to find out just how much I had observed and remembered about him during our long friendship on Stemple Pass.

Unlike the postal inspectors, Betsy and Charlotte occasionally shared information in return.

We established how Ted and I knew each other, that I gave him rides, that I had been to his home cabin but never inside it, and that he visited my Lincoln shop just to talk sometimes. I told them I considered Ted a friend, but said I didn't know what he really thought of me. Possibly, deep inside, he could have resented me since I had started logging, although he never showed it. They said Ted couldn't answer whether he approved of my logging and road construction because of possible self-incrimination.

They wanted to know about conversations Ted and I had about Betty and also about a woman I had dated earlier, and told me Ted had said he was jealous of me because I had a girlfriend and then a wife, and he didn't.

What else had we talked about? I briefly mentioned gardening, survival, technical skills, and different areas of the country near Lincoln.

Had I noticed differences in Ted over the years and, specifically, did his personality change? After saying yes to both questions, I added that I felt sorry for him because his home cabin area had become so built up and Ted had to have privacy. I also told them how surprised I had been when he applied for a job at the Blackfoot Market, because it would be so unlike Ted to work with the public. Betsy explained that Ted had become depressed and desperate about how fast his world was changing, or he never would have applied for work in town. The two women and I talked further about how much the area around Lincoln had changed since Ted's arrival in 1971.

At one point, Charlotte asked if Ted ate meat. When I replied, "Yes, he did," she was surprised because she thought Ted would be a vegetarian. I said he hunted on a regular basis, year-round.

Betsy and Charlotte asked if Ted ever told me where he had gone. I replied no, but that it was very obvious to me as I always could tell by his bike tracks or footprints, or by seeing him even when he didn't see me. I also mentioned his absence in 1978-79, when I assumed he had moved away. But I didn't mention anything about the great deal of time Ted spent in my gulch because too many unanswered questions remained about what he had been doing there.

As we concluded the three-hour interview Betsy commented that Ted wanted to know how much I remembered about him.

I chuckled, knowing that question really had come directly from Ted. My reply was: "Don't kid yourself, Ted knows I have a great memory and that I would remember everything about him."

Charlotte then turned and said maybe that was true, but I surely couldn't remember times and dates.

"Everything, including times and dates," I answered, knowing where my memory failed, the daily journal entries I had kept for years held critical information and would help me.

She was sitting to my left and I watched out of the corner of my eye as she turned to Betsy and whispered, "He will be the FBI's greatest asset."

Betsy turned to me and said I hadn't really told them much, even though we had visited for the last three hours.

I replied I was just being cautious, and not volunteering a lot of information; I planned to answer all questions simply.

As they prepared to leave, Betsy said Ted would like me to visit him.

I said I'd be happy to go to Helena to the jail and maybe he could answer some of my questions. I didn't know just what I would say to him, but I was eager to hear his side of the story.

Betsy told me to call her the following morning and she would make the arrangements. She and Charlotte were staying the night at Lincoln's Blue Sky Motel, room 6, if I had any questions later that afternoon. They'd drive back to Helena in the morning, and then she could be reached at Donahoe's office.

Why did Ted want to see me? I hoped he was looking for nothing more than a little support from one of the few people he could call a friend.

I was just starting to feel off the hook in the FBI's eyes as a possible accomplice. The agents, who just the day before had visited me at home and had discussed going out into the surrounding mountains together to conduct field investigations in McClellan Gulch, might view the meeting with Ted as a breach of trust. They would probably think I had told Ted everything they were doing.

I continued to wrestle with the decision to go to the jail, but Ted wanted to see me and he must have something important to say.

On Wednesday morning, June 19, I called Betsy Anderson's toll-free number in Helena to get directions on how and when to meet Ted that afternoon. She said normal visiting hours at the jail were from 1 to 4 P.M. and 7 to 9 P.M. Because of extra security involving Ted's visitors, his time didn't start until 2:30 P.M. and that would be a good time to talk to him. She continued by briefing me on the strict protocol for visiting Ted.

After hanging up the telephone, I nervously changed clothes and headed to Helena, timing it to arrive a little early. While driving up the steep hill along Broadway that leads east out of the Capital City's main street, Last Chance Gulch, and nearing the jail, I was filled with apprehension, still wondering if this was the right thing to do.

To make matters worse, even though I parked in a lot a block from the jail, a CNN producer spotted me as I walked toward the entrance on the north side of the detention center.

Throngs of media members were back in Helena because Ted was about to be shipped out to Sacramento, where he would at last be indicted for the Unabomber crimes and held for trial in federal court. Television cameras were set up across from the jail on the courthouse lawn. The actual time Ted was to be moved had been kept a secret, but nobody wanted to miss the opportunity to possibly get some additional footage of him being moved from the jail.

As I walked along the sidewalk, the CNN producer directed her camera toward me. The camera swung around and began to roll, following me to the jail's front door. Other reporters immediately noticed the activity and several followed me to the jail door, asking questions like, "Are you here to visit Ted?" and "What are you going to say to him?"

It was unnerving. I tried to be polite but refused to talk. I had the overwhelming feeling it would be better to be somewhere else, anywhere but there.

After following the entry procedure, I waited in a narrow room until 2:30 and then walked over toward the door that led to the prisoners' visitation room. Just then a deputy opened the door and Ted was sitting there behind a glass wall talking to another Lincoln man, who was just getting up from a chair, ready to leave. He had arrived just a few minutes before, as I sat in the waiting room, and had talked to Ted about five minutes.

Another deputy walked over to me and said new orders had just been received: Security had been heightened because of Ted's pending departure. A written request had to be submitted by Ted and then cleared by a federal magistrate before anyone could see him during the rest of his time in Helena.

I explained Ted had requested to see me through his lawyers and that all that should have been taken care of before my arrival.

They told me they had no written authorization from Ted or the magistrate and I would have to come back later; rules were rules.

I left the jailhouse confused, with the CNN crew following me all the way to my car.

The whole scene was upsetting and the more I thought about it on the fifty-mile drive back to Lincoln the more I started to feel like it had been a trick set up by Ted. He called me to the jail, calculating it would be a roadblock in my dealings with the FBI. If it were a set-up, then Ted's lawyer Betsy had been tricked as well, because she certainly hadn't known that morning I would be turned away.

The wheels of my mind were spinning furiously. With jailers and FBI agents watching Ted's every move, they would surely interpret my visit as friendly and want to keep their distance.

But why wouldn't he see me? Maybe he was trying to distance himself from me and discredit my story.

His ploy most likely had something to do with all the time he had spent in my gulch, I thought. Just two days earlier the FBI agents had made it clear to me they were expending a great deal of effort searching various areas around my home on Stemple Pass Road.

Or maybe I was making too much of Ted's gamesmanship and there was another explanation.

When I got home I called Betsy. She was just as confused as I was, and couldn't explain what had happened. She said she would find out, call me back, and set up the visit for the next day. But I didn't hear from her the rest of that day.

I knew from Betsy's conversation that she was unaware of a hidden motive. But did Ted possibly set me up to draw the agents' attention away from me and my gulch?

The following morning, Thursday, June 20, I phoned Betsy's office. She told me I couldn't see Ted. No explanation was given, but I could sense her confusion as well. I reminded her Ted was the one who asked to see me. But she wouldn't tell me anything further.

That Sunday, Ted was driven to the Helena Airport and then spirited away to Sacramento aboard a small jet operated by federal marshals. When he landed at Mather Field, he was moved in a black, armored four-wheel-drive Suburban in a seven-vehicle convoy to a special federal unit at the downtown jail near the federal courthouse.

That same day, the producer from CNN showed up at my door and I finally agreed to give her a short interview. That decision would turn out to haunt me as well, even though I said nothing new.

The interview, I found out later, was another major factor in the FBI agents' breaking contact with me that coming summer. They had it in their minds that anyone who talked to the press, or with Ted, couldn't be trusted with inside information.

I was sick of the whole mess. Being pulled from one side, then the other, was frustrating to say the least. But then being ostracized by both sides just didn't make any sense.

The FBI was hot on the trail to find evidence to convict Ted of being the Unabomber, with the death sentence in mind. I was convinced at this point my gulch held key evidence, something he desperately wanted to hide. Then agents suddenly pulled away, showing little interest in my gulch or me, and concentrated their efforts in the public lands and old mine areas north and east of my gulch. I felt Ted had accomplished just what he had wanted.

Then, in what seemed like a senseless move, I was sideswiped from a direction I least expected.

On July 9, a letter arrived from a person who had been close to me and whom I had worked with and respected a great deal. Butch Gehring and I were visiting in the yard when Betty came out of the house, livid after opening the letter and reading it.

It said I didn't even know Ted and that I had "sold my soul" to take advantage of his misfortune for my own benefit. The letter said Ted denied ever knowing me and that he had instructed the woman who wrote the letter and the other two named in it to tell everyone in Lincoln that he had never known me.

It was a strange twist and it certainly tightened the cap on my theory that Ted was trying to distance himself and discredit me.

The letter made me more determined than ever to find out about Ted's secrets that I was so sure were tucked away in the mountains behind my house.

But it was still hard for me to understand how the trio, especially the writer of the letter, could ever believe I was a liar and Ted was a pillar of truth.

He had succeeded in finding pawns to make this attack, but the chess game was far from over and his ploy would backfire. The FBI would come to understand his tactic, assuming it really amounted to an admission of guilt on Ted's part.

Even though at first I took things hard, the whole jail episode and letter had a positive ending. At times I had almost felt like I had betrayed our relationship not only with the media, but also with the prosecution; his betrayal released me from the loyalties of friendship. Now I could be free of regret, as I helped the FBI in every way possible.

I was now mentally armed and determined to spend whatever time necessary to help agents uncover Ted's secrets in my gulch.

The Secret Cabin and the FBI

Ted Kaczynski didn't realize it, but he had spurred me on with new determination and energy to spend every spare moment the rest of summer 1996 exploring my gulch. But the task was more difficult than looking for the proverbial flea on a long-haired dog's back.

Whatever the FBI had been searching for was overshadowed by the immensity of this Rocky Mountain region. I truly believed I had the edge. During the past twenty-five years, there were so many things I had learned about Ted and his habits that the agents could never know or understand.

So when they seemed unreceptive to any overtures, I buckled down to the task at hand and began my own search in earnest. Each excursion into the woods was carefully plotted on topographical maps so no area would be overlooked. It was intense and at times discouraging work, but I never considered giving up.

I had been ready to put the search on the back burner for winter that late afternoon of November 22, when some strange force pulled me through the deep snow to discover Ted's secret cabin.

I barely remember my trek back down the mountain that night, other than a last fleeting glance at the cabin's ghostly image in the dark, still discernible against the snow, and then opening the door at home and proclaiming to Betty that I had found it.

That evening another severe winter storm system was being slammed up against the spine of the Continental Divide just a few miles above our home. Another two feet of snow during the next few days would make a return hike to the cabin daunting, but I had to get back as soon as possible to see the cabin in the daylight and to take pictures.

I was determined to do it even if it meant snowshoeing the entire way after the weather cleared. It would be more than a week before that would happen.

DEC. 1, 1996 [WAITS JOURNAL]
I finally get to climb back up the mountain and go to Ted's secret cabin. Very tough trip. Take a couple of rolls of pictures. I saw many items inside. My first look inside during daylight hours. I didn't dare go inside in case of booby-traps or stepping on evidence. Can't wait till spring. Still wonder how to tell the FBI. I wish [agent] Dave [Weber] would call. Snow is waist deep now. I wonder what else is in there.

An incredible mosaic was coming into focus as the long Montana winter threw its heavy white cloak over the mountains near our home. At the center of the images was the secret cabin. Surrounding it were the many fragments of Ted's blurred life both in Lincoln and as the Unabomber, which were gradually starting to make sense.

But it was the cabin that haunted me. Every day I re-examined the photographs taken on the last trek through the deep snow where its stark outline was like a thumb-smudge of brown paint on an artist's landscape of snow and tree trunks. The small, log structure sat comfortably on a 40-by-40-foot shelf, cut like a stairstep in the steep mountainside, and looked out over three drainages and thousands of acres far below. From the looks of the hatchet cuts in the log butts, the cabin had been there at least twenty years. Its front door, covered by faded and ripped dark green plastic, was economical in size—a mere 24 inches wide by 54 inches high—but the view was majestic, looking between the widely-spaced trunks of lodgepole pine and Douglas-fir forest.

How many nights had Ted slept on the shelf-bed, built from small logs laid like matchsticks on a two-by-four frame across the back of the cabin? Was the makeshift stove, a five-gallon Phillips 66 oil can with a crudely cut front opening and sliding tin door anchored by a piece of wire, really big enough to keep him warm? When did he last drink wild herb tea from the gold-colored mug that still sat beside the stove on a flat hearth stone half covered by snow that had swirled in through cracks between the logs? How many grouse and deer roasts had he cooked at the nearby fire pit, which was surely a soot-filled grave for his burned, jagged-lidded tin cans?

The cabin, with its slanted roof and six-inch, bark-covered logs crisscrossed at the corners, was etched into my mind. Its role in Ted's life wasn't as clear, but that would change.

I knew from the moment of discovery it was more than a place where Ted camped out. It was surely a hideout or an escape shelter where he could look out but no one could look in, either from the air or the ground, unless they walked within fifty feet.

That winter would prove to be especially tough. Not because the weather was so bad, even though it was another season of extreme cold and heavy snows, but because I had to wait until spring to get back up there.

Before I left the cabin that first day of December 1996, I had carefully rolled up the light blue denim pants, which had been pulled half through the rear corner of the roof by rodents, and tucked them under the top of a lodgepole pine that had fallen on top of the roof during a summer windstorm. The pants were in good shape, not chewed by the small animals too badly, and I didn't want them to be damaged further.

Not knowing what else was inside, I wanted to preserve any evidence as well as I could until I took the FBI to the site in the spring. I knew the cabin and its contents would be important in the trial. The discovery phase of the investigation had involved positioning and surprises on both sides. Ted's home cabin had even been moved off its cement blocks, loaded on a flatbed and then trucked under the cover of a green plastic tarp to Malmstrom Air Force Base in Great Falls in the middle of the night on the previous May 15. It was being stored until it could be trucked to the trial site.

The immediate security of the secret cabin wouldn't present a problem because another storm had moved in quickly. The freshly fallen snow, combined with gusting winds, had obliterated my tracks; even down in the bottom of the gulch the snow looked undisturbed.

The only real hurdle that remained was how to tell the FBI about the discovery.

I hadn't had any contact with agents since they visited me at home on Saturday, July 20. But they occasionally called or visited Butch Gehring after they left the area about three months earlier.

Butch and I talked at length about the best way to tell them. We finally decided he should ask the agents to contact me and then I would tell them the entire story.

Butch and I kept in contact on a regular basis. I saw him at least once a week because I taught his daughter piano each Monday afternoon at the Lincoln Center. And whenever the FBI called he always let me know.

During the first half of December, Butch talked with agents on several occasions, but they never contacted me.

Each Monday I'd ask if he had heard from them and he'd reply that he'd had a call from an agent or a visit from Special Agent Max Noel and had told them repeatedly, "You better call Chris," or "Have you called Chris yet?"

He'd ask if I'd had any response.

"Not a word from them yet," I'd say.

DEC. 16, 1996 [WAITS JOURNAL]
Talked to Butch. I asked if he had said anything to the FBI. Butch said Max had called and he told Max, "Better call Chris," "Better get hold of Chris," but he didn't tell Max about the secret cabin. Maybe they will call me now.

Max started to get irritated about the repeated prodding to call me even after Butch gave him a strong hint I had discovered something important. But Butch and I decided, irritating or not, the tactic would eventually work; if for no other reason they would grow tired of the nagging to "call Chris."

The winter was proving to be as bad as the previous one, Ted's last cold season in Lincoln before his arrest. I hoped we weren't entering a cycle of hard winters. By mid-December the snow level was already over my head in many places, especially where the wind had drifted it into smooth white mounds with wave-like crests where plumes of white powder would swirl and settle.

The holiday season, then January and February, passed with little happening in the case. I was aware of the legal positioning behind the scenes as both sides prepared for Ted's trial, but in Lincoln things had quieted down considerably.

But I was confident the FBI would return in the spring, knowing their field work hadn't been a hundred percent successful. There were still many unanswered questions.

I turned to calendar watching, noting each passing day, and I found myself especially interested in weather reports and checking the snow level each evening. I busied myself with my piano students and preparation for their annual spring recital. But during their renditions of Beethoven's "Für Elise" or Mozart's "Sonata in C Major" it was hard not to let my thoughts drift back to the remote ledge and cabin.

Maybe there would be an early spring. But March came in like a lion with no spring thaw in the forecast. The first chinook winds, warming gusts that sweep down along the mountains, couldn't break winter's grip and we were destined to be locked in for at least another month.

It seemed as though I would never get back up there.

Betty was eager to go as well, and we often passed long winter evening hours speculating about what we might find and theorizing about the important role the cabin had played in Ted's hidden agenda.

I had spent hundreds of hours trying to fit the pieces together and, slowly, Ted's secret life both in and outside of Lincoln was beginning to show flashes of color. I had become obsessed with the case and had filled dozens of legal tablets with information obtained since the arrest—key items from my own experiences, the stories of my neighbors, and information from the media, the prosecution and defense teams.

One evening while poring over every detail listed in the "Unabom Chronology," certain facts and dates started to look different, almost like an optical illusion that suddenly makes sense.

I was trying to link key details from the bombings and the chronology to certain situations in and around Lincoln. That winter I found five such correlations.

Chronologically, the first was that my journals noted that Ted had disappeared from the Lincoln area during the late spring of 1978, and was gone for at least a year. I didn't see him anywhere and assumed he had moved away. He didn't show up again until the summer of 1979. Now I learned that he had been in his home state of Illinois.

During this time, the Unabomber's first and second bombs were mailed from the Chicago area. The first was found on May 25, 1978. A package turned up in the Engineering Department parking lot at the Chicago Circle Campus of the University of Illinois. It was addressed to an engineering professor at Rensselaer Polytechnic Institute in Troy, New York.

The package had a return address of a professor at Northwestern's Technological Institute. The package was given to the addresser, who then turned it over to the Northwestern University Police Department because he had not sent the package. On May 26, the parcel was opened by a police officer who suffered minor injuries when the bomb detonated.

On May 9, 1979, a disguised explosive device, which had been left in a common area in Northwestern University's Technological Institute, slightly injured a graduate student when he attempted to open the box and it exploded.

(After the first four bombs, the FBI organized the UNABOM task force, named for *un*iversity and *a*irline *bom*ber.)

When I read that the Unabomber's ninth device exploded at the University of California Berkeley on May 9, 1985, I recalled the third week of May that year. While driving my recently purchased Blazer home on Stemple Pass Road, I saw Ted hitchhiking and picked him up. It was the first and only time I ever saw him hitchhike. He didn't know I was in the Blazer since he had never seen the vehicle. He was fresh off the bus, probably from Missoula, and was in a hurry to get home. He was carrying his small travel pack.

That bomb had detonated in a computer room at Cory Hall on the Berkeley campus. A graduate student in electrical engineering lost partial vision in his left eye and four fingers from his right hand. The device was believed to have been placed in the room several days prior to detonation.

Near the end of February 1987 my wife, while out walking with her dogs, surprised Ted where he was camped at one of our old cabins about a mile up the gulch. It was morning and very cold. His tracks in the snow came from up the mountain, from the direction of his secret cabin. His beard was short, all new growth. He wasn't dressed for the weather and was on his way back to his home cabin.

The Unabomber's twelfth device had exploded at CAAM's Inc., a computer store in Salt Lake City, Utah, on February 20, 1987. Disguised as a pile of nail-studded boards, it was left in a parking space at the rear entrance to CAAM's. The bomb exploded and injured the store owner when he attempted to pick it up.

It should be noted that the Unabomber was spotted for the first and only time while in Salt Lake City. A woman saw him through a window at close range and a composite drawing was rendered from her description. He was clean shaven except for a mustache, was wearing wraparound sunglasses, a gray hooded sweatshirt and light blue denim pants like those found in the secret cabin.

Authorities later speculated that the sighting stopped the Unabomber activities for more than six years. Now I wondered if Betty's encountering Ted on his way home increased his furtive behavior.

In late spring, May or June of 1993, I attended two yard and garage sales and Ted was at both, purchasing large quantities of old silverplate flatware.

On the twenty-second of June, a well known geneticist received a parcel at his Tiburon, California residence. It was postmarked June 18, 1993, and later was determined to have been mailed from Sacramento. The doctor attempted to open the package, which exploded, severely injuring him. It was the Unabomber's thirteenth attack.

The fourteenth bomb was mailed from the same place on the same day, to the office of a Yale University professor and computer scientist. As he attempted to open it, the package exploded, severely injuring him.

It is significant these dates fall shortly after the yard sales. The explosive mixture in this later class of bomb included, along with other ingredients, metal powders—aluminum mostly, but silver as well.

The silver, added to the aluminum mixture, would have increased the power of the explosive, and would have made the aluminum

$50,000 REWARD

WANTED BY THE
POSTAL INSPECTION SERVICE FOR

MAILING OR PLACING AN EXPLOSIVE DEVICE

2/21/87

White Male
25 - 30 Years Old
5'10" - 6' tall
165 pounds
Slender Build
Blond hair (reddish tint)
(hair sticking out, not bangs)
Light Mustache
Ruddy Complexion
Wearing Blue Denim Jeans, Gray Hooded Sweatshirt
Tear drop Sunglasses (smoked lenses)

THE U.S. POSTAL SERVICE MAY PAY A REWARD OF UP TO $50,000 FOR INFORMATION AND SERVICES LEADING TO THE ARREST AND CONVICTION OF ANY PERSON(S) FOR PLACING OR MAILING AN EXPLOSIVE DEVICE IN A POSTAL DEPOSITORY.

ON FEBRUARY 20TH, 1987 A PACKAGE EXPLODED AT A COMPUTER BUSINESS AT 270 E. 900 S. SALT LAKE CITY, UTAH 84111. BOMBS HAVE BEEN EITHER RECEIVED IN THE MAILS AND OR PLACED IN THE FOLLOWING STATES: UTAH, PENNSYLVANIA, ILLINOIS, CALIFORNIA, MICHIGAN AND WASHINGTON. THIS INCIDENT HAS BEEN LINKED TO 11 OTHER INCIDENTS WHICH HAVE OCCURED ACROSS THE UNITED STATES SINCE 1978 INJURING 21 PEOPLE AND KILLING ONE.

IF YOU HAVE ANY INFORMATION ABOUT THIS INCIDENT PLEASE CONTACT THE UNABOM LAW ENFORCEMENT TASK FORCE BY TELEPHONE COLLECT (801) 359-1917 (24 Hr.)

impossible to track. It could also be added to the solder, rendering it untraceable.

The Unabomber's first devices had been quite crude; matchheads were the main explosive. They were weak, because the matchheads would deflagrate (burn suddenly) instead of explode.

The second-generation bombs were better, but still weak. The main explosive ingredient was smokeless powder, obtained from various types of ammunition, including rifle and shotgun shells. This was an expensive way to obtain enough powder to produce a device. However, mixing the various types and brands of powder made the bombs impossible to trace.

The problem with a bomb of this type is that smokeless powder from ammunition also will deflagrate unless it's packed just right, totally sealed and then detonated properly

As the years passed and Ted experimented in the mountains surrounding our homes and studied the near-deadly impact of the bombs detonated in his acts of terrorism, he learned how to boost the power of his devices, which became much more sophisticated.

His third-generation bombs were very powerful. Extremely explosive mixtures were combined with powdered metal, like aluminum and silver, to produce a combination that could produce lethal results when sealed in a pipe or similar structure and properly detonated.

The fourth and final generation of bombs was by far the deadliest. Ted had achieved a major breakthrough by eliminating the need for a pipe. Now he built a detonating cap from copper tubing, and placed it in an explosive mixture that was filled with shrapnel. These bombs were lighter, less bulky (so more easily concealed), and twice as lethal.

The devices used in the later attacks, including numbers thirteen and fourteen, were of this type.

Common to all the devices was they were constructed from materials that were untraceable.

In the spring of 1993, I moved all my heavy equipment home for the last time. Much of it was set up about a mile above my house in McClellan Gulch where I planned to operate a gravel business.

That summer thousands of yards of gravel were dug from the old

FEDERAL BUREAU OF INVESTIGATION

Date of transcription   **5/7/96**

The following is a decoded transcription of notebooks K2046C (A1) and K778F (B1).

"MAYABOUT1982 I SENT A BOMB TO A COMPUTER EXPERT NAMED PATRICKFISVER.HIS SECRETARY OPENED IT.ONE NEWSPAPER SAID SHE WAS INHOSPITAL?IN GOOD CONDITION?WITH ARM AN DCHEST CUTS.OTHERNEWSPAPER SAID BOMBDROVE FRAGMENTSOF WOOD INTO HERFLESH.BUT NOINDICATIONTHAT SHEWASPERMANE NTLY DISABLED.FRUSTRATING THATI CANT SEEMTO MAKO LETH ALBOMB.USEDSHOTGUN)POWDER INTHIS LAST HOPING ITWOULDD O BETTER THAN RIFLEPOWDER.NEXT IMUSTTRY ANOTHER GASO LINEBOMB,DIFFERENTDESIGN.THOUGH GASOLINEBOMB ITRIED L ASTFALLDID NOT GO OFF.REVENGEATTEMPTSHAVEBEENGOBBLING MUCHTIME,IMPEDINGOTHER WORK.BUTI MUSTSUCCEED,MUST GET REVENGE.NOT LONGAFTER FOREGOING,I THINK IN JUNEORJUL Y,I WENTTO U.OF CALIFORNIABERKELEY ANDPLACED IN COMPU TERSCIENCEBUILDING A BOMBCONSISTINGOF A PIPEBOMB IN G ALLONCAN OFGASOLINE.ACCORDINGTONEWSPAPER,VICECHAIRMAN OFCOMPUTER SCI.DEPT.PICKED IT UP.HEWASCONSIDERED TO BE"OUTOFDANGER OF LOSING ANY FINGERS",BUTWOULDNEED FU RTHER SURGERYFOR BONEANDTENDON DAMAGE IN HAND.APPAREN TLY PIPEBOMB WENTOFF BUT DIDNOT IGNITE GASOLINE.I DON T UNDERSTAND IT.FRUSTRATED.TRAVELINGEXPENSES FOR RAID S SUCHAS THE FOREGOINGAREVERY HARD ON MY SLENDER FINA NCIALRESOURCES.

---

vestigation on **4/25 - 5/7/96** at FBIHQ Laboratory   File # **149A-SF-106204**

Michael P. Birch - Cryptanalyst   Date dictated **5/7/96** *MPB*

With Kaczynski's key, the FBI was able to transcribe the coded journal entries originally written in numerals.

miners' stone and gravel piles, washed and then screened for various construction projects.

Looking back, I can see how this activity within the confines of Ted's sanctuary—namely my gulch and the surrounding country—would have had a disturbing impact on his psyche.

With each passing year, the world was closing in on him, choking his need for solitude. The activity around the gravel plant and the daily noise of machinery were things Ted could not tolerate. When the wind was right the grinding of rocks and gravel, along with engine sounds, could be heard far off in the valleys and mountains.

He faced a dilemma knowing he was unable to follow his normal recourse, which was to destroy any intrusive machines. Such a move would probably tip his hand.

I don't believe he thought I was part of the evil empire intent on destroying the country. He had listened to me talk too many times about my love for the land surrounding Lincoln and how I would always preserve my gulch. Even the gravel operation was a form of reclamation, an attempt to smooth out and level the mining scars left almost a century before.

He must have realized that if he alienated me in a violent verbal confrontation over the use of the machinery he would most likely be banned from my gulch and the privacy of the place he loved so much. So I am now grateful for our friendship, even if it evolved into a friendship of necessity for Ted. He could have easily destroyed every one of my machines before I realized who was responsible.

Yet, knowing Ted, he probably plotted some type of retaliation.

While studying the dates of the bombings and related letters compiled by the FBI, I discovered an intriguing coincidence. Or was it Ted's revenge? Starting in June 1993, a particular date appeared once, then again and again.

The date was June 24.

My mind flashed back to a conversation Ted and I had about my birthday back on June 24, 1980. I had given him a ride that day as I drove home to clean up for a birthday supper.

June 24 didn't appear in his chronology until 1993, the same period I began work in my gulch on a larger scale. After 1993, the date appeared as follows:

Ted Kaczynski's tiny home cabin had one room, a woodstove, and neither plumbing nor electricity.

Kaczynski on the way to one of his first appearances in Helena's federal court.

One of the roads to Kaczynski's home cabin, blocked off by FBI agents just after his arrest.

View to the west over Lincoln, Montana.

McClellan Gulch, the nearby wild area that Kaczynski treated as his own.
Photo by David Weber/FBI

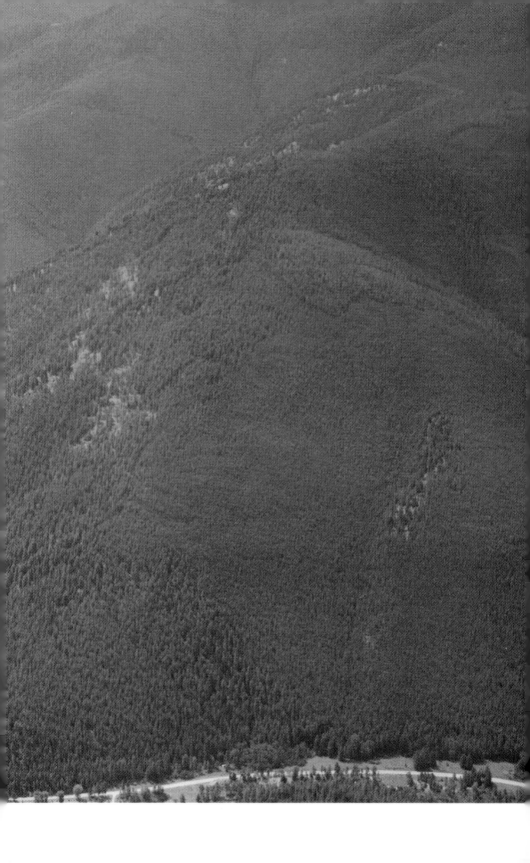

Above: By the time this photo of Kaczynski's root cellar was made, officials had fenced off his Florence Gulch home.

Left: Kaczynski's fair-weather shower.

Kaczynski's home-built fence stile shows his usual mixture of scrounged materials.

A typical Kaczynski trash dump, recognizable from the cans' jagged openings and attached lids and the fact that they had been burned.

Chemicals found inside Kaczynski's root cellar.

A buried food and ammunition cache.

Residents of Lincoln built their Community Center in the 1910s, using Model T's to raise the eight log walls.

Chris Waits' former shop where Kaczynski visited is now Waits' "true Lincoln Center."

Lincoln's Post Office.

Lincoln's small branch library.

Above: FBI agent Max Noel, left, with Chris Waits exploring the gulch.

Right: Tasha, the malamute adopted to replace the first of Betty Waits' dogs that were killed, would meet a similar fate.

Chris Waits' storage areas allowed him to recycle materials, but also provided "one-stop shopping" for the Unabomber.

A game trail through the woods near the secret cabin.

Kaczynski left tree blazes (left) that gradually would blend in and other blazes (above) that seemed like cryptic maps to special sites.

FBI agent Dave
Weber (right) and
Chris Waits explored
this old mine for
Unabomber evi-
dence.

The old miner's cabin that Kaczynski cannibalized to build his hideout collapsed shortly after this picture was made, because Kaczynski had stolen enough structural parts. Note the missing roof truss in bottom photo.

From inside the old miner's cabin, Kaczynski removed plywood (still in place at left) to roll up as chinking for his secret cabin.

Nearly invisible entrances to caves in the argillite cliffs, where Kaczynski stored materials.

This plastic container held solder and miniature wire connectors. Max Noel thought that Kaczynski had dropped it; Waits thought an animal had opened a cache.

To the casual observer, the remains of animals that Kaczynski poached might look like natural deaths. This site is near Ted's "most secret camp."

After months of disuse, the secret cabin was succumbing to weather and animals. Picture was made days after its discovery. Plastic tarp once had covered the roof; jeans were probably pulled out by animals.

The secret cabin's homemade woodstove (above) photographed through roof timbers, and the piece of Phillips 66 can cut out for its door opening.

Above: Going-to-town clothes were left to the elements, which included wild animals. Note fingerprinted brush handle at left.

Right: Gloves for bomb-building.

Inside the secret cabin, evidence emerged as the ice and snow melted, including a serrated hunting knife. Duff on the floor is from the camouflaging branches that once covered the roof.

Evidence inside the secret cabin was being destroyed for months before the FBI arrived, as the rodent-nibbled shirt below dramatizes.

Only very close to the secret cabin can you begin to see the "ghostly image of horizontal logs in a vertical world of tree trunks."

Above: Chris Waits, left, watches as Dave Weber sites the Global Positioning System unit near the secret cabin.

Right: FBI agents Max Noel and Dave Weber with Chris Waits.

The secret cabin and a trademark can-burning site.

Above: Kaczynski's mountain-top view onto one of Waits' logging sites, bare and snow-covered when this was shot.

Right: Betty Waits and Bobby Didriksen.

Low-level aerial of Stemple Pass area.

Typical of the country Kaczynski loved to hike.

Device #13, opened June 22, 1993. This device was mailed on the same date as Device #14, opened June 24, 1993;

New York Times letter, June 24, 1993. This letter was received by Warren Hoge, assistant managing editor for the *Times;*

San Francisco Chronicle letter, June 24, 1995. This letter was received by Jerry Roberts, editorial page editor;

New York Times letter, June 24, 1995. This letter was once again received by Hoge;

Washington Post letter, June 24, 1995. This letter was received by Michael Gretler, deputy managing editor;

Penthouse magazine letter, June 24, 1995. This letter was received by Bob Guccione, publisher;

Scientific American magazine letter, June 24, 1995. This letter was received by an unknown person working for the respected science magazine;

Dr. Tom Tyler letter, June 24, 1995. This letter was received with a copy of the Unabomber manifesto by Tyler, who was working in the Social Psychology Group, University of California, Berkeley. Another copy of the manifesto was mailed to *Washington Post* and *The New York Times,* also on June 24.

The June 24 coincidence continued when Ted floated a book proposal from prison. A story, published in the *New York Daily News* on June 24, 1998, and then picked up by The Associated Press announced "Unabomber Theodore Kaczynski is shopping for a book publisher from behind bars...Kaczynski's handwritten, four-page pitch arrived at Simon & Schuster offices earlier this month."

During the long winter of trying to figure out the enigma who I had thought was my friend, I began to wonder whether the recurring date was nothing more than a bizarre set of circumstances or maybe something more, a covert method of retaliation, a vendetta against me for violating his strict code of environmental ethics and also for disturbing his peace.

As March wore on the snow started to slowly recede, but bare ground was still weeks away.

Neither Butch nor I had heard from the FBI in months and I began to wonder just when they would contact me. Agents had come to

Lincoln on Wednesday, March 5, but they didn't take the time to talk to me.

I wanted to be patient, since I wasn't sure how they would react to the cabin news anyway—maybe they'd get a search warrant and confiscate all my notes and the cabin. I also wanted to prove to the FBI that I could be trusted with new sensitive information. At least I could document and preserve the evidence before there was any further damage caused by the small animals or the weather.

I certainly didn't want the press to catch wind of the cabin. A leak would cause a stampede of people and reporters either trying to pin me down or to sneak in and find the cabin site. The only people who knew about my discovery were Betty, Butch, and Bobby Didriksen. And I trusted them all implicitly.

Then finally, on March 26, I received a phone call from FBI agent Dave Weber, who was in Lincoln along with Max Noel and lead prosecuting attorney Robert Cleary. They were conducting pre-trial interviews with a few people who would be witnesses at Ted's trial.

Dave asked if they could drive up and interview me that same afternoon. I said I'd be free until my piano lessons, which began at 3:30 P.M. Dave replied they'd arrive shortly after lunch.

I didn't have time to run down to Butch's and he didn't answer his phone, so I wasn't sure if he had talked to them already.

A short time later they pulled up into the yard, knocked at the door and—after getting all of our barking dogs outside—we moved inside and sat down in the living room.

This was my first meeting with Max, who had been the lead in many areas of the investigation and was a member of the Unabom Task Force.

Max talked about the beauty of the country; Dave and Bob Cleary were in agreement.

After more small talk, Bob Cleary asked the first question: When had I met Ted? Cleary asked most of the questions and it was obvious he was preparing the case in earnest.

For the first time I began to volunteer more detailed information than I had shared with anyone yet. I talked about the frequency and duration of Ted's visits to my gulch and how much he loved it up there.

I then went on to explain the logistics and importance of not only the total privacy and Ted's exclusive access, but the gulch itself and its strategic location and easy access to the Continental Divide trail and also to the rail line, which was only ten miles across the mountains. Walking that distance meant nothing to Ted. From the Divide, it was an easy and fairly level jaunt to sidespurs and stops at Garrison Junction, Austin, or Mullan Pass where freight trains could be boarded easily.

I also told them details about Ted, his dress, the packs he used and the places he went.

Max asked me to describe one of Ted's packs.

I said Ted always carried a large army green canvas pack when out in the mountains.

Max then asked if it had a frame.

I replied that it did, but Ted didn't always use the frame.

He asked if the frame was wood or metal.

I realized he was quizzing me, not only to find out what details I might remember, but also to corroborate earlier interviews. I also felt he was testing me to see how I'd handle being questioned under pressure.

I described the frame of aluminum tubing—a metal frame—with braided white cord criss-crossed around the bottom. I apologized for adding the extra details, but Max said, "No, that's great," and commended me for being able to remember the details.

Cleary then wondered if I had talked to the defense team and if I had notes about what they had asked and when I had talked to them.

I said I had talked to the defense while Ted was still in Helena, but had adamantly refused to meet with the new defense team later in the fall when they asked for an interview. (Once the government set the first trial for Sacramento, the court appointed Sacramento-based public defenders for Ted.)

Cleary instantly lifted his head from his notes, looked straight at me and asked: "Why would you refuse to talk to the defense lawyers?"

I paused, but then told them in detail about what I felt was Ted's scheme to discredit me—when Ted refused to see me at the jail and the letter I had received claiming I didn't even know Ted.

They asked if they could have a copy of the letter, which I agreed to provide, and I also told them the names of the three who had sent me the letter. I said it felt like the whole mess was set up and once was enough.

They agreed.

Max said the woman who wrote the letter and signed it for the three had provided the defense with a sworn affidavit and then had tried to change details about her story, including how long she had known Ted, but a federal judge ruled what she said first was what she said. Max went on to say the letter I received, which contained information contrary to that in her affidavit, would help discredit her testimony.

I then saw her original affidavit, which stated she met Ted about four or five years after she started her current employment in Lincoln at the end of 1984. In her letter to me, dated July 8, 1996, she wrote she had known Ted for twelve years. The math just didn't add up and I could see what the FBI was talking about.

I went on to tell Cleary and the other two about several other uncharacteristic incidents, including the time Ted was hitchhiking, and the winter day my wife caught him at the cabin behind our house.

When I mentioned the cabin, Cleary instantly perked up and asked me what kind of cabin.

I replied it was an old miner's cabin.

He acted disappointed and put his head back down, returning to his handwritten notes.

I wondered if this was the right time, but I still didn't feel totally comfortable about how to bring up the secret cabin. I decided to wait because I knew they would be back and I had to get up there before anyone else.

Besides, I felt if anyone deserved receiving the information, Dave Weber was the one. I was sure he had trusted me the previous summer and was disappointed when he got orders to be guarded about any communications with me.

The conversation continued for a short while, centering on things I had discussed with Ted. As the three got up to leave I jokingly scolded Max for not taking the time to meet in person before making a character assessment.

As they left Dave informed me he would return to get the letter, which I told him I could copy at home, and also to jot down information about my background.

As I followed the trio out to their Ford Bronco I could sense Dave knew there was something I was holding back. They said their good-byes and said they were headed to Butch's house for a brief visit. I knew then Butch hadn't spilled the beans.

They said they were leaving town, so I was surprised to receive a call from Dave the next day, saying he wanted to come back up and double-check some of the details from our interview.

It was Thursday, March 27. I decided Dave would not leave without knowing about the secret cabin.

Dave arrived and I felt comfortable with him almost immediately. A Montana native who was named to the Unabom Task Force about two years earlier, Dave had a small-town easiness about him and was patient in building relationships. I also admired him for all the dirty work he had done the previous summer, spending hundreds of hours hiking in the rugged back-country looking for evidence.

As we talked I knew he didn't have an agenda or a long list of questions to go over. The conversation at times even slowed to the point of being awkward, but I had a strong feeling Butch had taken him aside and told him he better stop back and see me.

After giving him a copy of the letter I had promised, I said, "I've got something to show you, something I think you will find very interesting." I went to my office and returned with a photograph of the cabin in the snow taken the previous December and handed it to him.

Dave grabbed the picture, studying it intensely, and the questions started to roll. He immediately asked if he could have the pictures and negatives.

I could send him a set of pictures at a later date, I replied, but he couldn't have these because they were the only copies.

It was apparent from his excitement that this cabin was indeed what agents had been looking for in their long and tedious search of the mountains. He asked when and where I had found it.

I answered the when question, but stopped short of describing where it was located, other than to vaguely describe a remote area, fairly high up. He mentioned a specific area of the gulch, wondering if it was there. I said not exactly, but kind of across from there, and left it at that.

Dave sensed that was about all he would find out that day. He didn't press me further, but instead promised to send me a detailed map, actually a high-altitude aerial photograph of the area, enlarged to help me pinpoint the location.

"That'd be great," I said, eager to receive the map even though I knew exactly where the cabin was located.

I think Dave understood that as well, and he knew I was being careful and didn't blame me. He then said the FBI hasn't always had a glowing reputation in its dealings with people.

As he was leaving we talked about what had happened the previous summer and why agents didn't contact me after the CNN interview. Dave said he knew I could have helped greatly during the search and he had pushed hard to use me toward that end. But, as he put it, his words fell on deaf ears and he was ordered to keep silent and work only with the FBI team.

Dave went on to say his wife, Sue, had been right about the location of Ted's secret cabin. She had been with Dave and Jerry Burns that first time they stopped at my house. While Dave, Jerry, and I were talking in the yard, Sue sat in Jerry's pickup, scanning the huge expanse of country behind us.

Dave said that when he and Jerry got back into the truck, Sue said "if I were Ted, I would build my secret cabin up there," pointing up my gulch. She went on to talk about the privacy, remoteness of the land and how close it was to Ted's home cabin. Even to this day we occasionally laugh as she gloats about how her intuition was correct.

As Dave got into his truck he said we'd be in touch and then he drove off toward Lincoln.

I called Butch and said Dave had been told, but I hadn't divulged the location.

"Good," Butch replied.

I chuckled as he went on to say it was just like Columbo when they finally got the hint.

That night I received a phone call from Max Noel thanking me for sharing the information with Dave. He wondered when I might send pictures and when they would be able to get up there with a team.

Photos could be sent as soon as they were printed, I said, but it probably would be at least a month before the snow would melt sufficiently to hike up to the cabin.

We then talked a little about trust and I complained again about his not taking the time to meet me earlier. He agreed, but partially blamed Butch for not steering them to me.

I laughed as I told Max how Butch compared the whole scene to an episode of Columbo. Max didn't find too much humor in the comment and replied Butch watched too much television.

Max said he had to go, but would stay in touch. I replied I would take them up as soon as the conditions permitted.

As we hung up, I could sense the adventure was just beginning.

Secrets Revealed

The secret cabin was the touchstone of my new relationship with the FBI. I had made a solid discovery, and then sharing that information with agents had shown I could be trusted and was sincere about helping.

No longer would I have to wait for the chance to communicate with them. They would now be contacting me on a regular basis since I was the one with inside information.

Max Noel had told me I would be needed to help with their investigation once the field team arrived back in Montana, since I knew the country and terrain so well.

I told him I'd set aside the necessary time and I'd also monitor the snow conditions so we'd be able to hike to the secret cabin at the earliest opportunity.

As the year moved into April there was still no hint of spring. The few days the sun appeared were quickly offset by frigid nights; the snow level just wouldn't diminish.

Finally on Wednesday afternoon, April 9, 1997, I decided to force the season and hike up the gulch. I wasn't prepared for what I found.

The elevation change between home and the old miner's cabin just a mile beyond is only about 200 feet, but the snow around that cabin still was chest high, more snow than I'd seen there in a long time.

I snapped a roll of pictures for future reference and to document where Ted had removed boards, material, and nails. It took thirty minutes to dig down through the five feet of snow in front of the door to get inside.

I didn't realize how important the trip and the pictures would prove to be. That would be the last time I'd see the old miner's cabin standing.

The very next trip up the gulch the cabin was down, squashed flat like a toppled house of cards. The heavy snows of about seventy years had finally taken their toll and the structure just couldn't shoulder the weight of another winter. The missing piece of roof truss stolen by the joker, Ted, who had always been the odd card in the deck, had weakened the structure and contributed to the cabin's demise; Ted used the 2X4 as the side rail and frame for his secret cabin bed.

The leverage of the collapsing walls pulled up some of the cabin's floor boards, revealing where Ted had hidden a dry supply of split firewood. Also under the floor was a junkyard of old burned tin cans, all opened in his usual way with a survival knife.

Ted had helped himself to plenty of building materials taken right off the shell of the cabin, including boards, plywood, nails, and tarpaper. All were packed up the mountain and used in the construction of his secret cabin.

The old miner's cabin, built by turn-of-the-century prospectors who scoured this gulch for riches, stood all those years and was a handy shelter and ready supply of materials for Ted. But the first winter after his arrest, weakened by his pillaging, it wouldn't stand any longer.

Ted had used whatever he needed from it, just as he had used people. It was like he had some special privilege to take whatever suited him with no regard for anything or anyone.

His life during the Lincoln years was a dichotomy. He was a man of unyielding principles and was eager to kill for them, yet the rigid rules he devised for everyone else did not apply to himself. He was above the common man's law.

By the third week in April an amazing amount of snow remained in the high country. Everyone was worried it would melt quickly and severely flood Lincoln and areas down river. In some places even the twenty-foot-high snow poles used by the snowmobile club to mark trails were covered; several feet of snow had to be shoveled away to find the poles' tops.

That meant well over 240 inches of snow blanketed the mountains, the heaviest snowpack recorded for many years.

But every day the sun moved higher in the sky, finally traveling a path above the mountain ridges, and then it started to penetrate the snowbound valleys and streambeds locked away and shaded by the vertical, tree-covered slopes towering above them. Some sheltered valleys hadn't been warmed by a single ray of direct sunlight since the previous fall.

Chinook winds added their life-giving heat as the icy fortress and small rivulets began to be transformed into rushing streams.

On Friday, April 25, I told Betty I couldn't stand any more suspense—it was time to return to the secret cabin.

I laced up my waterproof, leather Chippewa hiking boots, grabbed a camera and fanny pack loaded with a few supplies, and started walking up the gulch, staying on bare or nearly bare patches of ground on the south-facing slopes as much as possible.

It was a struggle to traverse the rougher terrain, which was still snowbound. But I avoided most of it by choosing a longer, less direct route and I arrived at the cabin in remarkable time, considering the conditions.

As I stood there on the shelf in front of the cabin, it was more apparent than last November that Ted had chosen the location well. The only smell was the heavy scent of fresh-flowing sap invigorated by the warming weather. The only sounds came from the southwesterly winds brushing the treetops and the stream, far below, cascading over boulders and downed trees in its spring rush to Poorman Creek and then the Blackfoot River.

This was a piece of paradise, unusually buffered from the harsh winter elements. Not only was it secluded, but also the sun, even when it was low in the south sky during mid-winter, would top the distant ridge and warm the shelf through the tree cover. The snow cover right here was already melted, an oasis in the middle of a huge snowfield. It was a perfect location for a year-round cabin, one of the few in the high country.

The necessities of life—food, water, and fuel—were nearby. Any smoke from the small stove would be impossible to spot after it swirled above the treeline and mixed with the mountain breezes that swept up the small gulches and valleys. Any sign of a fire could be seen only from the mountain directly across the gulch, and that mountain slope is 70 degrees or more, heavily covered with brush and timber and very difficult to navigate.

Ted was calculating in choosing his spot; it was perfect in every way. If I hadn't been systematically looking for the secret cabin or something like it, it's doubtful it ever would have been found.

As I walked up to the cabin I had to shake off the same ominous feeling I had sensed before, both at Ted's home cabin and at the secret cabin the previous fall. It felt like an evil place and that its owner was still hidden among the tall lodgepoles, watching me invade his private domain.

Inside the small front opening I could see many curious items spread across the floor and piled under the bed, things you wouldn't expect to find at a campsite or mountain cabin.

Most out-of-place were several pairs of yellow latex-rubber gloves that immediately caught my eye. Some loose gloves were lying around, not only on the floor, but also near the stone hearth that supported the handmade stove. Others were still packaged in unopened clear plastic bags.

Without touching anything I got down on my hands and knees at the doorway and carefully looked at one of the packages. From the price tag and label I could tell it came from a Skaggs Alpha Beta, a chain that has never had a Montana store under that exact name.

There was a wide array of un–Ted-like clothing lying about on the dirt floor, probably pulled out from under the bed by small animals.

I had never seen him wear any of these clothes—a bright-colored striped sweater, a tan polyester Henley shirt, and designer jeans. I figured they had to be disguises he wore to blend into the crowds when he traveled to the cities. All the clothes were in pretty good shape and it looked like the cabin had been used right up to the fall before his arrest.

Many other items were still locked in stubborn mounds of ice and snow on the dirt floor.

The tall dead lodgepole pine that had blown down across the cabin's top the previous season had badly ripped a blue nylon tarp Ted had used to cover the roof and back wall. He had camouflaged the tarp with a layer of pine boughs, but they had blown off the roof and now lay strewn inside the cabin and around the outside.

Once the wind penetrated the blue roof tarp the gusts ripped away much of the black tarpaper, plywood plies, small boards, and small poles Ted used to chink the spaces between the logs.

The secret cabin was still intact, but without its builder close at hand to perform annual maintenance, it was in disrepair. Its condition surely would have irritated the proud builder who had penned many pages in his personal journals describing his creation and its interior fixtures, almost like a young father lovingly writing about his new-born infant.

Ted's journal entries not only described the construction of his cabin in detail and the amount of time spent on it, but also his original stove and the mistakes and problems he encountered building and then using it.

He also wrote about the pristine and secret location he had chosen for his hidden mountain chalet. What would seem to be nothing more than a crude survival shanty to most people was a luxurious, private alpine condominium to Ted.

I spent a little time hiking around the cabin, making mental notes about location, elevation, and other pertinent information. After taking a few more pictures, I placed my camera on a tripod and photographed myself standing next to the cabin so the FBI could see size and scale of the structure.

Then I headed home, eager to tell Betty that she could make the hike if we followed the route I had taken. She would be excited and her next day's schedule would be reorganized to include a trip to the cabin.

I deviated from my course slightly on the way back just to see how much snow remained in the creek bottoms. Walking across long snow-fields, I carefully tested each step to avoid falling into any snow-covered small ravines. Even though the wind-packed snow often looks level, it becomes rotten in late spring and a person can easily break through the surface and become stuck in wet snow over his head.

The forest floor in winter hides other potential dangers for the hiker. Fallen branches can cover a small chasm, ravine or old mining hole, become covered with drifting snow, freeze and look like the surrounding area. But as the melting ice loses its grip, such a hole can become a dangerous pit to trap either human or animal.

As I reached the bottom of the mountain, deep drifts still covered the creek, but I could hear rushing water undermining the last of winter's icy embrace.

When I arrived home, Betty asked: "How was it, did you make it up there?"

I told her it was a piece of cake. She knew me too well. She was eager and committed to go the next day, but she knew the trip would be more difficult than I let on.

We spent the rest of the afternoon talking about the cabin, what was inside, the trip up and how different everything looked this time of year. She was fascinated by my description of the cabin, the large chunks of snow-ice inside that still encapsulated many items, the clothing, and yellow latex gloves.

I added a pencil and tablet to my pack and Betty put some apples and snacks in hers. We wouldn't take any dogs because I was concerned about disturbing evidence and possible booby traps.

We went to bed that night eager for the trek.

The next morning, before we headed up the gulch, I called Bobby Didriksen so someone would know where we had gone. He was excited, too, and wanted a call as soon as we returned.

I wanted to carefully check out several areas spotted on my first trip.

Just outside the cabin door to the east Ted had dug a small firepit. It was still covered with patches of snow and ice, but some of his signature tin cans were starting to poke through the melting ice. Then on the west side, in a scrap pile, sheets of lead and pieces of angle iron were leaning up against the cabin.

The ice chunks held mysterious items. Some were unidentifiable, but there appeared to be at last two different pill bottles, some wire, and a round piece of metal that looked like a compact disc. Extreme care would have to be taken not to touch anything, because at least two pieces of threaded pipe—possible bombs—lay under the bed near a pair of pants.

The light blue denim jeans with beige pocket trim that had been hanging out through the back corner the first night I found the cabin had been pulled down by rodents once again, even though I had tightly rolled them up and placed them under the fallen tree on the roof.

During subsequent trips there would be time to document, map and make an itemized list for the FBI. More than likely, important evidence would be inside or around the structure and I felt responsible since it was on my turf.

As Betty and I started our climb up the mountain we speculated about what Ted would think of us going through everything in his secret sanctuary.

The summer after the arrest, prosecutors found a reference in Ted's journals about a booby-trap out in the woods that was designed to kill someone. They asked him if he had really hidden a deadly bomb out there and if he had, where it might be located.

Smugly, and with a sarcastic sneer on his face, he replied there was nothing. His arrogant look, however, said something different, like, "You'll never find it and I don't have to tell you anything, anyway."

It made me wonder if he still hoped someone would accidentally trigger the booby-trap so he could claim another victim. He probably wouldn't have minded if that was me, my wife or one of our dogs.

We'll never know, but I do remember an unexplained incident in the early '90s that was a sign of the evil things that were happening around us.

One afternoon Betty hurried into the house after a short hike and said, "I walked up to the first cabin and got an extremely uneasy feeling, the kind you get when you know someone is watching you." She said the sense was overwhelming; even the dogs felt it and the hair on their backs stood straight up. She turned around and rushed home.

She obviously wasn't joking, but I couldn't explain what had happened so I tried to play it down, attributing it to some passing feeling. Maybe that was the case. Or maybe Ted was watching her from an observation spot with his rifle sights leveled on her or one of the dogs.

As we worked our way up the mountain, I said to Betty, "One thing I do know is that it's been a little more than a year since Ted was arrested and there hasn't been one theft, vandalism, or strange unexplained occurrence around here since then."

Even though this hike took place before I was able to read Ted's own journals, where he defiantly took credit for most of those incidents, the suspicion of his guilt was already firmly rooted in my mind.

When we finally reached the small shelf, Betty was amazed by the way the cabin blended in to the mountainside.

We took off our packs and while she scanned the cabin and its interior I set up my camera to take pictures. The first picture was one of Betty and me by the cabin door. Then, after taking some more of the outside, I started to make a detailed list and map the location of any visible items for the FBI.

My first list wouldn't be complete because of the ice and since I was reluctant to move anything. It would take at least three more trips to finish the inventory. Even then, other items would be found after the FBI came.

While numbering and describing the visible items in the secret cabin I thought back to an evening phone call from agent Dave Weber on April 23, just three days earlier.

Dave had said Ted was acting as his own lawyer, ordering and then voraciously reading any law books he could find while planning his case. According to Dave, Ted's public defenders Quin Denvir and Judy Clarke were going along with the plan and were working with him.

I figured Ted probably had some trick in mind and would most likely discard these defense lawyers.

As my thoughts returned to the task at hand, it seemed like such a bizarre situation, me making a list of clothing, tools, parts of devices, etc., that belonged to Ted the hermit mountain man while he was in jail diligently studying law books in order to save himself from the death penalty.

I continued my list while Betty began a perimeter search, working away from the cabin in tight concentric circles, looking everywhere, especially in the juniper shrubs and other bushes.

The outside search wouldn't be completed on that trip. Many items, especially clothing, were found caught on bushes and tree butts later. Before the summer was over I would find nearly eighty items inside and around the cabin (see Inventory at end of chapter). Most were in plain sight, but some were intentionally concealed.

That April day, I finished packing away my pencil and tablet and after taking a few more photographs, Betty and I headed back down the mountain.

I was eager to call Dave Weber and share the news that the snow was melting and the secret cabin held many more intriguing objects than we had anticipated.

The FBI team had been delayed and wouldn't get back as early as planned. I made a trip—and more discoveries—alone on May 4. After talking to Dave Weber then, we decided it would be best if I returned and draped a large tarp over the cabin to protect it and the contents. Betty and I made this trip together on June 10, when we resumed perimeter searches and found many more items that had been packed off by rodents. Some were several hundred feet away and we wondered just how many things would never be found.

This time, I made a video tape of all the evidence before we covered the cabin to await the FBI. When agents arrived, much of our time was spent searching other areas, and we found nothing new at the secret cabin.

Every investigation at the secret cabin had been a juggling act between not disturbing important evidence and yet trying to preserve it.

Boards, pieces of tarpaper, and plywood pieces were used in the cabin construction. The plywood piece with handwritten penciled notes about the application of the insect-repellent flowers of sulphur was found on June 4, 1998.

The stove was full of charcoal and soot, and the aluminum stovepipe had been so hot at some point it had melted through in three places close to the ceiling and home-made roof jack.

From the looks of the holes, Ted had come dangerously close to burning down his chalet.

CHRIS WAITS' INVENTORY OF ITEMS FROM THE SECRET CABIN
1. Four-quart aluminum cooking kettle.
2. Two-quart aluminum cooking kettle.
3. Brown-gold mug with black-white floral design.
4. White plastic rectangular pill box with sliding top.
5. Green Bic-type lighter.
6. Aluminum frying pan.
7. Metal kettle bail with wooden handle.
8. Utility wire bail type handle for kettle and frying pan.
9. Light blue denim designer Levis with beige pocket trim.
10. Dark blue denim designer Levis with orange stitching.
11. Multiple pairs of yellow latex gloves open and used.
12. Unopened packages of Skaggs Alpha Beta Store brand yellow latex gloves purchased in Salt Lake City, Utah.

13. Plastic bag that contained Globe brand plastic utility drop cloth, 9-by-12-foot, from Seattle, Wash.
14. G.I.-type survival knife in sheath with whetstone in a snap pouch on the front of the sheath.
15. Five-inch-long thick aluminum pipe threaded on one end.
16. Heavy blue-and-white fine braid nylon rope hanging on a nail inside on the wall.
17. Coil of yellow nylon rope.
18. Hand-built stove made from a five gallon oil can.
19. Insulated stove board bent to fit the corner of the cabin, standing on edge to insulate the wall.
20. Short piece of eight-inch stovepipe opened up to form a door for the stove and held in place with wire.
21. Four-inch steel stovepipe crimped to fit into the large rear vent hole on the oil can stove.
22. Four-inch aluminum vent pipe.
23. Assorted tin cans, burned and with jagged open lids.
24. Large (64 ounces) plastic Dr. Pepper soda pop jug used for water, with date 12/06/94 stamped on the top of the lid.
25. One pair of about size 9 boots, Sorrel type (rubber bottom, leather upper) snow packs with felt liners.
26. Assorted angle iron scraps.
27. Assorted sheet metal scraps, some cut out.
28. Pieces of six-inch steel stovepipe outside of the cabin piled with numerous other pieces of metal.
29. Clear glass aspirin bottle with white snap lid.
30. One rectangular curved piece of sheet metal with Phillips 66 label on it. (The piece looked like what was cut out of the stove when it was built.).
31. Numerous pieces of olive drab rubberized nylon similar to the material used to build reinforced nylon rubber rafts.
32. Coils of wire, baling or stove-type steel wire.
33. Lengths of green nylon rope.
34. Lengths of blue nylon rope.
35. Small square glass bottle.
36. Metal split ring (keychain type).
37. One-inch threaded metal coupler.

38. Compass top for survival knife (glass broken).
39. Ten-pound potato sack from Stevensville, MT.
40. Flat round metallic metal piece, thin with hole in the center and black paint around the hole; resembled a compact disc.
41. Silver duct tape.
42. Aluminum, flat metal utility handle for use with fry pan and cooking kettles.
43. Small pieces of blue nylon tarp cut out into rectangles, possibly repair patches for roof tarp.
44. White nylon rope coil.
45. Fine-weave light-colored nylon rope tied to small tree and door frame for support.
46. Blue-and-white marbled plastic handle that had been sawed from a hairbrush or mirror. Handle had heavy black paint splotch with a well defined fingerprint clearly visible (probably why it was sawed off). The handle was hidden under the bed in pine needles.
47. Pieces of cardboard with printing on them, used as cabin wall insulation and covering.
48. Deer skull from buck shot right below one antler, with the other antler sawed off.
49. Numerous pieces of aluminum foil.
50. Pieces of olive drab plastic rain poncho.
51. Brightly colored striped longsleeve sweater.
52. Lengths of green nylon cord.
53. Metal clip, resembling small money clip.
54. Long blade from a bow saw that was hidden between the inside cabin corner and the metal stove board behind the stove.
55. Numerous pieces of bone.
56. Small pile of used nails (removed from miner's cabin).
57. Small oval metal piece with narrow slit and hole cut into it.
58. Small file, flat type.
59. Tan polyester Henley shirt, stuck in bushes outside.
60. Round green plastic holed base with a cone shape molded into the center. This piece resembles or even might be the

insert for a Tupperware lettuce container, the part that holds the lettuce head in place.
61. Lead sheets and scraps.
62. Numerous zip-lock bags with bottoms chewed and contents missing, no doubt eaten or removed by animals.
63. Empty bag for Skaggs Alpha Beta latex gloves, large, purchased in Salt Lake City, Utah.
64. Rabbit skull with small caliber bullet hole through it.
65. Metal flat washer.
66. Bic-type lighter, another green one.
67. Worm drive hose clamp.
68. Galvanized roofing nails.
69. Thin wooden boards from an old dynamite box.
70. Large blue nylon tarp used to cover entire cabin roof and down the back side; still partially covered with pine boughs.
71. Homemade candle holder, fashioned from a can or jar lid.
72. Homemade roof jack for stovepipe, fashioned from sheet metal.
73. Wood wedge for ax handle.
74. Part of a cooked-cereal or cornmeal box with small metal pullout spout on the side.
75. Pieces of pages from an American Heritage book or magazine.
76. Chunk of hardwood, oak or hickory.
77. Another pair of used yellow latex gloves down the mountain about 100 yards.
78. Remains of a gray hooded sweatshirt lodged in a juniper shrub, heavily chewed and pulled there by animals.
79. Small metal threaded ring.

Many other small items, bits and pieces of cloth, wood, and metal too numerous to mention.

Ted's Bed and Breakfast

About the time Ted Kaczynski turned thirty-three in the mid-1970s, a series of events in the Lincoln area had him churn in anger, nurturing his anti-technology philosophy.

One such event occurred early in July 1975 when one of his neighbors fired up a small bulldozer and cleared away trees knocked down by a heavy snow. To Ted's delight, the trees had blocked the road that ran past his home. But with the road's reopening Ted was furious, and he wrote passionately about it in his journals.

> JULY 5, 1975 [KACZYNSKI JOURNAL]
> Well I have some events to record. After I got back from the hike…I was feeling pretty disappointed and discouraged. After a day or 2 I started to feel better—then that [expletive] [name] took his caterpillar up along the Road that goes past the cabin. That road was sufficiently closed off by [name] (when he put in our new roads) to prevent the passage of ordinary vehicles, but it was still accessible for trail bikes and snowmobiles. Then when we had that extra ordinary storm of wet snow that broke so many trees, that road was so closed off by fallen trees that it was hardly practical for trail bikes and snowmobiles. Then that [expletive] [name] cleared it all out with his cat, though it is still blocked for ordinary vehicles. Makes me want to kill that [expletive]. Anyhow, it got me all upset and very depressed—all the more because the [expletive] is cutting pests [*sic*; probably posts] up along [name] and that cuts down still further the places where I can walk in quiet and solitude.…

This was about the time Ted began to "feel that there was no place to escape civilization," as he wrote in his journals, and started to lay plans to get away from the world around him by building his small, high-mountain secret cabin.

JULY 24, 1975

Today I hiked to a side-gulch of [name]. In a very secluded spot on a steep slope, I started building an 8 X 8 log cabin that I will be able to use year-round.

I have already packed in the stove that I made. After testing the stove I found out that the door was too large and it leaked smoke. I fixed the problem by blocking off part of the door with some old sheet-metal that I scrounged. It seems to work fairly well now.

I have been cutting trees for my cabin with my ax which I find works much better than cutting the logs with my bow saw. Using the ax was awkward at first but now I'm quite used to it.

It was imperative to do some digging to level up the floor for my cabin and I am almost done with this part.

I'm in a very good mood. Things are going well for me on this project.

JULY 27, 1975

My secret log cabin isn't going as fast as I had expected but I'm almost finished with cutting and building the walls.

JULY 28, 1975

Today I finished building the walls and cutting and erecting the logs for the framework of the roof.

JULY 29, 1975

My work today was temporarily halted by a rain storm. I still managed to get the cabin covered over by piling the tops of the trees used for the cabin against it. I built a stove hearth inside and firmly fixed the stove I have built to it by placing rocks and soil around it which also helps protect the logs in the wall from the heat.

I will have to leave tomorrow to replenish some of my supplies.

AUG. 5, 6 AND 7, 1975
On the fifth I returned to my little secret cabin I had been building.

I finished with all of the frame logs today. I haven't chinked the spaces between the logs yet but I will have time this winter to do that by placing small poles and boards between the spaces. I even began to do some of that today.

I was very pleased at how fast I was able to build this secret cabin. It only took me about seven and a half days total time not counting the time I spent cutting wood for my fire.

This last trip I worked more on the roof making it rain proof by covering it with a blue nylon tarp that I took from a place I had found it stored.

Then I cut as much wood for my small stove that I could comfortably store in my small cabin. When I finished I masked the secret cabin with pine boughs and branches from the trees I had used to build the small cabin so that it was camouflaged and could hardly be noticed or seen from more than one hundred feet, or maybe even less.

There isn't a very big chance of my secret cabin being found because it is in a very secret place far away from civilization.

He built his remote structure so he could get away from noise and people, but he also used it and its secret location to plan and plot his acts of murder and revenge. He not only had a hideout between bombings where he changed in and out of his disguise clothing and where he stayed while his beard grew back—apparent from his late-February 1987 encounter with Betty at the old miner's cabin and the disguise clothing found in the secret cabin—but he also had a refuge where he could sometimes build and test his bombs.

His arrest and the events that followed it led to the discovery of this most private part of his life, which was just starting to unfold in the spring of 1997, a year after Ted's arrest.

When Betty and I arrived home late Saturday afternoon, April 26, after our hike to the cabin site, I was eager to call Dave Weber and tell him about everything I'd found.

I had made the first detailed list of cabin contents, and taken two more rolls of pictures, and also drew a diagram to scale of the small hut's interior and where some of the more important evidence was positioned.

Dave had phoned the morning before to say he had just sent a two-foot-by-two-foot aerial photograph of the Stemple area taken from 32,000 feet, with approximately the same scale as topographical maps. He wanted me to mark important locations, including the site of the secret cabin, and return the aerial.

There were still things I hadn't been able to accomplish at the cabin site, such as checking out the scrap pile and the fire pit where Ted had burned and then buried his cans. Some items were still locked in the ice inside the structure, but I'd be returning soon.

Dave and I were now phoning each other almost daily and he was just as excited to get back to Lincoln as I was eager for him to arrive.

After the hard search the previous summer with few discoveries, his effort to find the cabin had become more like a quest. There wasn't anything Dave would like more than to consummate his many hours of toil by standing next to Ted's small log building. That desire was intensified by the fact Ted had taunted agents, calling the FBI a joke. They had a personal stake in the investigation: their pride and reputation.

While waiting that weekend for the FBI aerial to arrive in the mail, I spent my time mapping some of Ted's trails and campsites.

Finally on Wednesday, the postman delivered a long tube that contained the rolled-up photo-map. It was a beautiful, sharp, and very detailed photograph of the mountainous terrain between Lincoln and Stemple Pass, with every detail visible, from ridge and trail to the smallest little valley.

Kaczynski's home cabin in Florence Gulch.

4-24-97

Chris —

Well here we go — hope
this photo - map will help you
spot Teds bed & breakfast.
The scale is 1:24,000

Dave

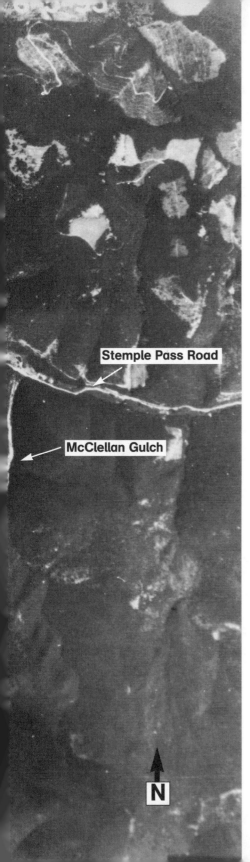

Stemple Pass Road

McClellan Gulch

N

Dave's note that accompanied it read:

> Chris,
>   Well, here we go—hope this photo-map will help you spot Ted's bed and breakfast. The scale is 1:24,000.
>   Dave

On Friday, May 2, I was home working on my notes right after lunch when Bobby Didriksen called and described what amounted to a disruptive morning at the Lincoln Post Office.

While he was picking up his letters, one of the postal workers pulled a package that resembled a mail bomb out of a large mail bag. It wasn't only its weight and composition that made them immediately suspicious, but also to whom it was addressed.

I decided to drive into town and talk to Postmaster Don Pearson. When I got there one postal worker still was shaken and upset.

The heavy package had been mailed in a cardboard Priority Mail envelope, designed to carry a pound or two. But this one weighed in at a hefty eleven pounds, stuffed to the breaking point with a sand-like material. It was wrapped with a clear packaging tape to keep it from rupturing.

It was addressed to none other than Ted, with a return address from a fictitious relative in California.

Don said he suspected it was a hoax; Ted's name was misspelled and the numerical address was not quite right. But he wasn't going to take any chances. He called the Federal Postal Investigator and was told to turn it over to the postal inspector who would drive up from Great Falls, and not to anyone else, not even the FBI. Because it was mail related, the Postal Service had control of this investigation.

The package was then marked with a forwarding address, since Ted no longer lived in Lincoln, and was given unopened to the Postal Investigator when he arrived.

Don was mystified how eleven pounds could be squeezed into a Priority envelope and wondered what kind of material would have that weight-to-volume ratio.

I told him there were many ground compounds, some explosive, that would weigh that much. Magnetite and hematite (black sand) would easily do the job. He said he wanted to bring up an envelope sometime and have me demonstrate.

That afternoon I called Dave Weber and told him about the excitement at the post office. He said none of the agents had heard anything about the package.

On Sunday, May 4, I hiked back up to the secret cabin to check the snow and ice level. On the return trip I followed a circuitous route lower on the mountain.

Directly below the cabin Ted had cut a blaze at least fifteen or twenty years ago on the trunk of a lodgepole pine. The old trail mark provided a new clue that would prove invaluable in future excursions.

As might be expected, Ted marked his forest trails and routes in a non-traditional manner. Old-timers normally blazed both sides of a trunk and cut their marks conspicuously into the trees, usually within eyesight of the next blaze along a trail, so they and others could easily follow routes through heavily forested mountain terrain.

Ted, on the other hand, blazed only one side of the tree to mark the route in, unless it was a special juncture in the trail, like a cut-off point. He marked his trees very carefully, barely nicking the heartwood. His blazes were often spaced several hundred yards apart and couldn't be seen from one another.

Ted traveled the blazed route below the cabin often and knew the general direction so he didn't need many markers to keep him oriented on the criss-crossing game trails. Plus, the infrequent number and positioning of blazes would make it difficult for anyone else to follow the route. After a few trips Ted became familiar with his trails through the timber and didn't need the blazes, which would gradually weather, turn gray, blend into the surroundings and almost disappear.

He took great care to disguise his trails and it took several hours to find all the blazes and flag his route into the secret cabin. The last blaze was located directly below the cabin. As I studied his system it dawned on me that he intentionally ended the trail with a blaze directly downhill of his destination. He knew that from the last marked tree he had to walk straight up the mountain's sixty percent slope quite a distance and he'd arrive at the cabin site.

All these precautions would have been tedious and time-consuming for the average person, but Ted had plenty of time and his cryptic methods virtually ensured that nobody would be able to follow him or locate any of his secret mountain places.

When Dave Weber called the following day, Monday, May 5, he was excited about the discovery of the blazes. He indicated they might be a key that would help unlock some of the remaining puzzles. As we talked about their importance, he started to share information about sketches Ted had drawn in his journals, including diagrams of secret caches and camps, marked only by vague points of reference like rocks, trees, streams, and tree blazes.

The agents knew the sketches were important maps and they had spent much of the previous summer trying to interpret them, but Ted delineated the maps in such a way that the caches and camps could have been located anywhere in the sea of trees surrounding Lincoln.

It would take someone with an intimate knowledge of the surroundings to break the code and find the areas that were mapped and described so generically.

Ted had an enormous advantage: he knew the general area being mapped so he didn't need to describe distinguishable features like mountains or streams.

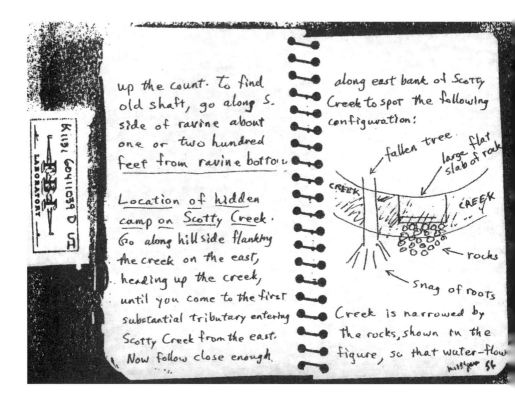

up the count. To find old shaft, go along S. side of ravine about one or two hundred feet from ravine bottom.

Location of hidden camp on Scotty Creek. Go along hillside flanking the creek on the east, heading up the creek, until you come to the first substantial tributary entering Scotty Creek from the east. Now follow close enough.

along east bank of Scotty Creek to spot the following configuration:

fallen tree   large flat slab of rock
CREEK
CREEK
rocks
snag of roots

Creek is narrowed by the rocks, shown in the figure, so that water-flow

But I knew the country as well as or better than Ted.

Dave also talked about a trip he took back to FBI headquarters in Washington, D.C., where all the Unabomber evidence was being stored, so he could study every note, map and description and possibly find a mark, a star, or any other small dot that would indicate where Ted had built his secret cabin.

He found no such mark.

I knew the cabin and the evidence inside were important in the government's case against Ted, but there had to be something more involved to trigger such a huge expenditure of manpower and money.

Dave acknowledged the Feds were concerned about public safety: Ted's bragging about setting a booby-trap out in the woods.

UNDATED JOURNAL ENTRY
Summer '77 I set a booby-trap intended to kill

172

someone, but I won't say what kind or where because if this paper is ever found the trap might be harmlessly removed.

But it probably doesn't have more than maybe a 1 in 5 chance of killing or seriously injuring someone.

FBI agents admitted later this journal entry, along with others about the secret cabin and what might be hidden in or around it, prompted their intensive search. Dave said their instruction from the top was, "You will find it."

I asked Dave if he'd send me copies of Ted's cryptic little drawings to help with my continuing search.

He said he couldn't, but he'd bring them when he returned to Lincoln. His need for caution was apparent. Dave said we had to keep our conversations confidential.

He also had a sense of urgency. He was afraid if we didn't find and gather these exhibits soon there might not be enough time to have them examined and entered as evidence by trial time in the fall.

It was astounding that such a high-profile case didn't warrant more expediency. There were other inner workings of the federal agency that were confusing and seemed counterproductive.

Dave had shared his disappointment and disgust that the agents in charge wouldn't allow him to come to Lincoln alone so we could start examining evidence found in the secret cabin.

As he sarcastically put it, "God forbid that we should find anything without them."

It didn't seem that professional pride, jealousy, and personal egos should have anything to do with this or any other investigation. He agreed, but admitted there wasn't anything he could do.

Dave was aware that if it wasn't for him the prosecution might not even know about the secret cabin's discovery, because they had repeatedly ignored my offers to help. At one point I had even considered letting them find out about my discovery from the press along with everyone else.

He was the one who had taken the time to build our relationship and had gone out of his way to enlist my help, realizing the enormous disadvantage they faced in working in an unfamiliar environment.

I was sure I could understand Ted's coded diagrams and find the secret locations plotted in the drawings if given a chance.

Dave said he was trying to put a team together for June 1 and asked if that would work. He and Max Noel were worried about invading our privacy and didn't want to bring too many people along.

As we hung up it was apparent Dave was ready and eager to leave California and come to Lincoln, but everyone involved with the case wanted to get in on the action; they didn't want to miss the first trip to the secret cabin. At one point, they said if they couldn't go, then neither could he, which seemed petty. While Dave was concerned with the integrity and deterioration of key evidence, other members of the Task Force seemed worried about missing out.

Later that day, Betty and I hiked to an old mine adit about three fourths of a mile up the gulch, thinking Ted might have used it as a cache site.

Several years earlier the portal to the mine had been nearly closed off by small rock slides, but there had been just enough space to squeeze into the tunnel. Ted was such a packrat, hiding things everywhere, that there was a good chance he had things stashed away inside.

His blaze line to the secret cabin was close by and the old mine site couldn't be seen from the double-tracked and seldom-used road that ran up the gulch. It was a perfect hiding place that I hadn't explored for probably two decades.

When we arrived at the old mine the opening had been recently covered by more slides of loose stones and gravel. I dug around by hand and finally enlarged the entrance just enough to squeeze through. But when I did, my body blocked the light and it was impossible to see past the first ten feet of the tunnel.

Betty didn't like the sight of me wedged into a small opening in the side of the mountain with just my feet showing and she implored me to pull out and return later with rope and better lighting.

I'm not intimidated by close underground spaces, but at her urging I backed out.

We would return to that spot when FBI agents came to Lincoln to begin field investigations.

On Wednesday, May 7, Max called from San Francisco to see if the cabin photos were back so he could get copies. They hadn't arrived yet, but they should show up any day, I said. The film had been sent to Seattle to avoid any possibility of a local film processor becoming curious about the secret cabin.

We then talked about some of the cabin contents, including the pairs of yellow latex gloves. Max said he would do some research on the gloves, so he wanted all the codes and sticker information from the packages.

Then he asked if there were any small steel ammo cans inside the cabin, which really made me wonder just what else the FBI expected to find hidden in the mountains.

None that I saw, I said, but they could be encased in the snow still inside the cabin.

That evening Betty and I hiked up the creek bottom about a mile and a half, and found the snow and ice were melting slowly.

It was almost impossible to concentrate on anything else during the next few days. Dave and Max had aroused my curiosity with hints of ammunition cans, secret cache locations, and maps from Ted's journals.

Dave called Thursday morning, May 15, and said Max had received the single cabin picture I sent. Trained in his job to be perpetually suspicious, Max promptly took the photo to Dave's office and asked if it was the same cabin Dave had seen a picture of.

"Yup, that's it," Dave replied.

We continued to have almost daily phone conversations and with each there was new information. It was like slowly turning the focus ring on a telephoto lens, changing the image from a total blur to one of enticing detail.

On Tuesday, June 3, I had finally received the photo reprints and mailed them to Dave, along with another set of maps, an initial list of cabin contents and the diagram of objects inside the cabin. I had called Dave the day before to inform him everything would be in the mail the next day.

Max called Wednesday and said he had determined the yellow latex gloves were purchased in Salt Lake City. The Skaggs Alpha Beta name wasn't around long, he said, because the company sold out to a larger chain after being in business a short time. But the store's brief period of operation and the purchase of the gloves coincided with a particular time when Ted was known to have been there.

Max said the original item numbers, bar-coding, and place of manufacture and sale were irrefutable, things Ted couldn't explain away in court.

Dave and I continued to talk almost daily. During one of our conversations he told me the prosecution had built a scaled-down, but true-to-life model of Ted's home cabin to use in the trial. The model had a side wall that could be removed to reveal everything inside, including Ted's work bench, bed, wood box, stove, shelves, and storage areas, even the small attic. I wondered if they would build the same type of model for the secret cabin.

By mid-June the FBI team decided they couldn't make it back to Lincoln until Monday, July 21. Max said it was the first day everybody could get away.

Several days later I suggested to Max that he should let Dave come up alone and get started with the investigation. He was irritated at the mere suggestion.

On June 24, I called Dave and told him another package was in the mail, including pictures of rock caves, campsites, firewood caches, and tree blazes located along some of Ted's trails, along with a map pinpointing their locations in the gulch.

A week later Dave called and said the package had arrived. As we talked I could sense there was something he wanted to share, another mystery that hadn't been solved. I had learned to read him pretty well and had become adept at paying attention to my intuition since the agents were always guarded about sharing facts.

So during the rest of that day I went back over my notes, looking for a clue to this newest mystery.

My 1996 journal entry caught my attention. The June 15 entry described a conversation with Butch when he had said the agents were looking for these clues: "Mentions cliffs, water dries up in the fall, rock slide, diagonal rock, herbs in vegetation, and that maybe firearms are involved."

Firearms had to be the key. So the next evening when Dave called we started to talk about what the agents wanted to accomplish during their time in Lincoln.

In the middle of the conversation I said to Dave we needed to take time to recover Ted's gun.

Dave said yes, most assuredly, then suddenly stopped, knowing he had been caught off guard. He told me to say nothing about the gun because it would get him into trouble. I assured him I wouldn't.

He then went on to talk about the six guns Ted owned, including his homemade zip gun, and how all had been recovered except his 30-30 rifle.

Agents were sure Ted had used the weapon in a Lincoln-area shooting crime many years earlier. Even though the statute of limitations had expired, Ted was now the suspect and they were trying to close the books on that case.

Ted had written in his journals that he had at times placed his 30-30 rifle in a special container and hidden it out in the woods. So looking for that would be another part of our work when agents arrived.

I finished my last map, gathered a new batch of photographs and mailed them off on Monday, July 14. This would be my last correspondence with the FBI before they arrived in Lincoln on the following Monday.

Dave had managed a quick trip to the area on July 7 and 8 to interview a couple of vandalism victims who had owned cabins near Lincoln and to go flying with a government pilot to take aerial photographs of my gulch and the surrounding mountains. He never did touch ground in Lincoln, but I waved as they flew overhead.

On Sunday, July 20, Dave made one last telephone call to me, saying they would depart the following morning. He'd call me Monday evening to make plans for the next day.

The agenda was full and I looked forward to helping the agents, because they were strangers in a strange land. And we were getting a late start.

Caught in His Own Trap

Often described as a lonely hermit, Ted Kaczynski had a penchant for recording details of his life in journals and also in small spiral notebooks he always carried tucked in his shirt pocket. It was as if he were fulfilling a basic human need to communicate, to tell someone about his life's deeds in succinct and descriptive handwritten notes, even if it were only himself.

As FBI agents and prosecutors read through the thousands of documents recovered in his Florence Gulch cabin, they knew those acknowledgments penned in his own hand would prove his undoing in a court of law if they could uncover corroborating evidence.

The journals were a dream for them, but had to be a nightmare for Ted. There would be little defense of his acts of terrorism, especially if prosecutors could link what he wrote to actual physical evidence and testimony from people who knew him.

Ted never intended to have his thoughts and writings fall into the hands of the enemy. According to federal agents, he had a detailed escape plan that included an incendiary bomb in his cabin loft to burn and destroy the structure and its contents at the first sign of trouble. He could trigger the demolition before he fled by pulling a cord that led from the device located by his bedside near the front door, behind which there was a rifle always loaded and ready for a quick escape.

From Florence Gulch, he could hike the short distance to McClellan Gulch and his secret cabin, which was a gateway to the rest of the world. There he could change clothes, cut his beard if he wanted, and grab food and ammunition from several nearby buried caches. Then, while investigators sorted through the burning remains of the home cabin, he could escape undetected into thousands of acres of wilderness through the rugged Rocky Mountains north into Canada.

But he had been tricked out of his cabin and arrested before he could set his escape plan into motion. Now Ted could do little to prevent the revelation of his secret life.

FBI agents were returning to Lincoln intending to link his journal writings to physical evidence found in the secret cabin and various hunting camps and caches buried in the woods, and thus thwart any defense that his journals were nothing more than the fiction of a fertile and literary mind.

On the morning of Monday, July 21, 1997, I awoke after a restless night, knowing agents were airborne and on their way to Montana. My stomach was jittery. I was anxious to see and try to decipher the mysterious maps Ted had drawn. Dave Weber and Max Noel had talked more than once about these hand-drawn sketches and their significance.

I was convinced, because of all his hiking trips and time he had spent in the hills, Ted knew the country around our homes better than any man alive—except me.

Dave had described some of the details from Ted's maps and drawings during our phone conversations. Even though the locations were ambiguous—the rock cliffs, talus slopes and large rocks Ted used as landmarks could be almost anywhere—I could call to mind several locations to fit each particular description.

Ted had used his cache system much like the old-time miners and mountain men who settled the West, burying ammunition and survival supplies in strategic locations safely hidden from animals and other humans. In case memory failed him, cryptic diagrams could lead him to any of the caches where he could grab rifle shells or non-perishable foodstuffs and quickly be on his way.

Dave said some of the drawings were marked with fallen trees and logs; others noted the dimensions of small trees. That bothered me because during the ensuing years the logs could have rotted away and the small trees and saplings would have grown considerably.

Only time would tell what natural changes might make the discoveries more difficult. One thing for sure, the cliffs, talus slopes, and streams would remain reliable and important clues.

Dave phoned Monday night and said he and Max were in Lincoln, had checked into a motel room and would be out in the morning.

The first task at hand was to take them to Ted's secret cabin. There they would use the Global Positioning System (GPS) to get an exact fix on the location. They'd have to set up the device and take the reading a short distance from the cabin because the GPS required a window through the tree canopy to take sightings off three satellites. The nearest suitable opening was probably 100 to 200 feet east of the cabin.

All through the night, Ted's journals, maps, and drawings flashed through my mind. As I lay there far too excited to sleep, I kept going over questions I wanted to ask and any information that I should share with Dave and Max.

Max already knew about the books and some other things that were missing from my home and I hoped he could tell me if they had been recovered at Ted's cabin. Butch Gehring also said Ted had gotten away with one of his books and we both were curious if we would recover our property.

Tuesday morning, I poured a second cup of coffee and checked over hiking gear one last time before the agents arrived. I expected them early, and sure enough, as I finished lacing my hiking boots I looked out the window and there they were, driving up to the house in a rented burgundy Ford Explorer.

Max and Dave got out of the car. They were alone and that was a surprise. They had wanted to limit the number of agents who came along but Joel Moss and Terry Turchie had talked like they would join the search, eager to see the secret cabin.

Max said something had come up so Joel and Terry weren't able to make it.

We shouldered our day packs and without further delay headed up the mountain, planning to reconnoiter near the secret cabin and scout some of the rocks and cliffs nearby that first day.

As I started up the old mining road I felt like a Boy Scout leader with a troop trailing behind; Max and Dave, always curious, asked questions continuously about the flora and fauna around us. It was apparent after a only short distance we would have fun, which would lighten the mood of the serious task at hand.

Max was keenly interested in the plants and asked the identity of any he saw. He wanted more than the plant's name, both common and scientific; he also wondered if each was edible, palatable or had medicinal value. In addition to satisfying his personal curiosity about the mountain plants, he wanted to learn as much as possible about the numerous species Ted had mentioned in his journals.

Both Dave and Max were enjoying the trip into the majestic western Montana mountains. Dave talked about how good it felt to get out into the field after sitting behind his desk for so long.

As we dropped over a small ridge and moved down along a stream bottom, Dave asked if there were any bears around, either black or grizzly.

I laughed and described a huge pile of bear scat, possibly left by a grizzly, that was right behind Ted's secret cabin the last time I was there.

Dave said he was glad he was packing his trusty, custom-built, .44 magnum, to use as a noisemaker if nothing else. Max was carrying his service revolver. With all their firepower in the woods it had seemed appropriate to leave my .357 magnum Ruger pistol at home holstered.

You rarely need a gun in the mountains anyway, since predatory animals in the wilderness are much less a threat than the two-legged predators found in some of our cities. But when the agents asked if they could carry their guns, I replied certainly, if it made them feel better.

The farther we hiked the more comfortable I became with the two of them, especially Max. Dave and I had spent a considerable amount of time talking, both in person and on the phone, so we had established a rapport, but Max and I had conversed only a few times.

Max was much more cautious about what he said. This was understandable, and I recalled how my friend Butch had said Max asked him what kind of guy I was, if I was "solid" and could be trusted.

As the summer morning wore on, the peacefulness of the mountains helped everyone relax and open up a little more.

I started to learn new details about the case.

We came to a small clearing and stopped for a short rest. I asked Max if he had found any wire in Ted's cabin that might match what had disappeared from my storage areas.

He replied it was very possible because Ted experimented with many different types of electrical wiring in the construction of his bombs. But he disguised the wire and other bomb components, using sneaky tricks to keep investigators confused.

Early on, Ted had wired his bombs with a common two-conductor "zip cord," the type commonly used for lamp and low-power appliance cords, Max said. But Ted altered the cord to throw the FBI off track and made it nearly impossible to trace by removing two or three strands from, for example, a 14-gauge, 16-strand wire, which transformed it into a type of cord no factory produced.

Max went on to say that after Ted ran out of two-conductor zip cord, he procured some extension cord wire, the type with three or four colored conductors encased in a black rubberized sheath. It was unlikely anyone would ever be able to trace the cord, but Ted didn't take any chances. He removed each black, white, green, etc., conductor from the outer sheath and altered them in the same manner, by pulling strands of wire. These deceptive actions demonstrated Ted's meticulousness in covering his tracks.

Max said a section of this black extension cord wire was found inside his home cabin and that, other than the missing strands, it matched perfectly the wire used in some of Ted's last devices.

I thought of the huge supply of surplus wire stored up my gulch. During the last thirty years, I had accumulated a half dozen large boxes of used wire, ranging in size from small automotive strands to wire large enough for welding leads.

Ted certainly could have taken whatever he wanted, unnoticed. I told Max and Dave about the wire and Dave said he would like to get some samples to see if they might match the different types found in the devices.

Once again that sick feeling came over me as I thought about all the ways I had unknowingly provided the means by which Ted carried out his acts of destruction.

As we hiked along the mountainside Dave started to describe certain large rocks and cliffs that were landmarks for Ted's buried caches and asked if I might be able to find them.

The caches, I was soon to find out, hid Ted's 30-30 rifle, many rounds of ammunition for all his weapons, food items, survival gear, and possibly bomb parts.

We neared the last extremely steep pitch just below Ted's secret cabin and paused so Dave and Max could catch their breath. While they rested I started to tell them about Ted's campsites I had found and the times and places I had seen him up my gulch when he hadn't seen me.

We were standing there within a hundred feet of the cabin, but they had no idea we were so close. I had told Dave more than once that "if you miss Ted's secret cabin by a hundred feet or more then you've missed it."

Then I told them how close we were, but as they scanned the mountainside they didn't believe me.

We moved several more steps up the slope and then the ghostly image of the horizontal logs in a vertical world of tree trunks started to take shape. It was clear both Max and Dave were excited. The moment of discovery raised their adrenaline level and helped them move quickly up the last steep incline to the small ledge and the front of Ted's hideout.

They both smiled broadly, relishing the conquest as we reached the front door of the cabin and the end of their year-long quest.

As we removed our gear and set up for the work at hand, we had to wonder how horrified Ted would feel if he knew his secret site was in the hands of the very law enforcement people he had taunted in the past. As recently as April 1995, Ted had made fun of the FBI in his letter to *The New York Times*. "Clearly we are in a position to do a great deal of damage," he wrote. "And it doesn't appear that the FBI is going to catch us any time soon. The FBI is a joke."

While Dave removed the GPS from his pack, Max decided to explore the perimeter. I stayed with Dave, eager to ask him more questions.

He looked for a spot on the forest floor to set up the GPS and he quickly understood the paucity of locations for a window through the tree cover large enough to get a multiple-satellite fix.

By the time we settled on a small grassy opening east of the cabin, Max had vanished. Dave moved the GPS, a compact olive green rectangular unit with built-in dual satellite tracking rods, several times before he settled on a spot where he could align his sightings.

I continued to quiz Dave about the maps and other documents they both were carrying in their packs. Finally he looked up from the GPS and said: "Go ahead and read the notes for yourself."

He pointed to a black loose-leaf notebook inside his pack.

I couldn't believe what I had in my hands as I leafed through copies of dozens of journal documents penned by Ted that had been organized in the binder.

My mind was locked on the pages while I mentally catalogued and memorized each one.

Dave concentrated on setting up the GPS as I read. I even gained a little extra time because the GPS was a new model and he wasn't sure how it operated, aggravated by the fact he had left the instruction manual in their Lincoln motel room.

As I studied Ted's documents describing the buried caches, it was impossible not to notice the meticulously detailed and descriptive legends included with each hand-sketched diagram. Each tree and sapling surrounding a cache was identified by species and measured to within a quarter of an inch. Ted not only measured and noted the depth of the hole he dug to hold an ammo box, for instance, but he also precisely measured the distance from the top of the container to ground level after it was placed in the hole.

Then he carefully inventoried the ammo box's content in minuscule detail. Food was identified and then equated into the caloric intake needed to sustain a person in the wilderness.

The basic human needs and the staples stored in the cache were calculated to within 1/100th of an ounce or gram, "3 bags flour, each containing 2 days' ration of flour at 5.33 oz per day, being 75% whole wheat, 25% white flour, total 32 oz. flour." He used mathematical symbols to describe stored food amounts, e.g.: "1 bag milk ($\approx$ [approximately equal to] 6.7 oz.)."

Ted also kept track of every round of ammunition for each of the four calibers of gun he owned, not only the live rounds in his possession, but every spent cartridge as well.

He never fired unless he thought it was a sure shot, whether at a running rabbit at night or a standing coyote at long range. He kept a tally of his ammo supply, how each round was used and whether it was a hit or miss. That information was entered into mathematical

<u>Sack contains</u>
big shelter cloth
sweater
pot
gizmo for | <u>pot contains</u>
 hanging pot | pot holder
 | plastic dish
 | knob
 | 8 teaspoons baking powder
 | 3 bags flour, each containing 2 days' ration of
 | flour at 5.33 oz per day, being 75% whole wheat
 | 25% white flour, total 32 oz flour

<u>Ass pack contains</u>
4 books matches
fat pine
sunflower seeds
10 oz sugar
compass
1 bag milk (≈ 6.7g)
1 pack Koolaid
Additional ties for
  large shelter cloth
Papaya Ensyme
<u>Also Take</u>
Rifle (.30-06)
Scope
hatchet
sheath knife
blue notebook

<u>White Sack contains</u>
35 rounds 180-grain .30-06
Several boxes waterproof matches
Skin medicine
radio
All relevant maps
2 fishhooks and line
Extra string
iodized salt

Canteen
Oil bottle
Plastic water bottle?
Extra blanket?
Dried bread

equations so he could track percentages of success and failure and the cost of each round per caliber.

July 14, 1975 [Kaczynski journal]
One morning I went down from my camp to the lower areas to look for deer. While sitting on a stump to rest, I heard some noise in the woods, and then a large cow elk broke out into a logged over area—followed by 3 coyotes! The elk was clearly upset—but the coyotes left off the chase probably having concluded that that big old elk was too tough for them, and stood around as if trying to decide what to do next. I tried a shot at one from a long way off—didn't want to try to sneak up too much since coyotes are so sharp. I thought I ought to hit it, but I missed, probably because the rifle went off before I was ready for it. The trouble is that the .30-06 has a lighter trigger pull than my .22. Unconsciously following my practice with the .22, I put a certain amount of pressure on the trigger before I was quite ready to fire. Anyway, I got all depressed again, over wasting a 30¢ cartridge like that.

[from Kaczinsky's Spanish-language journal, translated by Language Services Unit. Words in italics were English in the original.]
June 23. [1981]
It was maybe 4 weeks ago I shot a ground-hog; (*ground-hog; i.e., yellow-bellied marmot*), near my cabin.
I shot it at the head; knocked it out and got blood at the site; but before I could get it, he recovered enough to go to the burrow. Although I spent a lot of time digging the burrow, I could not get it....[Expletive]! This puts my average (*average*) under 90%; I mean, my average since last August. So, without a doubt, I will raise my average again...

I was amazed when I read further and noted the detailed information regarding the ammunition Ted had stashed in one of his buried caches or carried with him. He not only recorded the number of rounds for each caliber, but also the grain weight and composition of each bullet, e.g.:

KACZYNSKI'S HANDWRITTEN AMMUNITION INVENTORY
74 rounds 180 grain .30-06, 12 rounds 220 grain .30-06, 10 rounds 150 grain .30-06, 5 rounds 170 grain .30-30.

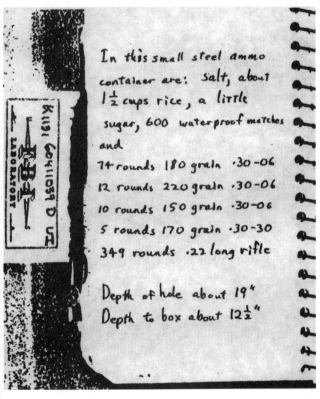

If that wasn't enough, he went on to describe the type of bullet as well, e.g., bronze point, silver tip, soft nose, etc.

The more I read the more the inconsistency of Ted's life unfolded. Here was a person obsessed with neatly organizing and assigning mathematical detail to everything around him, yet the design and construction of his root cellar, for example, was a feeble attempt at construction. It lacked signs of even the most basic building skills, resembling more a child's fort than an important structure necessary to store and protect food.

Time seemed to stand still as I studied the documents. But then I was nudged back to reality as I looked up and noticed Max taking our photograph from a spot slightly below us.

Max walked through the lodgepole tree trunks to the GPS and he couldn't say enough about the beauty, solitude, and tranquility of my gulch. It was apparent he fully understood the reasons Ted had spent so much time up here. What a contrast to their hectic lifestyle living and working in San Francisco. I couldn't imagine trading places with them.

Dave and Max were invited to come back any time. They both said they'd love to return with their wives for a vacation after the Unabom saga concluded.

After Dave obtained the GPS coordinates we all moved back to the secret cabin, set up my tripod, and prepared to take pictures of the cabin with all three of us standing in front of it.

As we stood there the agents joked and exchanged lewd remarks, which shocked me, ranging from one suggestion that we all drop our pants and "moon" Ted from his secret cabin, to other options much worse.

I wanted no part of the whole affair and was even less impressed when the conversation shifted to speculation about how Ted might accept the presentation of some "special photographs" if they were anonymously sent to him in his prison cell.

To me, it wasn't that Ted didn't deserve a taste of his own medicine, but rather that I didn't approve of lowering myself or the agents to his level.

The more I learned about Ted and his secret agenda of hatred and revenge the harder I found it to understand him and also the motivation of a small number of Lincoln people who were forming Ted's "bleeding hearts club," corresponding with him on a regular basis and projecting him as a gentle and misunderstood genius. They were either blinded to the truth or refused to look at it. I wondered what their feelings would have been if a spouse or child had been Ted's victim.

After posing for pictures in front of the cabin and studying some of the more important evidence inside, we talked about moving on to a couple of Ted's campsites and returning to the cabin at a later time. They felt it would be time well spent, allowing Max and Dave a chance to become more familiar with the terrain while looking for new clues.

We dropped straight down the mountain searching for sites that fit the descriptions in Ted's drawings.

The more we hiked and talked together, the more I learned about

Ted's writings and the containers he used to conceal things. They ranged from waterproof steel ammunition boxes to glass and plastic jars and bottles.

Most of these caches were dug deep, a foot and a half or more beneath the forest floor, e.g., "Depth of hole in which cartridges are buried, 18". Distance of uppermost part of jars from surface of soil, about 15"."

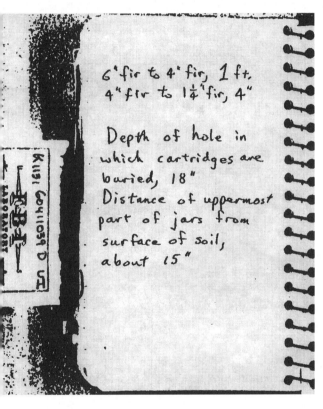

The FBI agents were anxious to find at least one of the caches. Its discovery, along with that of the secret cabin, would help prove in court that Ted's journals were valid and reliable descriptions of his life.

Such evidence would also lend credence to some of Ted's other writings, that is, if he wrote about burying an ammo can and it was there, then when he wrote about sending a mail bomb to somebody it was arguably a fact and not just fantasy or a symbolic entry.

We all were convinced that what he wrote he meant, down to every ounce of salt he used.

The irony of it all! In spite of his efforts to live in obscurity, his methodical practice of recording nearly everything now exposed his entire life to the very FBI team he had just a few years before called a joke. The agents were definitely enjoying this role reversal.

As we reached the creek bottom Max stopped for a second and

pulled out more notes, descriptions, and drawings and began reading them slowly. One particular passage caught my attention and I told them it fit a spot nearby.

We headed up the next mountain, split up and began to search small caves and crevices located within some rock outcroppings.

The next hour or two passed slowly. We found nothing. Spirits were still high though and we knew if we could find even one cache it would be a major victory.

As I neared the edge of a ridge that ran like the tail of a *T. rex* upward to the summit of the mountain, I spotted quite a few small animal bones strewn about in the soil and duff of a crevice in the rock outcropping.

I picked through the bleached remains and noticed something out of place, a small plastic bottle.

I shouted down to Max and Dave, "I've got something, come on up."

As they neared, I said it wasn't clear what I'd found and that I couldn't take all the credit for the discovery because some digging and burrowing animal had helped reveal the buried stash.

We stared at the small cylindrical plastic bottle, translucent white in color, but nobody wanted to touch or move it, fearing it might be one of Ted's hidden forest booby-traps.

Finally Max grabbed a long stick, stepped back as far as possible and nudged the bottle slightly. Nothing happened, so his confidence grew and he carefully slid it onto a rolled-up piece of his notebook paper and then onto the top of the notebook.

Max removed the waterproof snap lid from the container, which was about three to four inches in length and an inch and a half in diameter, and we all stared in amazement at what we saw inside.

Bomb components! Along with small coils of solder the small bottle was packed with miniature wire connectors, the uninsulated, flat, fold-over type designed to crimp two wires alongside each other. The thin exposed edges of the connectors also would have doubled as deadly shrapnel in an explosive device.

"This is exactly the kind of thing that Ted would have and carry," Max said.

He was convinced Ted had stopped to rest and scan the country from atop the large rock outcropping directly overhead and had accidentally lost the container from his shirt or coat pocket.

Max's theory made sense. But there were a couple of other plausible scenarios.

I thought back to the late afternoon of October 1, 1996 when, after shutting down the dragline, there was a loud blast that sounded like it came from the exact area where we stood. Had this container been thrown through the woods by the explosion?

It seemed unlikely Ted would have been careless enough to lose the bottle, since he obviously kept meticulous track of every item in his possession.

A second theory was logical as well. The small bottle of bomb parts could easily have been part of a larger cache carefully buried for future use, and a small animal burrowing through the earth brought it to the surface.

Later we scanned the area with a metal detector, but didn't find anything. The search wasn't conclusive, though, as it's difficult to obtain detector readings from metal items stored in heavy plastic containers.

Even though Max made up his mind Ted had accidentally dropped the bottle, I was determined to return another day. One way or other I would solve this mystery. Not only was the site located on my property, but I had vowed to the agents earlier that by the time we were finished Ted would have no remaining secrets in my gulch.

Max and Dave encouraged me to send Ted a package with pictures of his secret cabin with the three of us posing in front of it, pictures of his secret camps, and a letter describing our discoveries.

I thought about it, but knew he would continue to deny the truth.

Max carefully placed the small bottle of parts into his pack, and as we continued our search around the ridge our conversation turned to Ted's firearms and the types of ammunition he used.

Earlier, while I studied contents of an ammunition cache listed on one of the daily journal pages, one entry had stood out. It pertained to the number of rounds in a cache for his 30-30 rifle and it made me think of a discovery many years before.

It was clear at this point that Ted always meticulously described the caliber, bullet weight, and most of all, the number of rounds in each cache.

Yet this particular entry read:

> …log lying along a contour line of the hillside. About fifty, .30-30 cartridges are buried under…

The word "about" jumped right off the page. It wasn't like Ted. Unless he arrived at the site and discovered his container was open and later, when he made the journal entry, thought he might have lost a round or two as he hiked through the woods.

I told Max that years ago I had been walking in an area near where I now thought this cache might be located and had found a single 30-30 round lying in the rocky gravel alongside the game trail. It was a live round and I picked it up, curious about its origin since I didn't own a 30-30 and nobody but Ted and I had been in the gulch for years.

"I wish that you still had that round," Max said. "Maybe we could match it up not only to other unfired rounds, but to spent bullets recovered as well."

Both Max and Dave were amazed when I told them I had run across that very bullet a couple of weeks earlier while cleaning out an old camper where parts were stored.

Max asked if I could find it, and I replied I was sure I'd be able to as soon as we got home.

It was late afternoon so we decided to work our way back down the mountain and search along the way.

Max continued his questioning about the flora on the mountain.

While pointing out the variety and abundance of wild herbs and vegetables in the area, I identified, among others, the lomatium, erythronium, and yampa nearby.

"Yampa, Ted liked yampa," Max blurted out after recognizing the name.

He said Ted had written in his journals about using yampa in some of his stews.

Sept. 8, 1975
Today I went up in the meadows west of here to get

yampa. Digging was tough, but I got perhaps 3 cups anyway.

I dug some of the roots to let Max and Dave taste them. The lomatium (also called biscuitroot), and yampa (also called Indian carrot) smell just like carrots, but are bitter and pithy. Cooking removes some of the bitterness. The roots also can be cleaned, dried and ground into a flour for making cakes.

WILD CARROT
BIG YELLOW
1992

Plant these just as you would regular carrots. Some will probably put up seed stalks the first year. Pull these out, since the roots get tough as soon as they put up seed stalks.
The white roots have only so-so flavor. The tasty roots are the pale-yellow ones. If you like them and want to grow the seeds, dig around the plants in the fall to see which ones have large, pale-yellow roots. Leave these in the ground over the winter, with soil mounded up over them to prevent mice from getting at them, and the second year they will put up seed stalks.

Ted had experimented with cross-pollinating some of these wild varieties of carrot with domestic ones. He found fair success with one cross-strain he called "Wild Carrot Big Yellow." He gave away some of the seeds obtained from his field experiments.

Max was especially fascinated by the abundance of wild herbs, vegetables, and plants and the idea they could provide not only excellent vitamins and nutrition, but were tasty in salads as well.

Those facts, coupled with the medicinal values of many of the plants—e.g., willow bark tea contains salicylates (compounds similar to that used in aspirin), an effective wilderness analgesic—proved to both Max and Dave the importance of understanding the endless larder and pharmacopoeial supply the wilderness could provide.

We finally reached the bottom of the gulch and worked our way back to where the agents had parked their vehicle.

Betty greeted us as we walked into the yard and asked questions about the day's excursion and what we had found.

"We weren't skunked," I said smiling.

Dave and Max started to share stories about the day and I disappeared for a minute to find the 30-30 bullet.

It didn't take long and when I walked back to where the three were talking, Max jumped up, looked in my hand and exclaimed, "Is that it?"

"You bet, do you want to take it with you?" I replied.

He nodded enthusiastically as I handed it over to him.

"It may not mean much to you, but it certainly does to us," Max explained.

We wrapped up the day with a lengthy discussion about our discoveries and then talked about our plan for the next day.

Being an eternal optimist, I was confident we'd have continued success. Max and Dave, both more conservative, tempered their optimism with a healthy dose of reality.

After they left, I wrote out detailed notes of our conversations and pages we had read from Ted's journals. Betty and I talked into the late evening hours. When we finally went to bed I was mentally mapping all the places we could go the next morning.

I got up early, prepared my gear and waited for Dave and Max to arrive. After making their morning phone calls they drove the seven miles from town to our house, ready to hit the trail.

Our agenda included plans to explore some of Ted's secret camps, several of which I had already located. I also knew about many of his favorite haunts since I had cut his tracks frequently or had seen him at other times, without his knowing I was anywhere near.

Ted shouldn't be surprised I was watching him. If our roles had been reversed and he had owned the gulch, he would have watched it and me like a hawk as well. But he must have been shocked and surprised to learn how much I knew about his secret places and trails.

I marvel to this day how Ted, the person who once said "Who's

Chris Waits?" could begin to convince anyone, even a total stranger, that he never knew me. Having heard a rumor that I might write a book, he wrote from his Colorado prison in 1998 to a television journalist in Denver, changing his story and admitting that he accepted a few rides from me and visited occasionally, but playing down everything else. It takes quite a leap of faith to believe that, considering he virtually lived in my back yard for more than twenty-five years and owned his home cabin nearly across the road from me in 1971 when only three other people besides Ted and me lived in the area. And he wrote extensively in his personal journals about the many places he loved and often frequented in my gulch, the gulch that he penned had "special magic" and "is a glorious place."

The more I learned and read from Ted's own pen in his journals only confirmed what I had suspected since he refused to see me at the jail in Helena. He wanted to distance himself and discredit me so authorities would not search and find the many secrets in my gulch.

I marveled even more when I read that when Ted arrived back in Lincoln after his long absence in 1978-'79, after returning from Chicago and his early bombings, the first place he went for peace and solitude was my gulch. As his journal entries show he immediately reacquainted himself with areas in and near my gulch.

TUESDAY, JUNE 26, 1979
I started out before dawn this morning and am now at an old campsite of mine overlooking McClellan Creek. It feels very good to be in the wild country again. I especially value the silence here. (It is now so noisy around my cabin.) The only disruptive sounds this morning have been caused by the 9 evil jet planes that have passed within my hearing.

WED. JUNE 27, 1979
Am now camped at another of my old campsites in the McClellan Creek drainage, high up.

TUESDAY, JULY 10, 1979
This morning moved to my camp on the other fork of

McClellan. Took a walk up on hillside, then climbed up through beautiful parks of old Douglas firs. Shot a big blue grouse rooster. On the ridgetop enjoyed the magnificent views. The one good thing about this campsite is that it is especially well hidden from the eyes of man. It is also comparatively good picking for wild herbs, for this altitude.

SATURDAY, JULY 14, 1979

Today I had the most wonderful morning I've had for a long time. At this beautiful dark, densely wooded spot, the Wisp began calling me, so I followed it to an oxen meadow. I slowly climbed to the top of the mountain through this strip of magic meadow. I gathered some mint along the way and felt as if it would bring me luck to drink tea from mint gathered in this enchanted landscape. (I didn't believe it, of course; it was just a feeling.) At the top of the mountain I looked down on the ridges below and contemplated the sight for some time. Then I climbed down through the Douglas Fir parks, over to the meadow strip again, and sat for awhile looking at the blue lupine and yellow flowers of some plant of the composite family, both of which dotted the meadow. Then I climbed back down to camp, looking at the plants. Only 2 jets passed, and those when my walk was nearly over, so that I was able to forget civilization and the threat it poses to these wonderful solitudes. Thus I was able to drink in the things that I saw with full appreciation. This gulch is a glorious place. It has special magic. I never get tired of seeing these fine old parks of Douglas firs around here.

As Max, Dave, and I embarked on the second day's journey, I described the places we would be exploring, starting in a side gulch that was one of Ted's favorite campsites. I had already given them a map showing the location.

We talked at a steady pace as we moved through the forest, talking about all the wild plants and all the pertinent information.

Max mentioned Ted's diet and how he was extremely health conscious. He said that when Ted was first arrested and taken to Helena by agents, Max asked him if he was hungry and if he needed something to eat.

Ted surprised Max by replying he wanted a peanut butter and jelly sandwich. His selection was unavailable on the jail menu, so he had to settle for grilled cheese, a sandwich he said he hadn't tried for years.

He ate the grilled cheese with gusto, Max said.

Dave started to talk about Ted's teaching career and said that his former students who had been interviewed said he was a poor teacher. They disliked him because he didn't explain things well and had no patience for slow students or ones who asked for extra, one-on-one, after-class assistance.

We were probably a mile and a half up the mountain when we saw a huge, very fresh pile of bear scat. I explained it probably was left by a grizzly bear while Dave knelt down, bent over to within several inches of it with his camera and snapped a picture. A scat pile was something they weren't used to seeing.

I chuckled and asked Dave what the FBI crime lab would think of a close-up picture of a wild forest beast's defecation.

They laughed, too, and Dave replied this wouldn't be the first bizarre picture sent to the lab for developing.

As we moved on after the photo shoot, Max explained how Ted had driven the FBI lab experts crazy with all his home-blended alloys. Metallurgists had an extremely difficult time breaking down the composition of the metals used in the devices.

At one point, technicians in the crime lab, with Ted's own blueprint at hand, decided they would recreate one of the devices. Using power tools, it took them more than twenty hours, while Ted had created the original device with crude hand tools.

Ted had taken the old tried-and-true term "handcrafted" to a new level.

Just down the trail a short way I showed Max and Dave a rock pointer, a triangular piece of granite, about ten inches long, six inches wide and five inches tall, that sat atop a natural stump at least four feet high and pointed off to the west. The top of the stump had been leveled by hand.

The arrow-shaped stone had been placed there for a significant reason, because rocks just don't fly, and Ted had been the only one in that area besides me. When we moved on I said I'd come back later and check it out.

It could be something was buried nearby, Max said. Ted was a great believer in the secrecy and safety afforded by a few feet of Mother Earth. Back at his home cabin FBI agents had literally uncovered a great many items, including ammunition under a corner post near his garden and other bullets near a large tree. Things were even found buried in his garden.

Max talked about the difficult time the FBI language translators had with Ted's Spanish, which was used in some journal entries as well as to label containers of chemical mixtures. They were so used to interpreting "street Spanish" that they had a difficult time deciphering Ted's.

FROM FBI INVENTORY OF ITEMS SEIZED
AT KACZYNSKI HOME CABIN
B-163—One metal can, with aluminum foil pressed over the top, with white paper label secured with masking tape, with handwritten notations. "Cuidado muy sensibilizado mezcla C de exp. 90 esta esta la misma que la mezela [*sic*] #5" [Chris Waits translation: "Be very careful of the sensitiveness of the mixture C of Exp #90 this, this what is the same mixture of #5"]

But why would he write anything in Spanish in his own journals?

Even though he did correspond with Juan Sanchez Arreola, a friend introduced by David Kaczynski, in Spanish, his motive for using a foreign language as he wrote to himself within the pages of his journals was much different.

MAY 6, 1981
From now on I think I'll write my confessions on illegal hunting in Spanish because it'll be safer in case someone sees these notebooks by accident.

*   *   *

I was amused by this entry, knowing that the "someone" Ted referred to was probably me. And Ted didn't have a clue that this someone also knew Spanish.

The two agents and I eventually dropped off the game trail we had been following, just down the mountain from one of Ted's old campsites. I pointed out the hard, red Douglas-fir stump where he had often cut kindling. We found many dead, dry poles, large limbs that had been hatcheted into small lengths and stumps, all signs of Ted's firewood gathering.

As we studied those jagged remains, Max brought up Ted's strange aversion to breaking glass. He wondered if I had known about it, witnessed it, or heard Ted talk about it.

I replied no to all three parts of the question, but said he must have made exceptions when he was really mad.

"What do you mean?" Max asked.

I told him about all the windows Ted had broken out of the small, tin-covered cabin located in my gulch during the late seventies.

Even though I didn't know at the time who had trashed the cabin, Dave had recently said Ted bragged in his own journal about being the culprit.

I said I had gone up the gulch right after the owner had found the cabin vandalized and had personally seen that every window had been shattered.

Max seemed surprised and looked over to Dave, who nodded in agreement, saying he had interviewed the owner of the cabin, who had told the same story.

Max said Ted must have been furious, because he had written often about his glass-breaking phobia.

UNDATED JOURNAL ENTRY

Somebody used to have an oldish house-trailer parked at an abandoned mine up Fields Gulch; it seemed to be used only in hunting season. In Summer '75 I broke into this trailer by unscrewing some screws and prying off a metal window-frame, ruining it in the process. (I had a strong psychological inhibition against breaking the window, even though it's very unlikely anyone could have been within earshot.) I stole a few cans of food from the trailer....(Next summer I noticed the trailer had been removed.)

Spring '77 I went back to this same cabin [mentioned in an entry not quoted here]. There was a diesel earth-moving machine parked near it, and I sugared the fuel tank. Then I unscrewed a window from its frame (still that inhibition about breaking windows), entered the cabin, stole a trail axe, slashed the mattresses of 6 beds they had there, slashed a sofa, and poured out a 1/3-full bottle of vodka.

We continued the climb to Ted's hunting camp.

Max kept saying, "We've come so far," but I assured him the distance we had hiked that day was nothing more than a little nature walk for Ted. The country was huge and uninhabited; walks of several miles or more were mere jaunts.

Max thought we had gone too far, saying Ted wouldn't camp so high up the mountain.

Just the opposite, I replied, saying we still had a way to go.

Max had a difficult time grasping a sense of scale in the mountains, even though he carried one of Ted's hand-drawn maps that traced all the trails he had hiked over the years.

Seeing them on a map was one thing; following them on foot in the rugged terrain was quite another.

As my father-in-law had often said, "A mile is a long way in the woods." I always agreed with him, knowing how true it was: the climbing, stepping over fallen logs, walking through slippery mud and rocks.

We topped the last incline and reached Ted's hunting camp, one he had used often and had written about extensively.

Many bleached animal bones and pieces of firewood with the tell-tale chop marks from Ted's ax were strewn about the area near the well-disguised firepit where he had cooked meals.

Dave thought perhaps the bones were from a winter kill or left over from a predatory attack, but those theories were quickly dispelled when they saw the distinct knife marks left as Ted stripped meat away from the bones with his hunting knife.

Dave thought it was interesting how Ted's personality had changed since his arrest. While this had been his special place for many years, he had adapted to prison life well and was now in "heaven" playing the part of a jailhouse lawyer.

On top of it all—ordering every law book he could find to prepare his defense and making his lawyers follow his lead—he now required everyone to address him as Doctor Kaczynski.

Dave painted quite a graphic picture as he described the Doctor, with his head high, smiling and obviously in control, while a clique of "groupies" followed his every move.

I said the gullibility of people mystified me; it's amazing how quickly a criminal is transformed into an icon, to be almost worshipped. It's a given that criminals have rights, but what about the victims and their rights? Somehow I feel our nation's sense of values has become skewed.

The agents both agreed, especially considering the many lives Ted shattered and destroyed.

What bothered me above any other thing then, and still bothers me now, is Ted's total lack of remorse.

Max and Dave went on to tell me how Ted had written in his journals about some of the laws of men and how good they were for everybody else, but they didn't apply to him.

While we were examining the bones lying around the campsite, I told them about the rabbit skull I had found at the secret cabin with a small caliber hole through it.

The conversation then shifted to our dogs that were brutally killed. They both shook their heads as I described the gruesome details of how our malamute, Tasha, had been shot by a .22 caliber in the rectal area and had bled to death internally. She was no doubt killed by Ted, using his .22 pistol or his homemade .22 zip gun.

Max said the zip gun was fairly sophisticated for a weapon that was made entirely by hand, but it was crude at best when compared to some of the machined but home-built guns commonly confiscated when the agents arrested street criminals.

Since they can't be traced, home-built street weapons are made almost exclusively to commit crimes. Ted's was no exception.

A few days ago I finished making a twenty-two caliber pistol. This took me a long time, for a year and a half, thereby preventing me from working on some other projects I would have liked to carry out. Gun works well and I get as much accuracy out of it as I'd expect for an inexperienced pistol shot like me. It is equipped with improvised silencer which does not work as well as I hoped. At a guess it cuts noise down to maybe one third. It is said that it is easy for a machinist to make guns, but of course I did not have machine tools, but only a few files, hacksaw blades, small vice, a rickety hand drill, etc. I took the barrel from an old pneumatic pistol. I made the other parts out of several metal pieces. Most of them come from the old abandoned cars near here. I needed to make the parts with enough precision but I made them well and I'm very satisfied. I want to use the gun as a homicide weapon.

My days in the woods with the agents weren't without incident. Max soon discovered I was just as stubborn as he, and we argued more than once about things as simple as logistics and which end of a fallen log was the butt.

Every "discussion" ended with a laugh, though, and I knew both Dave and Max were having a good time, in spite of the seriousness of the whole matter. Our arguing was little more than stress relief. There was plenty of stress, considering all the loose ends and the trial looming just months away.

I could understand the tension felt by the whole prosecution team. Just sorting through approximately 22,000 pages of documents written by Ted and found in his home cabin would be daunting enough. Add to that all the physical and lab evidence documenting the past eighteen years and the task grew to epic proportions.

We finished scouting around Ted's old camp and decided to move down and around the ridge to another area matching a description Max had given me from Ted's notes.

As we climbed up and around one of the main forks of the creek, we neared the small cabin covered with sheet metal that Ted had bragged about trashing. His journal entries described how he broke out all the windows, stole things from inside and vandalized the small bulldozer parked nearby. He also stole the magneto from the Cat and buried it, although he didn't describe where, so it was never found.

Dave and Max looked in awe at the sorry remains of the cabin Ted had vandalized nearly twenty years before. The ruins were a stark reminder of the severity of Ted's rage when it was leveled on members of the industrial-technological society who irritated him.

The more I visited with Dave and Max, the more we were able to resolve many of the Lincoln mysteries that had puzzled area residents during the past twenty-five years. The solutions were simple as they poured out of journals, where Ted bragged about most of the acts of destruction.

> KACZYNSKI CRIME JOURNAL [A SEPARATE NOTEBOOK FOR "BRAGGING" ABOUT HIS CRIMES; SEE DESCRIPTION BELOW]
> There is a small, functioning mine—I'll call it Mine X for future reference—a few miles from my cabin, on the south side of the ridge that runs east from here. They had a large diesel engine mounted on the back of an old truck, apparently for running a large drill for boring holes in rock. In Summer '75 I put a small quantity of sugar in the fuel tank of the diesel engine and also in the gas tank of the truck. Sugar in the gas is supposed to severely damage an engine because it gets into the cylinders and acts as an abrasive. But I don't know if this works in diesels (maybe sugar is soluble in gasoline but not in diesel fuel—or something).
> ...Summer '76 I went back to Mine X and put a generous quantity of sugar in the fuel-tank of the diesel engine and the gas-tank of the truck.
> ...Still in Summer '75, I went to the camp—apparently it is an outfitter's camp—along the [name] trail east of the [name] drainage. They have a corral there, and, a little way back in the woods, a kind of lean-to with equipment stored in it. I stole an axe (this is the axe I still use), poked holes in several 5-gallon plastic water-containers, took the

stovepipe and hid it off in the woods, smashed 2 thermometers, and scattered most of the other stuff around.

...Summer '77 up [name], I shot a cow in the head with my .30-30, then got the [expletive] out of there. I mean a rancher's cow, not an elk cow.

FBI TRANSCRIPTION FROM CODED JOURNAL [To further complicate his numerical code, Kazcinski used no apostrophes, created misspellings, and altered word breaks.]

SOME [expletive] BUILT A VACATIONHOUSE A FEW YEARS AGO ACROSS [name]...SO ONE NIGHT IN FALL I SNEAKED OVERTHERE,THOUGH THEYWEREHOME,ANDSTOLE THEIR CHAINSAW,BURIED IT INA SWAMP.THAT WASNOT ENOUGH,SO COUPLE WEEKS LATERWHEN THEYHADLEFTTHE PLACE,I CHOPPED MY WAY INTO THEIRHOUSE,SMASHEDUP INTERIOR PRETTYTHOROUGHLY.ITWASA REAL LUXURYPLACE.THEY ALSOHADA MOBILEHOME THERE.I BROKE INTO THAT TOO,FOUND SILVERPAINTED MOTORSYCLE INSIDE,SMASHED IT UP WITHTHEIR OWN AX.THEYHAD4SNOWMOBILES SITTING OUSTIDE.I THOROUGHLY SMASHED ENGINES OF THOSE WITHTHE AX.THINKTHEYWERETHE ONES I CUTCYCLE TRAIL AT [name],SINCE SILVERPAINTED CYCLEISUNUSUAL.WEEK OR SO LATER,COPS CAME UP HERE AND ASKED ME IF IHADSEEN ANYONE FOOLING AROUNDWITH ANY BUILDINGS AROUND HERE.ALSO ASKED IF IHADHADANY PROBLEMS WITHMOTORCYCLES.THIS LASTQUESTION SUGGESTSTHATTHE TRUTHCROSSED-THEIR MINDS.BUTPROBABLY THEY DIDNOT SERIOUSLY SUS-PECTME,OTHERWISE THEIR QUESTIONING WOULDNOTHAVEBEEN SO PERFUNCTORY.THIS WINTER (1982TO1983) VERYFEW SNOWMOBILESHAVECOME BY.I SUPPOSE EITHERTHOSE [EXPLETIVE] HAVENOT GOTMACHINES FIXED YET,ORHAVEREALIZEDTHAT-THEREISSOMEONE WHOWILLNOT LET THEMGET AWAY WITH TERRORIZINGTHE AREA.WHO SAYS CRIME DOESNT PAY?I FEEL VERY GOOD ABOUTTHIS.IAMALSO PLEASEDTHAT I

Standing there with Dave and Max, I now understood why the
FBI agents had been carrying a boat around these forested mountains
the summer before. Dave said they'd been prepared to search "the
swamp" where Ted said he had buried the chainsaw.

Dave now told about journal entries that described a hair-raising
story of three young motorcycle riders who violated Ted's code of not
riding off-road.

As they playfully climbed the steep mountain trails, riding comfortably on top of their noisy two-stroke machines, they didn't have
a clue that their young lives were almost snuffed out on that bright
summer day.

Ted, hiking nearby, saw them through the trees and was so enraged
that he raised his rifle, leveled the sights on the first rider, took aim
and prepared to fire. Then he paused momentarily and lamented that
one of the riders might escape before he could kill them all.

That, coupled with the proximity of his home cabin and the intensive manhunt that would surely ensue if the boys were missing or
found dead, saved their lives. Ted also wrote that the shootings would
undoubtedly have ended his bombing campaign, so he backed off and
allowed the forest desecraters to escape.

The thought of that near-fatal experience made me cringe and
led the three of us into a discussion about Ted's cowardice: If he
couldn't carry out an act in a pusillanimous way he wouldn't carry it
out at all.

Dave had another equally chilling example: Ted wrote about a
wire he had stretched across a mountain trail at neck height to snag
motorcyclists.

I had found a similar wire many years earlier, and took it down
and wrapped it around a tree, I said.

Dave said Ted had written about stretching a wire between two
trees across a trail, and described the location. FBI agents had found
it the previous summer. But Ted wrote about setting more than one
such trap. We wondered how many more deadly wires could still be
out there in the woods.

At the end of Summer '75 after the roaring by of motorcycles near my camp spoiled a hike for me, I put a piece of wire across a trail where cycle-tracks were visible, at about neck height for a motorcyclist. (Next summer I found someone had wrapped the wire safely around a tree. Unfortunately, I doubt anyone was injured by it.)

UNDATED JOURNAL ENTRY
Summer '77…I strung a neck-wire for motorcyclists along the divide trail above [location]. Later I found the wire was gone. Whether it hurt anyone I don't know.

Another mystery solved.

Max, Dave, and I hiked farther south upstream until we came to a fork in the creek. We hopped across the side fork and followed it through a flat area loaded with wild herbs.

As I started naming some of the vegetation, including yellow mon-keyflower, bog orchid, arrowleaf groundsel, and pink penstamen, I also noted the thick carpet of light-green sphagnum moss covering the ground.

Max broke in and told me about one of Ted's accounts that men-tioned sphagnum moss. I replied it was a common form of vegetation found in many areas near Stemple.

We moved on, explored briefly some of the historical areas of the gulch and decided to head back, since the day was wearing on. Even though we hadn't found anything monumental that day, there were successes, and Dave and Max were satisfied to have stood in the place Ted had described as his "Most Secret Camp."

We made good time hiking down the mountain, which left enough of the afternoon to explore the old mine tunnel. We stopped at one of my sheds to grab extra lighting, climbed to the old mine adit and carefully crawled inside the body-sized opening I had dug out sever-al weeks earlier.

I led the way with Dave close behind. Max would have no part of the underground adventure and waited outside. We followed the tun-nel, dark and musty because of the stagnant air, some seventy-five to one hundred feet. We couldn't find anything that could be clearly linked to Ted, even though many objects littered the inside. They could have been carried in by pack rats as well as Ted.

Ducking under overhanging rock and crawling through the tunnel, which was chiseled and blasted out of sedimentary shale, made one appreciate the hard work and danger hard-rock miners faced as they followed veins of gold into the mountainside.

As we crawled back through the small adit, squinting as our eyes adjusted to the sunlight, Max snapped a couple of photos. He suggested that the pictures would probably end up on the safety bulletin board back at FBI headquarters, an example of what an agent shouldn't do in the field.

We climbed down from the old mine and returned to the house, where we settled into a discussion about more of Ted's strange characteristics. Max said he was amazed by the vile language Ted used in his writings and how viciously he attacked friend and foe, even members of his own family.

Finally, as the early evening air cooled, Dave and Max drove back out the gulch to Stemple Road and to Lincoln, eager to reach their motel room.

Over supper, Betty and I conversed about the day's events and what I had learned. One piece of information really embarrassed her. As we came back down the mountainside, Max, Dave, and I had stopped along the trail where we could easily look down on our house. I jokingly said Ted could have peered into our atrium windows from that spot and watched us climb into our large spa, night or day. It wasn't a joking matter, they said. Ted had watched people frequently and wrote about it, which really surprised me.

But even that little bit of information left an indelible mark on us and our lifestyle. My wife would never again enter our spa while the lights were turned on.

The next day we had planned another trip to the secret cabin. After Max and Dave arrived, I piloted them back to the shelf high on the mountainside by a roundabout route, actually passing the cutoff point and then backtracking on an oblique angle.

We approached from a different direction, walking in to the east side of the cabin site. I wanted Max and Dave to fully appreciate the secretive location Ted had chosen and that it had all of the qualifications of a hideout and none of a campsite.

We took off our packs and started to carefully remove all the metal items from the inside of the cabin and then searched both inside and out with a metal detector.

As we worked I really noticed the decomposition of some of the more fragile items I had tried to protect so diligently while waiting for the FBI to arrive. That confirmed my theory that things deteriorated quickly when left unattended in the harsh mountain elements, so Ted had surely used the cabin on a regular basis, right up to the fall and winter before his arrest.

Nothing new was found during this search.

Then I was surprised, and disappointed, as was Dave, when Max said this would be our last day out in the field.

Dave wanted to stay and continue the searches, feeling we were just getting a good start.

I argued we could find Ted's missing 30-30 and try to link it to the shooting many years ago of an area miner as he stood on the top of his washing plant. Authorities had retrieved the slug from the victim and could perform a ballistics test if we could find the rifle. The statute of limitations had run out, but Dave especially wanted to close the book on yet another unsolved case.

The sneaky shot certainly fit Ted to a "T," and when I informed Dave just how quickly the crime scene could be reached from the secret cabin site, his suspicions grew. Even though proving Ted shot the miner wouldn't add to the sentence he faced, it would be comforting for people around Lincoln to know the case had been solved.

But Max had already made up his mind the field search was coming to a close that day and there would be little time for us to look for the 30-30. Almost as if to settle any argument, Max started to read from Ted's journal pages, which mentioned another cabin, an old miner's shack that the agents had found during the summer of 1996.

The discovery, a few gulches to the west, had been one of their few field successes that first summer after the arrest, but it proved to be a hollow victory because Ted had mapped the cabin as nothing more than a reference point and possible emergency shelter.

We made one final sweep of the area around the secret cabin with a metal detector, this time in a larger perimeter. The agents used a random method that was pretty much hit or miss and we found nothing more that was earth-shattering.

I wasn't the least bit discouraged, though, because as we searched we talked and I was continuing to learn more about Ted and the case.

I was shocked, but not totally surprised, when Max said Ted had often shot at airplanes and helicopters overhead. The rumors that had circulated in Lincoln in the past were true.

Ted had even made special excursions into the mountains with the intent of shooting a helicopter or plane.

CODED-JOURNAL ENTRY
EARLY AUGUST I WENTANDCAMPED OUT,MOSTLY INWHAT
ICALL [name]GULCH, HOPINGTO SHOOTUP A HELICOPTER IN
AREA EASTOF[name]MOUNTAIN.PROVED HARDERTHAN
ITHOUGHT,BECAUSEHELICOPTERSALWAYS INMOTION,NEVER-
KNOWWHERETHEYWILLGO NEXT, TALLTREES IN WAYOF-
SHOT.ONLY ONCE HADBEHALF [*sic*] A CHANCE.2QUICK-
SHOTS,ROUGHLYAIMED,AS COPTER CROSSEDSPACEBETWEEN-
2TREES.MISSEDBOTH....FORGOT TO MENTION,ON TRIP-
WHERE I SHOT AT HELICOPTER,I CHOPPEDDOWNWOODEN-
POWER LINE POLE,[name]CREEK AREA.

It was obvious that the more time I spent with the agents the more I learned about the Lincoln mysteries of the past twenty-five years.

On one hand I felt good that Ted had been removed, so there would be no further damage or violence here. But on the other hand, the more I learned the angrier I became. I found myself begging Max for an opportunity to be alone with Ted in his jail cell for even five minutes, knowing it would never happen.

They humored me, saying they wanted Ted to be alive and healthy when he was tried for his crimes. I was joking, anyway, but I had to wonder what the cowardly Ted would think if I was placed in his cell. If nothing else, it would lead to some interesting conversations.

If Ted didn't approve of my occupation or had concerns about it, why didn't he have the guts to discuss things with me? Actually, he would have found I shared many of his views and concerns about the environment, and would have loved to talk about the issues.

But as I mulled over his secret years and acts in Lincoln, it became apparent his motivation to carry out his acts of terrorism really had little to do with saving Mother Earth. His true motivation was nothing more than hatred and revenge.

His self-conceived superiority even extended to a feeling that hunting should be banned. Of course, he hunted daily and killed scores of forest birds and animals for sustenance.

> SEPT. 11, 1975
>   I just heard 2 shots, a few minutes apart, maybe 1/4 mile away; something light, but heavier than a .22 I'd say. Made me nervous lest they see the smoke from my fire (no chance of their finding my camp otherwise). Makes me about ready to join the ban-hunting crowd, just to keep these disgusting twerps out of the woods. Of course I'd hunt anyway.

We finished at the secret cabin site, packed up our gear after taking a few last photographs and headed down the mountain. As we walked along the game trails toward home, I was perplexed that Dave and Max hadn't packed up any of the evidence and taken it with them. I didn't say anything, though, and felt satisfied about the week's work.

Everyone would like to have found more evidence, but considering the time parameters, I was especially pleased about all the new things I had learned. We had worked together well and they knew all the sensitive information was safe with me; I wouldn't be responsible for a leak that could jeopardize the trial.

I told Max and Dave that I wanted to continue the investigation on my own and wondered if it would be possible to procure some of Ted's journal entries to assist me. I had plenty of information to continue the search. I had already written down our daily conversations almost verbatim and had redrawn most of the maps and landmarks from memory. They hadn't realized that was part of my nightly routine.

I explained my motivation was to find hard evidence to corroborate the things about our friendship and Ted's use of my gulch I had talked about from the start, especially since my character was being assassinated by Ted and his few sympathizers who were calling me a liar.

Max and Dave understood and said they would see what they could do. I didn't want them to jeopardize their jobs since I knew about the non-disclosure statement each had been required to sign.

When we arrived at their vehicle Dave surprised me with a gift, a full-color, computer-enhanced satellite photograph of my gulch and much of the country surrounding me.

After loading their gear, Max and Dave said they wanted to drive down and make a quick stop at the area where I stored wire, solder, pipe, copper tubing, and electrical switches, among many other things.

As we got out Dave showed me another one of Ted's intriguing hand-drawn maps. It charted, starting in the fall of 1971, all his foot routes through the mountains. I was astounded to see all the places Ted had hiked in the various drainages of my gulch. It was another piece of irrefutable proof that Ted had spent an incredible amount of time living and hiking in the gulch.

We dug through the various boxes of electrical wiring and other materials as the agents looked for something that might match evidence recovered in Ted's cabin or that he used in his bombs.

I mentioned the gold and the black sand found in Ted's home cabin, and wondered if it was the material pilfered from my sluice box a few years earlier.

If I could just see a few flakes of gold and a small amount of the black sand, I would be able to identify its origin.

Max and Dave were intrigued when I went on to tell them that placer gold and the black sand that accompanies it have individual characteristics as unique as fingerprints.

They thought it would be interesting if I could see the gold and tell where it came from, but that wouldn't be possible since nearly all the evidence taken from Ted's home cabin was still back at the FBI crime lab in Washington, D.C.

They examined the contents of the last box of wiring and found several pieces that caught their eye. Ted obviously could have used some of the material, they said, since it was the same type of wire. He garnered what he needed from dozens of places and much of it would never be traced to its origin.

We headed down to the house. When we got there Dave pulled out several more presents—a couple of FBI glass mugs and two ball-point pens with "FBI" embossed on them.

They encouraged me to continue the search and keep them informed.

It was almost anticlimactic, watching them turn onto the Stemple Road and roll out of sight toward Lincoln. We had waited all summer for this exploration, and now it was over.

I was back on my own. Armed with a plethora of new information, I could hardly wait to get back out there.

My first order of business would be to return to the secret cabin, gather up all the evidence and protect it before it deteriorated further.

I wasn't sure why the agents hadn't taken anything with them, but I had a theory. Maybe the prosecution thought they could circumvent the laws of discovery by not gathering any of the evidence.

Certainly Ted's defense lawyers would return to talk to me before the trial. What would I tell them? I just hoped I wouldn't get caught up in the middle of charges of failure to disclose evidence.

It was aggravating and puzzling they'd go to such efforts to find evidence to corroborate Ted's journals and then not want to take it and process it for the trial.

Interviews and
Trial Strategies

Flattery won't buy you much in a mountain community like Lincoln, especially if you're a stranger. Small-town people get right to the point.

"How's the weather?"

"It's 20 below zero on the old barn thermometer this morning. The dogs won't even go outside."

Talk all you want about the splendid scenery in the Upper Blackfoot Valley, the rustic charm of the town of Lincoln and its stores, the friendliness of the people, but it won't buy a cup of coffee at Lambkin's.

Any conversation laced with profuse compliments immediately draws a suspicious look: "You want something?"

That's pretty much the way it went in those months of late 1997 during the final interviews as both sides prepared for Ted's trial. Attorneys and experts were in Lincoln, and there were plenty of compliments being handed out, sometimes almost to the point of embarrassment, as the defense tried to learn about the strategies of the prosecution, and vice versa.

After agents Max Noel and Dave Weber returned to California, I continued my field investigations whenever possible, trying to solve the remaining mysteries in my gulch. Dave and I both shared a keen interest in gathering every possible detail relating to Ted's life in the Lincoln area and his survival methods in the uninhabited wilderness.

We talked on the phone regularly. When Dave referred to Ted's plan to escape to Canada, I thought Ted was well aware other criminals had been quite successful evading the law in Montana's high country. Two cases received extensive coverage in the Montana press during Ted's Lincoln years.

The most notorious was that of the father-son duo of Don and Dan Nichols, who kidnapped twenty-two-year-old world-class biathlete Kari Swenson July 15, 1983 while she was on a training run in the mountains near Big Sky Ski Resort.

During a rescue attempt the next day, she was shot in the right lung by Dan Nichols, and a rescuer was shot and killed by Don. They dumped the wounded Swenson, who had been kidnapped to be the "mountain bride" of Dan, the younger Nichols, out of a sleeping bag and left her for dead at the camp.

Don and Dan then evaded a small army of law enforcement officials—in helicopters and planes, and on foot and horseback—for the next five months in the rugged Madison Range in southwestern Montana. They were finally arrested near Bear Trap Canyon along the Madison River as winter set in.

A second case involved the murders of Lincoln-area ranchers Kenneth McLean and his wife, Marion, in September 1977.

Andrew Sunday and his small entourage of ruffians from Nebraska had stolen horses and tack from the McLeans' beautiful resort ranch east of Lincoln and ridden off into the mountains. The McLeans were shot and killed after they discovered the theft and tracked the group into an open meadow some ten miles away in the Alice Creek drainage.

The horses were spooked during the shoot-out, so Sunday and his two companions took the McLeans' pickup and fled. They were arrested several days later east of Spokane when they attempted to pick up a money order that had been wired to them. Ted surely noted their fatal mistake, knowing their chances of escape would have been much better on foot in the wilderness areas to the north.

Ted must have been acutely cognizant of the Nichols' superior escape plan. Lawmen found it almost impossible to apprehend fugitives Don and Dan in the rugged terrain. Ted, so cunning and well versed in wilderness survival, would be even harder to find.

As the summer days shortened and another Montana winter loomed, I had to break off field work to build a new garage with guest quarters overhead.

But the investigation had taken all my time and I wasn't able to pour the concrete for the floor and foundation until August 19.

We designed the garage as a two-story structure, almost like a small chalet. Since I had to fell and skid trees and mill out all the lumber on my one-man sawmill, the job ahead was huge, especially considering the mountain seasons are so unpredictable—winter can arrive to stay almost any time after the end of September.

Nervous that I would be subpoenaed to testify, I kept asking Dave when the witness list would come out. Butch Gehring and I also discussed the trial every time we saw each other and both wondered what we'd be asked to do.

I absolutely didn't want to go to California to testify, but that wouldn't be a matter of choice.

Finally Dave said the witness list wouldn't be released until November. I breathed a sigh of relief, knowing that should give me enough time to enclose the garage for the harsh winter. If it wasn't sealed in by November, it'd be too late anyway.

Dave also mentioned another piece of surprising trial strategy during that conversation. He warned me I might also be called as a defense witness.

That brought to mind a sobering scenario: being grilled on the witness stand by both sides. I wasn't afraid to testify, but I was nervous about a prolonged, drawn-out trial keeping me away from home during the winter months because Betty would have to manage everything at our remote mountain home alone.

Dave and I continued our phone conversations several times a week through the early fall. He said he wanted to get back to Lincoln by himself so we could conduct more field work. We knew there were unsolved issues. Also, there was Ted's secret cabin and all its contents.

Dave said he wanted to pick up the evidence and wrap up the final details.

At that time it wasn't clear why he and Max hadn't taken any evidence with them in late July. But whatever they decided to do, or not to do, the cabin and its contents were documented. Every item was safe and preserved for the short term at the cabin site.

I called Dave in September to get his new address since the entire Unabom Task Force—its offices, computers, everything—had been moved to some anonymous offices located in the Sacramento federal building. They made the move as discreetly as possible to avoid media attention.

On Thursday, October 2, Dave called and described a website, named "Soft Kill," recently posted on the Internet. It gave names of people in Lincoln who had talked to the press or had been interviewed by the FBI. The website called for harassment of those listed. Dave said some threats had been posted. The site's creator had been traced and arrested for obstruction of justice, he said.

Nothing really was surprising anymore. There seemed to be no break in the ominous cloud that hung over us all as Ted's legacy; new manifestations surfaced on a regular basis.

I was furiously working on the garage, trying to beat the winter weather. Rain and snow flurries made roof work impossible on several occasions, but then a beautiful late fall high pressure system built over western Montana and I knew, even though working alone, that I'd be able to button up the roof and finish the framing and sheeting—if only the phone would stop ringing.

As Ted's trial neared, the media attention again intensified. There was one distraction after another.

On October 14, Dave called and left a message while I was working on the roof. He caught me by surprise, saying government psychiatrists were on their way up to see me. He apologized for the short notice, but explained it had been planned that way so the press wouldn't get wind of the visit.

I returned his call, wondering when they would arrive, since I was trying to complete the roof and the weatherman was now predicting snow and colder weather that night.

This might be the last nice day for roof work, but Dave didn't have any more information other than to say the doctors were on a tight schedule and needed to interview Butch and me that day.

I climbed back on the roof and screwed down waferboard sheeting until a rented Ford Explorer drove up into the yard a couple of hours later.

Four people got out as I climbed down the ladder. Max Noel was the only familiar person. He was extremely cheerful.

He introduced the others as FBI agent Kathy Puckett and two doctors, Philip Resnick and Park Dietz, both psychiatrists working for the government.

Max spoke glowingly about the beautiful and unspoiled country and all the places we had explored during the past summer. Then he turned and asked if he could hike around and enjoy his time while the doctors conducted their interview.

"Certainly, you know you're welcome," I replied.

With that Max disappeared and the rest of us sat down outside. It was a beautiful late fall afternoon, one of those almost-too-good-to-be-true days that usually ride the leading edge of an approaching cold weather system.

Drs. Dietz and Resnick pulled out their tablets and pens and started the interview. I kept close mental notes of everything that was said.

Agent Puckett said very little, and Dr. Dietz asked the bulk of the questions. He cycled through the questions on Ted's apparent mental state, returning again and again to the same basic question phrased slightly differently: what were Ted's "emotions" like when I first knew him and more recently, his "temperament," his "demeanor." Were his actions "open or secretive," were they "paranoid"? Did he seem "irrational," or "coherent" or "abnormal" or "unfriendly" or "withdrawn"? With each new phrasing, Dr. Dietz asked whether the change had been gradual or abrupt. Another series of questions pursued what "obviously upset him": things I did or said, things others did or said, complaints Ted may have made about people or events around us, any time I saw him lose his temper.

Dr. Dietz wanted to know about our conversations, also: four questions on the quality and occurrence of Ted's eye contact (in general, while he spoke or I spoke, and how direct it was), his vocabulary, what we talked about and what he said that I found unusual, who initiated our talks and who dominated them.

Interspersed were questions about Ted's wardrobe and grooming. I described his two kinds of clothing, his somewhat nicer going-to-town clothes and his everyday garb, which he never washed and wore until it was "indecent" and would no longer stay on his body.

When asked if Ted had an offensive odor, I said it was a smoky, musty, musky smell. Other people had noticed it, too. I said that when Ted would leave the library one of the workers, or the librarian herself, would liberally spray the interior with a deodorizer to mask the strong pungent smell that lingered. Dietz asked whether this odor ever prevented me from offering rides or visiting, and I said "Absolutely not." I knew that Ted's heat stove leaked smoke and ash. He had no bathroom facilities and when the weather was bad he would relieve himself in a newspaper and then burn it in his stove. Dietz later returned to this topic to ask whether Ted's physical state seemed to decline.

Another point Dietz pursued was the quality of our friendship, whether it seemed genuine or whether Ted was using me. Was it one-sided or mutual, and had it deepened or become strained over the years? Had our contact increased or decreased over the years? When asked whether Ted ever was unfriendly, I explained that he hadn't been so to me, but had towards Betty.

The other area Dietz asked about was how much of his personal history Ted had revealed: home, family, education, girlfriends. I said I knew he had gone to college, but not for how long, or where.

They didn't stay long after the interview concluded. Max said they still had to stop down the road and visit with Butch. Then they'd drive to Lincoln before heading back to Helena to catch their plane.

The whole interview lasted several hours and that time proved to be a crucial loss on the roofing project. After they left, I worked late into the evening before calling it quits in the pitch dark.

The next morning a fresh, wet snowfall draped the forest with an early winter look and made roofing extremely dangerous. Disappointed, I drove to Lincoln to pick up some nails and screws at the hardware store.

I ran into a few Lincoln friends and quickly discovered the town was buzzing—the shroud of secrecy regarding the psychiatrists was a joke. Not only did everyone seem to know they had been in town, but after leaving Butch's, the entire group spent the rest of the late afternoon and evening dining and socializing at a local steakhouse.

There are few secrets in a small town. Whom they interviewed was not one of them. Once again the leaks came directly from the very source that demanded secrecy on our part.

Back at home, I checked the answering machine and found new media messages and more calls coming in at a rapid pace. The word had spread quickly that the psychiatrists had visited.

Some secrecy!

During the next two weeks I faced a juggling act between spending every possible moment working on the garage, in spite of the inclement weather, and fielding the continuing barrage of phone calls.

The psychiatrists' visit had only intensified interest.

Everyone on the outside seemed to know. Calls poured in from all over the country, including ones from the *Los Angeles Times*, *Time* magazine, and *Newsweek*, with reporters wanting to know every detail about the interviews.

Finally, I let the answering machine be the secretary, noted who left messages and when, but refused to return a single call because of the confidentiality of the case.

Working on the roof gave me plenty of time to mull over some of the puzzling actions of the past several months.

The things of most concern were the secret cabin and why the FBI had left vital evidence behind. Clues gleaned from the psychiatrists seemed to support my theory that the defense didn't know of it. They didn't ask any direct questions about the secret cabin, as if it didn't exist. At one point I brought up the subject, but they passed over it and went to another question like they hadn't heard anything.

During our phone conversations, I often asked Dave if Ted and the defense team were aware the secret cabin had been discovered. His usual reply was "No, I'm pretty sure they still don't know."

It seemed strange. The prosecution had so much evidence against Ted, why would they risk the potential damage of going against the basic rules of discovery in a criminal case?

But it would be hard to refute evidence to the contrary. A fingerprint, which I felt sure was Ted's, had been left clearly imprinted in the black paint on the brush handle found in the cabin, locked there like a fossil, and much of his clothing was found inside. Plus his journal entries and other pieces of evidence, including Ted's own handwritten notations on a cabin wall, were convincing proof he used the cabin often.

There was one thing for certain: I wouldn't lie if asked about the cabin by the judge or even the defense.

It seemed the prosecution still wanted the 30-30 rifle because of the serial number. But they didn't want to examine anything else, figuring then they wouldn't have to inform the defense about the secret cabin. The only plausible explanation seemed to be they were going for the jugular and wanted the death penalty.

It was no secret that an insanity defense was probably Ted's only chance to escape the death penalty. The defense's plan to use his home cabin to show a pattern of isolationism, and thus his mental state, was widely reported. They had trucked Ted's home cabin from Great Falls to Sacramento so the jury could examine the oppressive structure and even walk through it.

At one point, defense lawyer Quin Denvir said that to enter the cabin was to enter the troubled mind of Kaczynski, who Denvir believed was a paranoid schizophrenic. The defense wanted to show he wasn't an evil person, but a sick one.

The prosecution indicated it would oppose an insanity defense and the use of the cabin as evidence for that reason.

If Ted's 10-by-12-foot home cabin, which had been located near other homes and cabins, portrayed paranoid schizophrenia, what would an 8-by-8-foot secret cabin, located high on a mountainside miles from others, do to help the defense's case? It was obvious to me the prosecution didn't want to find out. It seemed as though it had become personal. They wanted Ted executed.

These theories and ideas were supported further when on Wednesday, October 29, a woman parked out on the main road and approached as I was working out in the yard. She introduced herself as Susan Garvey, a member of Ted's California-based defense team. Knowing I had refused to meet with defense lawyers the previous fall, she wondered if I might now be willing to talk.

It seemed like the situation had changed, and I definitely wanted to confirm my theory about the secret cabin, so I said we could. We ended up standing in the yard for the better part of two hours, discussing Ted and the case.

She described in great detail the need for jurors to learn as much as possible about the area where Ted lived.

Of course, she wanted to know if I liked Ted and considered him a friend. I told her I had, until he refused to see me after inviting me to visit him in the Helena jail, and asked her to tell Ted I had forgiven him for that. She covered the ground of what our interactions had been over the years. I mentioned that I had trusted Ted and was glad to have him roaming about my gulch, believing he would tell me if he noticed anything unusual happening.

She asked what I thought about the supposedly secret visit from the "shrinks," and what they had asked; I wouldn't answer. Later she inquired what I thought about Ted's refusal to submit to a psychiatric exam, and I said it didn't surprise me; knowing Ted, I thought he wouldn't want to be accused of being crazy. I also explained that Ted's lifestyle wasn't that unusual for this area and I had lived much the same way early on, before I was married. She referred to Ted's dirty skin and torn clothing at the time of his arrest, so I told her I thought he may have been sheltering in his root house during the cold nights.

We discussed many other topics that others had wanted to know about, but the time was fleeting and there was plenty to cover, so we decided to talk more the next day. She was working with another person from the defense team, Courtney Bell. I was sure they would take the information shared and use it to structure trial questioning. With jury selection slated to begin in mere days, time was of the essence for both the defense and the prosecution.

Evening came with the usual phone calls. Despite the intense media pressure there was little new information in stories about Ted. It was apparent no one else knew about Ted's twenty-five-year secret life in Lincoln. Certain reporters also realized that and were beginning to zero in on me. There wasn't much I could do about it, so I was just glad to live within the boundaries and safety of my gulch, shielded by my answering machine.

Betty and I turned in early that night. I was really feeling bad about what the case had done to her. It had not only been causing a huge disruption in our private lives, but it also had affected Betty personally. She wasn't able to go anywhere without being asked questions. It also was taking much time away from things that needed to be done. She was very understanding, but would be glad when it was all over.

The following morning the weather had changed for the worse—disappointing, but not surprising. A cold wind was blowing from the west and light rain was trying to turn into snow, especially higher on the mountainside where it started to cling to the trees. Bad weather was inevitable, as it was the end of October. We were living on borrowed time, weatherwise.

Around noon Susan drove up into the yard. I met her outside and said I had to go up into the woods about a mile to check on some things. If she would go along we could talk up there as easily as we could at the house.

"Great," she replied.

As we headed up along the old miners' road I told her she was one of a select few who had entered the area in recent years.

She jokingly asked if she should be blindfolded.

But soon she was looking open-eyed at the mountain peaks in awe. "Now I know why Ted loved this gulch so much; it's beautiful up here."

I checked to make sure some of my equipment was properly covered and then we went into one of our campers parked there and resumed the interview. It was an expanded version of our discussion the afternoon before, and covered many now-familiar paths of the prosecutors' and psychiatrists' questions about certain topics. But some of her questions went in new directions.

Susan asked why I had kept such close track of Ted and the places he liked to hike. Not to violate his privacy, I said, but to be there in case he got sick or hurt—it's just part of the old-school, mountain-man code of ethics to be there if your neighbor needs help.

When she asked what I thought about Ted's cabin, I said its size wasn't unusual for a mountain cabin. There are several smaller ones right here in my gulch where old-time miners lived. She acted surprised. It was a matter of efficiency, I went on. The smaller the cabin, the less area to heat during our long Lincoln winters.

We talked in detail about certain acts of violence and vandalism that had occurred around Lincoln, but I didn't say Ted was responsible or that I had already read his admissions of guilt in his journals.

We talked extensively about the country, its present condition, the mistakes of the past made in logging and mining, and the government's polices about logging and mining. I gave a brief history of my work—logging, road construction, mining—and described some of the environmental benefits, like eliminating bug infestations in the woods by logging selected stands of trees.

Later on, she returned to environmental concerns and asked about the huge new mining venture planned for the Lincoln area and whether I was for or against it. I explained I wasn't against mining if it was conducted responsibly, but I was against reckless operations. She asked about logging, and my response was much the same. Any activity conducted in the forests, even recreation, needed to be managed in accordance with responsible guidelines. Recreationalists can literally love the forest to death.

She inquired about the large piles of gravel and rocks that lined parts of Stemple Pass Road along Poorman Creek, what they were called and how they got there. I explained they were called tailing piles or dredge piles and were the remains of earlier placer mining operations.

She wondered when the piles were made and when the placer operation was running. More than forty years ago, I said, and then told her that hand-placer mining dated back more than 130 years, starting in this area as early as 1863 and changing little until mechanized methods took over well into the present century.

She asked why the piles were still here and I explained reclamation during the earlier years was non-existent. I said nature is in the business of slowly healing the wounds inflicted by man, noting the many trees and shrubs growing on the tailing piles. Education and public awareness has helped forge modern reclamation methods.

She asked if I ever discussed Ted with others. Rarely, I replied, except occasionally with Butch Gehring, as when Butch was sure Ted had vandalized his sawmill, but I had defended him.

She talked extensively about the separate guilt and penalty phases of the upcoming trial and asked if I had any questions about procedures. Surprisingly, she said the prosecution had a "very strong case against Ted," indicating a guilty verdict was very likely. She said the defense would be focusing a great deal on the penalty phase and that I would probably be called as a defense witness.

As we headed back down the gulch to her car the light rain spattered on the windshield of my old work truck and the wipers worked in a rhythmic whine.

From her questions, it looked like the defense wanted to portray Ted's mental state and use environmental issues to help show the jury some of the outside influences that spurred his progressive mental decline.

Dave Weber called that afternoon and was pleased to learn about the two visits with Susan. He said chief prosecutor Robert Cleary would be interested in what she had asked. He would talk to Cleary and call the following day.

I said, "Okay," but as I hung up the phone that uneasy feeling of being caught in the middle returned. I wanted to do what was right, but was anyone else's sense of right the same as mine?

The next day a break in the weather allowed me to work on the garage in earnest while struggling with what might happen in the case.

Dave called that afternoon and said since it was Friday, Cleary would contact me next week. He wanted to talk about Susan's line of questioning to help understand the direction Ted's lawyers were going with his defense.

I told Dave more pictures would be on the way soon, and then asked if he had heard anything new regarding the secret cabin and when he would return to Lincoln. He was vague about the cabin and said it didn't appear he'd be able to return. That didn't surprise me. I decided not to mention the secret cabin again.

As soon as our conversation ended I went into the next room and told Betty we had to go on a hike that weekend. She asked where and why.

"To Ted's secret cabin—you'll see why."

Sunday morning we packed up a half dozen large, strong plastic sacks. I grabbed my camera and a jug of water, and we started along the trail above our house to the secret cabin.

If the FBI wasn't going to gather and preserve evidence, then I would. I already had placed many items inside Ted's cooking pots, but that was only a temporary fix. The rubber gloves and clothing would disintegrate or be used by animals for nesting material. They wouldn't survive the winter. The FBI already had a complete set of photographs, and if anything was needed for the trial I would have it close at hand.

A main concern was the important items—like the plywood with his handwritten note on it, the fingerprinted brush handle, rubber gloves, gray hooded sweatshirt, and light blue denim pants like those he was wearing when spotted in Salt Lake City—be preserved indefinitely. It was all an important part of Lincoln's history and should be shared with the rest of the country.

Before long Betty and I were standing outside the secret cabin door. The day was gray and overcast, so we didn't waste any time. We filled the bags with everything we could carry, concentrating on the most important and fragile items. Then we headed back down the mountain.

On Wednesday, November 5, Dave called and said he had received the pictures. I didn't breathe a word to him about moving the evidence.

He said the new Unabom office was located high above and right across from the courthouse where the trial would be held, a great vantage point for everything that was happening.

He said the media had pooled resources and rented a half-block parking lot from the city. It must have been expensive, he said, considering the cost of just one downtown parking space. The power company had moved some new main feeds into the media area and mobile satellite uplinks were being set up. The total price tag for all this, Dave said, was a staggering half a million dollars a day.

He said Cleary had been caught up preparing his opening statement, filing motions, and other important trial work, so he hadn't been able to call me.

Then Dave surprised me by asking if I would send them all my notes from the defense interviews. I didn't respond immediately, feeling uncomfortable. Answering questions from Cleary over the phone was one thing, turning over notes was another—something that didn't seem ethical.

I told Dave it would be better if Cleary called, especially since the notes were condensed and would be extremely hard for anyone else to decipher.

Jury selection was scheduled to begin in a few days, but Dave said he hadn't seen the witness list from either side. It probably would be compiled at the last minute.

The next week flew by as I continued construction on the garage. Dave didn't call again until November 14, a Friday. He was back in San Francisco. They'd been swamped. The office spaces in Sacramento were very small and the media pressure was "unbelievable."

Robert Cleary hadn't had time to call, Dave explained, because he was caught in the middle of a pre-trial tussle over disclosure about the so-called "unchargeable offenses."

He went on to explain that unchargeable offenses were crimes Ted had confessed to in his journals, but from which he was protected by the statute of limitations, or else the offenses had never been reported.

The defense was trying to persuade U.S. District Judge Garland Burrell these offenses had nothing to do with the federal crimes for which Ted was being tried. The prosecution wanted them made public and entered into evidence to portray a pattern of violence and a propensity for killing.

Dave said there wasn't a hint which way the judge would rule. So Cleary had to prepare two opening statements, one that included the unchargeable offenses and one that excluded them. The judge might make the ruling before the trial started, but Cleary and the prosecution had to be prepared either way.

Dave, sensing I was about to ask him my usual question, beat me to the punch and said, no, the witness lists had not yet been released. He promised to call as soon as he knew.

We both laughed.

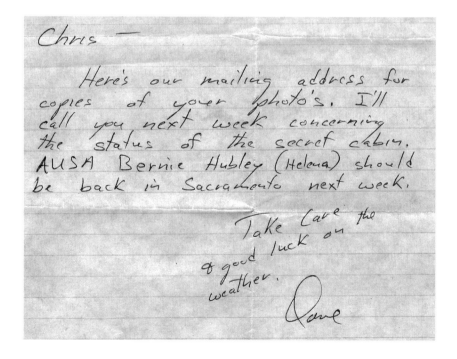

Chris —

Here's our mailing address for copies of your photo's. I'll call you next week concerning the status of the secret cabin. AUSA Bernie Hubley (Helena) should be back in Sacramento next week.

Take care & good luck on the weather.

Dave

Dave said he would call the following week when he returned to Sacramento.

Betty and I continued work on the garage and every day media phone calls increased.

Jury selection was under way and Dave had said the way the process was progressing, the jury should be seated by the first or at least the second week of December. I tried to avoid the phone and work on the garage as much as possible. Once again, real work helped get my mind off the upcoming trial.

The "Queer" Scale

On Monday, November 24, as I studied some of Ted's journal pages and compared them to my field notes from the previous summer, I found few differences. There were cryptic diagrams of cache locations mapped with pertinent landmarks, trees, rocks, and streams, fodder for many days of exploration. These documents included additional information, but several important pages studied during our field trips were missing, including Ted's hand-drawn map of all the trails and places he had explored.

The Montana winter had been coyly holding back, almost like a mountain lion on a talus slope sizing up its prey. But it was looming right around the corner, just like Ted's trial.

In final attempts to save him from the death penalty, Ted's attorneys were working furiously to reach a plea agreement with prosecutors. But U.S. Attorney General Janet Reno seemed steadfast, refusing to deal.

No one cared to argue Ted's innocence or guilt. The case instead centered on his mental health. Was he an insidious calculating murderer who deserved the death penalty or a deranged madman desperately in need of confinement and treatment?

Ted seemed resolute; he wouldn't take shelter from the storm, much as he often had defied nature's harshest elements in the backcountry mountains of western Montana. A defense of mental illness wasn't an option in his mind, so he was trapped in a snare, like the small mountain rodents he often killed for digging in either of his Florence Gulch gardens. Yet he didn't want to die.

While "Doctor" Ted directed his defense team from a California jail cell, I pored over many secret details of his years in Lincoln.

With a set of blank topographical maps spread out across the kitchen table, I methodically plotted every conceivable route and location; I was convinced my gulch held the answers to these final riddles of hidden caches. It was possible to zero in on the areas that looked like the best places to search.

That Wednesday I talked to Dave Weber. Events in Sacramento were confusing and fast-paced. Dave said media members were buzzing with new information; rumors surfaced almost daily, including a disturbing one that Ted's secret cabin had been found.

I was surprised, and assured him the leak didn't come from me. He said he knew that and was sure the loose lips were among their own people; one reporter mentioned photographs showing agent Max Noel, Dave and me standing in front of the cabin.

"I have all my pictures," I said. Dave replied he had all of his as well. Max was the only other person with pictures and we were both sure he wouldn't give any of his to the press.

Dave thought the whole thing would probably blow over. I knew otherwise.

Journalists are the best bloodhounds in the world and regularly put law enforcement investigators to shame. I knew that if the press had a clue about another untold aspect of the story, they wouldn't rest until they had dug it out.

I worked through the weekend on the garage and took breaks to explore areas of the woods that seemed promising; the activity kept me busy, easily the best way to ignore media phone calls and avoid the fury building in Sacramento.

When I talked to Dave the next Monday, he mentioned that prosecutor Robert Cleary had seemed excited about "cleaning the board" and resolving the remaining mysteries, showing a pattern with the unchargeable offenses.

Dave asked if the fingerprinted brush handle, the rubber gloves, and clothing from the secret cabin were protected. I told him they were secure; I think he sensed all the important evidence was now safely out of the cabin, but he didn't ask me where it was.

But later that week, when I again called Dave, he said Cleary now felt it might be too late in the game to add evidence to the case. It was still a possibility, Dave said, but the prosecution would have to look at things long and hard before making any decision.

The following week I tried to call Dave, who was out, and talked to a woman at the main desk instead. She switched me over to Max Noel. I excitedly told him I was pretty sure I had located an important buried cache site and asked if it should be dug up.

I was disappointed, mostly by the nonchalant tone in his voice, when he responded, "Well, that's great if you think you can find it."

He cut the conversation short; it almost felt like he didn't want me to continue my exploration. Discouraged after Max's negative reaction, I was determined to go out and find the cache and then I'd share that information with Dave, and Dave only.

As I sat inside near the fire during a couple of days of light snow and freezing rain, I studied and pondered the journal notes, which contained fascinating information about Ted's devices, acts of terrorism, and secret life.

It was clear he had gone to great lengths to throw the FBI off track and avoid detection. His life was a montage of plotting, designing, building, and testing bombs, all with one goal in mind—to kill. Then he made every conceivable effort to conceal his identity so he could kill again.

Not only were his devices built with home-mixed metal alloys and solder, wiring that was altered by removing strands, and parts obtained from scrap piles, but also he applied even more devious methods in his attempts to trick the FBI and to make sure no bombs or packages would lead them back to his home cabin.

Among the more than 200 books found in Ted's home were volumes on chemistry and electrical circuitry, and there also was a FBI manual on fingerprinting. The manual was his graduate-level textbook on the process, and taught him how to avoid detection.

Ted learned his lessons well, evident from all those years he remained free in the Montana wilderness while people suffered and died.

For starters, he carefully wore rubber gloves any time he worked on a bomb. You have to wonder how many devices he constructed at his secret cabin, where all the pairs of rubber gloves were found. Then, to remove any fingerprints, he hand-sanded every part that went into his bombs and every piece of copper tubing used for his hand-made detonators.

The tube should be worked over with fine emery
paper to remove any fingerprints—wiping is not enough.
Even if your own prints are not on the tube, store employees' prints may enable FBI to trace tube to store where it
was bought.

As Ted packaged his armed devices, he carefully wrapped, sealed
and weighed each one so he himself could apply the proper postage
in stamps, rather than allowing a post office to weigh and meter the
parcel, which could be traced
But the stamps weren't just any stamps. He didn't want to take
any chance they might be traced either, so he went to great extremes
to soak every one in a homemade solution to remove any potentially
incriminating marks. Then he'd apply a glue. He chose every stamp
carefully and refused to purchase any stamp that was embossed.

NOTE FOUND WITH STAMP CONTAINER
These stamps are *CLEAN* and do not bear the
impression of this writing. They were purchased from a
vending machine in one of the two Missoula post offices
between March 1995 and May 1995. They have been
treated.

These stamps are CLEAN and do not bear the impression of this writing. They were purchased from a vending machine in one of the two Missoula post offices between March 1995 and May 1995. They have been treated.

Ted took the added precaution of wearing disguises when he mailed a device or purchased any materials.

His measures to deceive and mislead any investigators were layered like a cat's cradle.

He placed a human hair found in a Missoula bathroom inside one of his devices, knowing if it was discovered by FBI agents as they studied the shards of the exploded bomb, they would have a field day testing and studying it. He chose hair with a different color and texture than his own.

FROM BOMB NOTEBOOK

A while back I obtained 2 human hairs from the bathroom of the Missoula bus depot. I broke one of these hairs into two pieces and I placed one piece between the layers of electrical tape I used to wrap the wire joints inside the package. The reason for this is to deceive the policemen, who will think that the hair belongs to whoever made the device.

When he broke the hair in half, he saved one piece to use in a later device.

Ever methodical, Ted compiled a chart of pros and cons.

PLUS	MINUS
1. Confuses them about hair	1. May make them suspect we're not from CA.
2. Removes their idea we may have brown hair	2. May make them suspect we wore wig
	3. May make them doubt false verbal clues

Ted's deception wasn't relegated solely to the physical. Like a multi-level chess game, he constantly was trying to outwit the FBI in the psychological arena as well, twisting information used in his letters to enhance his smoke-screen, writing as if several people or a group were responsible, rather than an individual, or by implying that he resented people with advanced degrees so agents wouldn't look to the academic world for suspects.

In a letter say that, "scientists consider themselves very intelligent because they have advanced diplomas (advanced degrees) but they are not as intelligent as they think because they opened those packages." This will make it seem as though I have no advanced degree.

The very essence of his subterfuge can be seen in a letter sent to Yale University computer scientist Dr. David Gelernter, who was injured by one of Ted's bombs in 1993.

FROM LETTER TO GELERNTER POSTMARKED APRIL 20, 1995
...People with advanced degrees aren't as smart as they think they are. If you'd had any brains you would have realized that there are a lot of people out there who resent bitterly the way techno-nerds like you are changing the world and you wouldn't have been dumb enough to open an unexpected package from an unknown source....any college person can learn enough about computers to compete in a computer-dominated world. Apparently, people without a college degree don't count....

As usual, this piece of correspondence was written as if several people were responsible so authorities would think it was a terrorist group at work (FC, Freedom Club). At one point, Ted came up with an idea that he should write a letter to "Dear Abby" in Spanish, referring to his membership in the "Freedom Club," the supposed group behind the Manifesto.

Ted's explosive mixtures found in his cabin were often prepared from common objects—first matchheads, then black powder from shells and bullets, and then from common household chemicals, making them untraceable.

He was constantly at work developing mixtures that ranged from flash powder to incendiary thermite, which he carefully stored in containers with numerical identifying labels. Ted even prepared and built his own detonating caps; the mixtures used in the caps were logged and numbered as well.

Ted kept careful, laboratory-like records of his experiments—"Igniter charge mixture #8," "Tube mixture #5"—a practice ingrained during his days in academia.

His experiments extended to ingenious devices used to house his bombs, including books that exploded when opened, gas cans that would detonate upon lifting the handle, a bomb disguised as a stack of research papers, electrical testing equipment, or even a road hazard.

It seems he left no stone unturned, though he apparently overlooked one important item—the DNA left in saliva from licking glue

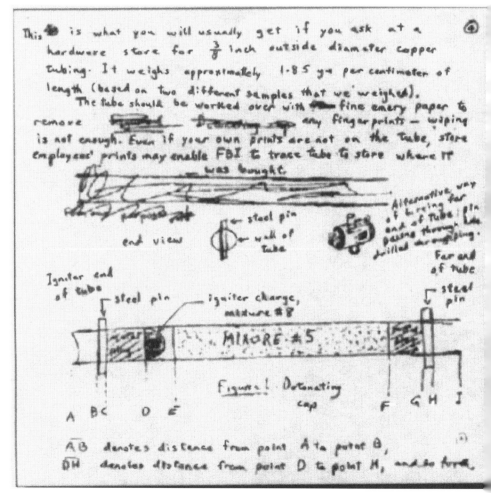

Kaczynski the scientist carefully tracked materials and methods he used in bomb-building.

on envelopes. But even the DNA samples frustrated the FBI, since they did little good until a suspect was apprehended.

On Monday, December 15, Dave called and left a message since I was outside. He missed me the next day as well. On Wednesday, we finally made contact and he said rumors about Ted's secret cabin had resurfaced and the two of us discussed possible leaks.

It became apparent the leak was in Sacramento. Dave explained some people in law enforcement can't keep information to themselves; they become those "unnamed" or "reliable" sources often quoted by the media.

The whole process was starting to frustrate me and I let him know as much the next day when we talked again.

To make matters worse, it seemed like I was being accused of the leaks by a few in charge. At one point I even said to Dave I was going to stop helping them because of the distrust and manipulation brought on by some of his superiors.

It also was upsetting that the FBI had never offered to reimburse me for film, processing, more than $500 worth of long distance phone calls, plus countless hours spent on the case, including some sixty days helping them with field investigations.

I felt I was being used. If the FBI could hold a party at a local steakhouse after Ted's arrest, then they could be more appreciative of all I had done. I told Dave I was tempted to take everything I had and knew to the press.

He encouraged me not to, and he knew I wouldn't.

"You can trust me," he said. "The FBI hasn't always treated people the way they should and have taken some bad press because of it, but we've tried to change that."

Dave was sincere, but I wasn't so sure about the people in command.

I told him when I solved the remaining pieces of the case that I might just keep the items and not even send them more pictures.

"Don't do that," he replied. "They are still interested in the help only you can provide."

Dave encouraged me to send copies of any bills and a list of hours and days spent working for the FBI and said he would try to obtain reimbursement. I didn't have much faith that would happen since I barely had received a thank-you from anyone other than Dave.

After we hung up, I studied Ted's hiking-trail map. Even though I had caught glimpses of the map during our field work in July, it was astounding to be able to carefully study all the miles Ted had covered, and how he had hiked virtually every accessible area around our homes, everything that wasn't a sheer vertical cliff. He left few places unexplored.

Looking down at the paper I could visualize every trail, ridge, and gulch he had crossed and could almost see a bearded and long-haired Ted standing there in the forest, protected by a poncho, a pack on his back, oblivious to the sleet and snow.

While leafing through some of Ted's other documents, I began to understand the unusual structure of the journals themselves and how they were organized.

His writings were voluminous, to say the least. More than 22,000 pages were found in his cabin after the arrest, all organized in three-ring binders and spiral notebooks. They chronicled his entire life from early childhood to the time of his arrest. Much of his work about lifestyle—what he ate, details about the weather and country—was written during his early years in Lincoln; it tapered off in the '80s and '90s when he was spending much more time building better bombs, testing them, then delivering them.

Ted's early life was described in an unpublished autobiography, which documented every important aspect up to the age of twenty-seven.

That's when he started to keep a daily journal, which early on was written in great detail. His notebooks quickly became his constant companion and best friend as he carved a new life for himself as a mountain hermit. He carried on conversations with himself in them, expressing his feelings, frustrations and most of all, his plans for revenge upon society.

Ted's daily journal entries described where he hiked, camped, and what he ate, and elaborated his views about everything from philosophy to environmental issues.

As his precious papers and journals grew in volume, he developed a library-like system that organized everything from his autobiography to secret documents written in sophisticated numerical code, a code that Ted the mathematician had devised.

This substantial library of his own work was divided and organized into series and volumes, including his autobiography; then Series I, Volumes #1 to #7; Series II, Volumes #1 to #6; notebooks with bomb experiments, tests, and diagrams; a notebook containing entries written in his own numerical code; and a notebook written partly in Spanish to disguise "misdeeds": vandalism and illegal hunting activities.

This was a fairly academic way to organize his documents, which contained the bizarre and twisted stories of a serial killer. Much of the writing was extremely dangerous and sensitive if ever seen by outside eyes. Ted realized that and knew in the military they deserved at least a "CLASSIFIED" or "TOP SECRET" stamp. Top secret didn't appeal to Ted, though, so he devised his own system, classifying his writings according to his "Queer Ratings," based on the sensitivity of the material, and were assigned as follows:

Queer #1—embarrassing but not dangerous;
Queer #2—embarrassing, not dangerous, but past the
statute of limitations;
Queer #3—embarrassing, not dangerous, past the statute
of limitations, but very bad public relations;...
Queer #10—Most sensitive, embarrassing, incriminating,
and dangerous.

If in a hurry, he also used a quick-and-dirty rating system with two letters maximum.

It read as follows:

S—Slightly Queer
R—Moderately Queer
Q—Very Queer
QQ—Super Queer

Other notations used in the documents addressed the disposability of items:

B—Burnable
NB—Not Burnable

There was another classification system devised to help him quickly decide how to deal with all his jars, containers, documents, maps, drawings and journals.

Class #1, Hide carefully, far from home
Class #2, Hide carefully, far from home, but can be destroyed at a pinch
Class #3, Hide carefully, far from home, but can be burned at a pinch
Class #4, Burn away from home
Class #5, Burn in a stove, eventually
Class #6, Burn with glass jars
Class #7, Destroy with glass jars
Class #8, Treat to make safe
Class #9, Burn in stove, then dispose of remains
Class #10, Dump in trash far from home

Ted's systems and classification codes seemed to cover every conceivable possibility: how to treat postage stamps, what to do with refuse, how to dispose of a container of chemicals, the sensitivity of a particular document or complete notebook, where to hide or stash a document or writing, and finally how to burn or dispose of "Top Queer" items quickly.

FROM FBI INVENTORY OF ITEMS SEIZED AT KACZYNSKI HOME CABIN

L-31—Two rolls of brown paper marked "3QQ," can containing wire marked "QQ" and documents...

L-32—Box marked "All 1 or 10 Q or QQ" (Handwritten), metal tubes, wiring, springs, ball trigger in tin foil, stapler, 9V battery, and small copper color tubing....

L-33—Books with "5Q" on container...

L-52—Five bottles labeled "SaltPeter" and plastic bag "3Q"

Despite this all-encompassing system, Ted occasionally found it wasn't enough, so he also wrote special instructions for certain journal sections.

Series I, #3   pp. 261-262 . queer 9
      #   p. 276 - 283   queer 10

   Almost all the rest of the notebook is queer 8

   Series I, #4. Might as well call the whole
notebook queer 8.

Series I, #5. pp. 111 - 115 queer 10
               pp 138 - 139 queer 10

Might as well call all the rest of the notebook
                  queer 8

   Series I, #6   Queer 10
   Series 3, #7   Queer 8

   Series II, #1, no queer

Series II, #2, no queer

   Series II, #3, p. 29   queer 1 (embarrassing, not dangerous)
                  p. 56   queer 2 (but past statute of limitations)
                  p. 64   queer 7
                  pp. 82-86 queer 7
                  p. 102   queer 1
                  p. 105   queer 2
                  pp. 120-121 queer 2 (but past statute of
Bad Public relation   limitations)

   Series II, #a   Call this notebook queer 3. But
very bad public relations.

       Series II, p 5,
up to p. 121, queer 2 (but past statute of limitations)
p. 122 - end, queer 9

Here I am going to confess to—or, to be more accurate, brag about—some misdeeds I have committed in the last few years.

He ended this multi-page section of confessions (which are quoted throughout the present book) with this entry:

By the way, my motive for keeping these notes separate from the others is the obvious one. Some of my other notes contain hints of crime, but no actual accounts of felonies. But these notes must be very carefully kept from everyone's eyes. Kept separate from the other notes they make a small, compact packet, easily concealed.

Just as he switched between English words and Spanish, in his numerical code certain words and non-sensitive phrases were written in English, then he would revert to the sophisticated numerical code for the rest of the text.

It was a marvel, the great effort and thought that had gone into all his codes, classifications, methods, and categories set up to conceal, and yet at the same time protect, his legacy. Ted explained in his journals that the reason he kept such meticulous notes was to prove that his acts were planned and were not random acts committed by a crazy person, or as he labeled it, a "sickie."

Yet he was writing his own detailed exposé about a secret world that he also tried so diligently to conceal. There was a conflict raging inside his mind, pitting Ted the master criminal, who was making every effort to deceive, and Ted the scientist and historian, who wanted to archive his work so that at some point the world could marvel at his ingenuity and see him as a jungle fighter in a war against the modern world.

As if all this wasn't enough—the codes, Spanish, Queer Ratings—Ted also had a "No Queer" rating for benign information.

It was nothing more than a non-rating, and it helped complete the classification of almost every aspect of his life.

His system did have one practical application; it enabled him to quickly find a sensitive page or group of pages, containing embarrassing or incriminating information. Once the FBI understood his system, it was a time-saver for investigators. Coupled with the fact Ted conveniently had placed the key to his numerical code within the walls of his home cabin, his organizational skills were greatly valued by the FBI.

FBI agents admitted his numerical code was sophisticated and would have been difficult to crack, requiring a great deal of time and resources.

Time was critical, but resources didn't seem to be a problem. At one point certain agents in Lincoln said money was no object. I was told that, in all, upwards of $70 million was spent on the Unabomber case, not including final court costs.

Monday, December 22 arrived, and even though it was almost Christmas, the weather was incredibly mild. It just didn't seem like the holidays. I was still building outside, making a final effort to enclose our garage for the winter.

I walked out to the mail box and found a Christmas card containing notes from both Dave and his wife, Sue. It was a nice gesture, and made me feel good.

In Sacramento, jury selection had been completed and Ted's trial was slated to begin before the New Year. That seemed unlikely, though. Ted and his defense team were determined to delay the trial and would probably file some sort of motion or plot another tactic to compel Judge Garland Burrell to postpone opening arguments until after the holidays.

The upcoming trial promised to be fascinating for technocrats around the world and feature never-before-seen methods. I had learned all the exhibits, documents, interviews, supporting evidence, etc. had been recorded on CD ROMs, a first in U.S. criminal trial history. Kodak, I learned, was working with the prosecution on the technical details and how the evidence would be presented.

This technological advance was to be initiated in the trial of a man who epitomized anti-technology.

Dave told me Ted had been held in the Bay Area's Dublin Federal Correctional Institution from September 3 to November 6, then he was moved to his Sacramento County jail cell near the federal building. Dublin was a high-security, low-profile women's prison where Ted was housed to answer his complaints about noise in the Sacramento jail, but mainly to avoid excessive media attention.

From everything Dave had told me, Ted had apparently adapted remarkably well to prison so far, and if convicted and sentenced to life, incarceration would mirror his reclusive mountain ways—quiet, contemplative, a place where he could write extensively and communicate with himself through those writings. His punishment would be not roaming in the wilds.

At the time of his arrest Ted was still plotting more acts of terrorism, despite the vow in 1995 to stop if the manifesto was published.

It was hard not to think about the people who were on the "hit list" found among his papers in the home cabin. By fate's hand they were now spending Christmas with their families.

The list consisted of a cross-section of people with diverse occupations, but all were employed in technology-related fields. For instance, the list included people working for Pegasus Gold, which operated mines in Montana; Potlatch, a large wood-products manufacturer; and a helicopter-charter business. Along with the list were maps of the cities where these targets lived, with their neighborhoods marked.

Everything found in his home cabin, my gulch and the secret cabin clearly pointed to a life of continued violence. Also, he seemed prepared for nearly every conceivable situation, except his arrest, which truly caught him off guard. Because of the surprise, he wasn't able to carry out his plan to destroy the plethora of evidence in his cabin with an incendiary device and then escape.

All the carefully documented schemes proved useless once he was handcuffed. He didn't have a clue as he walked out his door when lawmen pretended to need his help interpreting a map that it would prove to be the last time he would ever step out of his cabin.

He moved too far from the cabin door that April day in 1996, while his .25 caliber Raven automatic sat just inches away behind the door. If he had just reached inside, he could have grabbed the gun and held law enforcement officials at bay.

A completed device lay under his bed. It lacked an address and name, but seemed to be earmarked for an airliner or an airline-affili-ated person. Written on the wrapping was a misleading note that inside was a "Newell Channel Reamer," a tool commonly used by aviation mechanics.

Was Ted planning another sabotage attempt on an airliner, like the one in 1979—where not one, but hundreds of lives could be taken at once? Who knows? But one thing is certain, he wouldn't have labeled the package as containing an airline related tool if he were planning to send it to a microbiologist. Maybe his threat to blow up a plane at the Los Angeles airport by July 4, 1995, wasn't as much a hoax as he claimed.

Ted was extremely careful about formulating precise plans to make "hits" on people who represented technological industries he hated.

One of his plans explained how to murder an oil executive.

Kaczynski's typewritten letter to the FBI that followed the 1995 Los Angeles airport incident.

UNDATED JOURNAL ENTRY

How to hit an Exxon exec:

Send book-like package preceded by a letter saying I am sending him a book I've written on oil-related environ-mental concerns attacking environmental position—and I'd like to have his comments on it before preparing a final version of manuscript. Also put in the letter a disclaimer stating that the book represents my own personal views and not those of the company I work for. This gives a touch of realism and it also explains why the letter is not on the company's [letterhead?].

Ted had spent plenty of time working on every detail of his plots. Now, incarcerated, he had nothing but time on his hands. After his arrest, one project was to create a chart that showed the mathematical probability of his being found guilty.

But in some ways Ted was prepared even for being arrested. He had acquired a copy of a publication on civil liberties and civil rights with precise instructions detailing the rights of an accused prisoner.

Ted knew every right, and followed to the letter every trick, that the booklet spelled out—right through all the pretrial actions.

His manipulation of the court system eventually tested the patience of Judge Burrell, who after the plea agreement would accuse Ted of "trickery" to preserve his life; grandstanding "antics" to delay and disrupt the trial proceedings; "contriving conflicts" to affect the process; and staging an "alleged suicide attempt that was merely one attempt among many rational and ongoing attempts to delay the trial he dreaded."

The judge also described Ted's "conflicts" with his attorneys as "purposeful attempts to delay" and cause chaos in the courtroom.

As Dave once put it, Ted was running his lawyers, not the other way around, and he was upset when he discovered they were planning an insanity defense.

His defense teams reluctantly went along with everything, but what else could they do?

Christmas seemed to come and go in a flash and I hoped the trial would as well. I knew better, though. Dave had told me the state of New Jersey would become the site of a second trial. He said a federal magistrate had ordered this trial and also told the prosecution to be prepared for it in no more than seventy days, which allowed little time to get ready for such a complicated case.

A second trial would have its advantages for the prosecution: in the event of a hung jury or a mistrial, there would be another chance to obtain a conviction.

On Monday, December 29, Dave called and left a message saying he had something important to tell me and would call again. I missed his call the next day and then decided to work near the phone until he called again. The next day, Dave reached me.

His important news disturbed me deeply. He said he was leaving the Unabom Task Force, and transferring to a job as a firearms and weapons instructor at a military base near San Diego. Dave seemed sad to leave, but excited about the prospects of his new job. He'd miss coming back to Lincoln on the case but would return for a vacation later with his wife.

Dave would work on Ted's case until the trial was over, but I knew we wouldn't be able to stay in touch as we had in the past.

I asked Dave what his boss, Joel Moss, thought about his transfer. Joel seemed upset, Dave said, and asked why he was leaving and what they should or could have done differently to keep him.

Dave's answer surprised me. He told Joel there were numerous things they should have handled differently. He was tired that every word and idea he uttered had fallen on deaf ears, and still believed that he should have been allowed to remain in Lincoln the past July to explore my gulch with me.

He also told Joel the shroud of secrecy imposed the first summer (1996) served no purpose, as I could have helped them greatly. Working together we could have wrapped up all the details before the pressure was on. He then said he had gone to the trouble of building a relationship with me, which they cut off. Yet the leaks they were so concerned about came from within their own organization.

I mentioned I had decided to do a short interview with NBC to clarify a few details about Ted, but the interview contained no sensitive information. He promised to watch for it.

Dave said he would call me again the following week, and we both agreed it was nice to get a few things off our chests.

The first Monday of 1998 dawned. Opening statements in the Kaczynski trial were scheduled to begin that morning. But shortly into the session Judge Burrell called both sides and the court reporter into his chambers and they didn't return until after 12:30 P.M. The jurors were sent home.

That afternoon I called Dave, to find out what had happened in the courtroom. He said Ted had wanted to address the jury, then was allowed to approach the bench and to speak to the judge privately. The on-the-record meeting lasted for four and a half hours. Ted told Judge Burrell he wanted to fire his lawyers because he didn't approve of the insanity defense they planned.

It was an interesting but not surprising development, considering how Ted had written of his extreme concern about the public perception of himself and his ideas. After all, if his ideology was being advanced by a "sickie," then it would be easily discounted and cast aside.

On the other hand, if his ideas were perceived to be the enlightened philosophy of an intelligent revolutionary, then Ted would gain respect in some quarters and possibly even develop a following.

Dave said it had been interesting to watch Ted during the short public court session. He refused to even look at his mother or brother, who were in the courtroom, or acknowledge their presence.

As Dave and his boss, Joel, were waiting for Judge Burrell and Ted to finish their discussion in chambers, Joel said, "That friend of yours, Chris, is going to be on TV doing an interview," a comment that implied I couldn't be trusted and was going behind Dave's back.

Dave immediately shot that theory out of the water, replying, "I know. Chris already told me."

There was no further comment, Dave said.

I asked Dave how Joel knew about the interview before it even aired. Dave said they had a public relations spokeswoman, Leesa Brown, who monitored every facet of the media, from tabloids to talk shows to mainstream television and newspapers. Besides finding out what was coming from the press, her job included making statements to the press regarding the trial.

Dave said he was busy and couldn't talk anymore, but that he would call again on Wednesday. He was soon to be in San Diego training for his new job.

Earlier, when I had asked him about the witness list, he said Robert Cleary planned to first lay the foundation for the case, then call expert witnesses—lab technicians, forensic analysts, and agents involved with the investigation and arrest—and finally call civilian witnesses to the stand. The flow and direction of the trial would determine when and who would be called.

My thoughts during those early days in January were often directed to Ted, trying to understand his adult life between his move to Montana in 1971 and the fight for his life in a courtroom.

Some of the things I had learned about my friend and neighbor of twenty-five years were incredible, to say the least.

It still stunned me to feel I had been blind to what was going on right under my nose, especially when it came to his bombs.

In scientific fashion, he had developed them from crude devices into sophisticated, anti-personnel weapons. Included with detailed design diagrams were test results, charting the impact of different components.

He calculated mathematically the heat transfer on the bridge wire inside his home-built detonator caps. He tested different types of detonator designs, chemical mixtures used in the devices, and different currents supplied for the batteries used, e.g., 9 volt; 1.5 volt C cell, and 1.5 volt D cell.

He field tested prototypes and calculated results like the distances of fragmentation, weighing different designs and various types of shrapnel. Using all this information, he could determine the effective killing zone of each type of device or detonator built.

He was extremely careful with the shrapnel he used, burning and soaking every piece in acid to destroy any traceable marks.

Ted achieved technological breakthroughs in some of his later devices by experimenting with explosive mixtures and detonators until he discovered lethal combinations that more than doubled the deadliness of a device while maintaining or reducing the weight of the finished bomb.

He learned how to eliminate the heavy, cumbersome, and more easily detected metal pipe and produce more easily packed and concealed bombs. The shrapnel in these was made of untraceable materials.

Even when he still used pipe, Ted learned how to make the bombs explode with greater fragmentation, causing more damage. His designs showed a gradual learning curve, the result of continuing experiments.

He obviously was obsessive about the very technology he loathed as he built and tested his devices right under my nose.

The whole case had dominated my thoughts since Ted's arrest, but it was so bizarre and unreal that at times I had to pinch myself to determine if it was real or nothing more than a bad dream.

The more I thought about the bombs, the more often strange incidents from the past popped up. My mind seemed to be making endless correlations, Ted things that were puzzling at the time, things I hadn't thought about for years.

For example, I remembered an incident related by a delivery truck driver. He knew Ted and I were friends, he'd seen me talking with Ted.

The driver told me one day he had delivered a package to Ted. It was the first and only time he ever had one for Ted.

Surprisingly, Ted opened the package right in front of him. It contained a blood pressure monitor from a hospital or doctor's office in Missoula. Ted grabbed the instrument, wrapped it around his arm, pumped it a little bit, and replied, "This should work." He smiled, removed it, placed it back in its box and then walked off.

The incident had always been an enigma to me. Ted was health conscious, there's no doubt about that, and he tried to take care of himself physically. But buying a blood pressure monitor, especially from a health care provider instead of a more economical source?

I found out later he was taking his own blood pressure on a regular basis. He thought his heart was going bad, especially when he was consumed with anger.

FROM CODED JOURNAL

    ...MOTORCYCLE AND SNOWMOBILE FIENDS.THEYWOULDBUZZ UPANDDOWN ROADPASTMY CABIN ON MOST WEEKENDS,SUMMERANDWINTER.LAST SUMMER SEEMEDTHEYWEREWORSE THAN USUAL.SOMETIMES MADE IT A3DAYWEEKEND.WHEN THEYWERENOTBUZZING UPTHISROAD I WOULDHEAR THOSE CYCLES GROWLING ANDGROWLING OVER BY THEIR PLACE,ALLDAY LONG.ITWASGETTING ABSOLUTELY INTOLERABLE.MY HEARTISGOINGBAD.TAKES EXERCISE OK,BUT ANY EMOTIONAL STRESS,ANGER ABOVE ALL,MAKES IT BEAT IREGULARLY [*sic*].ITGOT SO THAT THATCONSTANTCYCLE NOISEWASCHOKINGME WITH ANGER,HEARTGOING WILD.

Concerned about his heart, Ted wrote that during 1991 he went to see Carolyn Goren, a doctor of internal medicine/cardiology in Missoula.

She saw Ted in person twice and found nothing irregular about his heart or anything else, but prescribed a low dose and quantity of sleeping pills for stress and to help him sleep.

Ted sent her a record of his blood pressure readings every six months for the next five years.

But now I thought of another possible use for the gadget. What better piece of equipment to test an atmospheric pressure trigger switch? By the time he received the monitor, Ted had already attempted to use a barometer in one airliner bomb, unsuccessfully in that it detonated but did not destroy the plane.

Did he plan to use his monitor as a trigger switch? At the least, it would be a handy and reliable way to test barometric or atmospheric pressure trigger switches in order to gauge how much pressure would be required to complete the circuit and detonate the explosive.

In his journals, he had complained about using a barometer to complete this function.

CODED JOURNAL

DEC29,1979.INSOME OFMY NOTES I MENTIONEDAPLAN-FOR REVENGEONSOCIETY PLAN WAS TOBLOWUP AIRLINER INFLIGHT.LATESUMMERANDEARLYAUTUMNICONSTRUCTED-DEVICE.MUCH EXPENSE,BECAUSEHADTO GOTOGR.FALLSTO-BUYMATERIALS, INCLUDINGBAROMETERANDMANYBOXESCAR-TRIDGESFORTHEPOWDER.IPUTMORETHANAQUARTOF-SMOKE LESSPOWDERINACAN,RIGGEDBAROMETERSODEVICEWOULD-EXPLODEAT2000FT.ORCONCEIVABLYASHIGHAS3500FT.DUE-TOVARIATIONOFATMOSPHERICPRESSURE.LATE OCT.MAILED-PACKAGEFROMCHICAGOPRIORITYMAILSOITWOULDGOBYAIR.U NFORTUNATELYPLANENOTDESTROYED,BOMBTOOWEAK.NEW SPAPER SAIDWAS"LOWPOWERDEVICE".SURPRISEDME.

Scientifically, Ted analyzed the problem. "Possible explanations...defective barometer. Light touch of barometer needle on contact not absolutely reliable in transmitting current. I will try again if I can get a better explosive. At least I gave them a good scare."

Where is the blood pressure monitor now? It wasn't in his cabin, and to date it is missing. Did Ted create a device from it that is still out there somewhere in a deadly state of limbo? Or did he dismantle the monitor and use the parts?

One thing for certain, Ted did write he would again attempt to blow up an airliner once he came up with a better and more powerful explosive. The bomb found under his bed, marked as a Newell Channel Reamer, certainly could have been designed for such a commercial plane.

On Wednesday, January 7, NBC began airing my interview early in the morning on *Today*. I wasn't able to watch the piece, but they sent me a tape.

It was apparent when it had aired, though, because of an immediate increase in phone calls from the media, which I avoided.

Wednesday afternoon, Dave called and said opening statements were now scheduled for the next day, Thursday, January 8. Ted was in court as we were speaking, in a private meeting with Judge Burrell where the judge was trying to convince him to keep his present counsel. Dave and I agreed it was just another attempt to delay the trial.

Robert Cleary was hoping the judge would make his ruling on the admissibility of the unchargeable offenses before the trial resumed, so he'd be able to choose between his two opening statements.

Dave said he hoped the judge would get the issues regarding Ted's lawyers resolved that afternoon.

"They just don't get it," he said.

Ted's refusal of an insanity plea made perfect sense to Dave and me. Ted would rather accept the death penalty and go down in history as a martyr for his cause than spend the rest of his life in a mental institution labeled as insane.

The next morning, I received a call that Ted had tried to commit suicide by hanging in his jail cell. He was immediately placed on "suicide watch" twenty-four hours a day.

I had to wonder if it had been a serious attempt or just another ploy to delay the trial.

I went outside to clear my head with some good honest physical work—cutting firewood, milling boards, and working on one of my Cats. More than anything, it got me away from the phone. The whole affair had really changed our lives. Betty would no longer pick up the telephone for any reason and I didn't blame her.

That evening, while going through all the messages, I was startled to hear something new—a phone call threatening my family if I cooperated with authorities further. It didn't intimidate me, though, and I was even pretty sure who had made the call.

"Don't you dare go and confront them! Just let it go, they're not worth it," Betty said.

I had to agree, but how dare they try to intimidate me?

"Turn it over to your friends in the FBI," she said.

That was a good idea.

A few days after Ted had staged his suicide attempt the thing I feared most happened. On Wednesday, January 14, the defense learned from an unnamed media source that Ted's secret cabin had been found.

I dreaded the stampede that would ensue.

I thought about the buried caches of ammunition and food I had uncovered barely two weeks earlier and wondered if that would leak out, too. The agent I had shared the most information with was Dave, because I was trying to get him back to Montana to finish the job with me.

I really only wanted to turn things over to him, but now he was gone except for his contributions to the trial. I knew it was only a matter of time before other agents would want all the evidence from the secret cabin and caches.

And, the very next day, Thursday, January 15, Helena-based FBI agents Tom McDaniel and Terry Wade drove up to pick up the items from the cache and other evidence.

It wasn't a shock, since we had played phone tag during the last couple of weeks. I had mentioned it to Dave, knowing the purpose of their calls.

"At least they can't say you haven't been returning their calls," he replied.

Before the agents arrived, my friend Bobby Didriksen called and said they were in Lincoln looking for me.

None of the evidence was at home, but was safely protected. I didn't want to withhold anything, but I knew I wanted to talk to Dave before making any move.

A white Ford Bronco showed up in my yard and the two agents got out.

Both were nice. Tom, the senior agent, and I talked about some mutual friends. After inviting them in and visiting for the better part of two hours, I said I knew why they came, but I wasn't prepared to turn over the evidence yet. I had been working closely with Dave and needed to talk to him first, and also, the things they wanted weren't at home and would have to be retrieved from the place where I had them hidden.

I told Tom I wasn't refusing to give up the items, but I wanted to be careful and get Dave's advice. Mistrust had developed between others on the Unabom Task Force and me, and because of the way I had been treated regarding the secret cabin, I didn't want a repeat of events. Tom understood.

When they left I knew there would be repercussions and that Dave would be calling soon.

Sure enough, Dave called Saturday. I told him about the threatening phone call and he said to tell Tom McDaniel so there would be a record.

I already had told Tom and also had saved the tape from the answering machine. I would probably let the incident slide, but if it happened again the young man would be held responsible.

Dave said some of his bosses were mad at me for not turning over the things they wanted. He had advanced that possibility earlier to his boss, Joel. "Why do you want this stuff now?" he had asked. "What if Chris doesn't want to give up the things?"

The truth was the prosecution had withheld information about the secret cabin and caches from the defense and that risky strategy was now coming back to haunt them.

I told Dave that if I turned over the items it would only be to him, as I trusted him and he trusted me.

I asked what he wanted me to do.

"I can't tell you what to do," he replied. "You'll have to do what you think is best." He added that he thought I should probably turn over what they wanted and fill out a claim paper so that after the trial I could get the things back.

I still had reservations. I knew the possibility existed that if I gave them everything, it could be hidden or destroyed, or they could deny the items ever existed.

Now that the secret cabin story had leaked out, I was in a position to embarrass the agents and maybe even get them into legal trouble. That was the last thing I wanted to see happen, but now that mistrust had developed I wanted to protect myself, too.

I told Dave to call me in a few days and I would let him know what I would do.

I felt as though I was about to get swept into the middle of a conflict between the defense and prosecution. I also found it interesting that, after all this time, the agents had come to my house unannounced now, when they knew that the secret cabin story had leaked out. I certainly didn't blame Tom or Terry, who were following orders from the Task Force in Sacramento.

I had no idea what was going on at the trial, but as it turned out the defense team had spent the weekend preparing a motion to compel the prosecution to disclose the location and other relevant information about the secret cabin.

On Monday, January 19, the motion was filed by fax and delivery; the trial was set to resume that Thursday, but on Wednesday the motion was argued in federal court in Sacramento before United States Magistrate Gregory G. Hollows.

According to the hearing transcript, the defense motion stated: "On January 14, 1998, the defense learned from a media source that the secret shack had been located by the government. Based on that information the defense has requested that the government provide all information in its possession concerning the location, contents, and other matters regarding the shack. Although not denying that the government has located the shack, the government refuses to provide any further information. Regardless of whether the government intends to use evidence regarding a secret shack, the defense is entitled to discovery of all information in the government's possession regarding the shack. The shack, the location, the method of construction, and the contents are all potentially relevant to the issues of the defendant's past and present mental status, and thus may be admissible on these issues in either the guilt or penalty phases of the trial."

The secret cabin certainly fit into the defense's mental defect plan, supporting the argument that Ted lived a pathologically isolated life. But disclosing this kind of evidence didn't fit the prosecution's game plan of seeking the death penalty.

The prosecution maintained to the court they weren't going to use the evidence of the cabin and its contents in the trial, so they didn't have to disclose the information.

Judge Hollows didn't buy the prosecution's argument and came down hard on them, saying the defense had the right to see the evidence. One of the problems facing the prosecution was that the bulk of the relevant photographs were ones taken by me and they had neither extra copies nor the negatives. I had both. Along with the cabin's contents.

Defense attorney John P. Balazs, answering the judge's query about what this evidence would add to the defense, stated:

"Well, I think it's significant....[T]wo points I could make. One is that...Mr. Kaczynski said that he built the shack because he felt there was no place to escape civilization. I think it's directly relevant to his mental state. We've already told the government, and they've brought a motion to preclude, which was denied, that we wanted to present information in the guilt phase, and maybe in the penalty phase as well, of his writing, of lay witnesses and other information that could go to his mental state at the time of the offenses. And second, it's not just a matter of the shack itself but what is in the shack and in the surrounding area. And so we need to know whether or not they found anything in the shack."

Now Judge Hollows asked prosecutor Stephen P. Freccero whether the defense had been shown the photos. Freccero answered, "No. We're prepared [pause] the point I want to make is, we don't know whether these [pause] We have never known whether...[pause]"

The prosecution's lawyers all of a sudden found themselves facing embarrassment. They hadn't bothered to get a complete list of the cabin contents, even though I had offered it to them. I had sent them a preliminary list the previous June, but the final one had more than double the entries.

How would they explain that? As the hearing continued, there were a lot of "oh's," "um's," and pauses in their answers.

"I want you," Judge Hollows told Freccero, "to define 'no' for me. Did you have any knowledge that this might be a shack related to defendant Kaczynski?"

"Absolutely," came Freccero's answer. "These are locations which could be or might be or sound similar to locations mentioned in Mr. Kaczynski's writings."

"And have you acquired any confirmation that one place or another is probably related to the defendant?" When Freccero hesitated over his answer, Hollows went on, "In other words, have you interviewed the neighbors? Did you talk to any…"

"Yes, we have."

"All right. And that's the information that they [the defense] want."

Freccero turned to legal technicalities of defining the information that would satisfy disclosure, and the judge answered in kind. Then Freccero tried to excuse the delay: "…[W]e have protected the confidentiality of the people who have given that information."

Judge Hollows was not buying that argument, and replied, "But if they've already talked to them…what difference does it make? I could say tongue in cheek, perhaps, inquire of the media; there are probably people crawling all over that place right now as we speak, talking with people. I don't think privacy's an issue anymore."

Judge Hollows pursued photographs and reports, but Freccero almost slipped, in his response to the question about "any other documentation": "No, nothing besides what we've already turned over to the defense. There is no physical evidence. We have seized no evidence from these locations."

Freccero caught himself by specifying "seized."

"You seized no evidence," Judge Hollows asked, "from locations outside of the cabins themselves but that relate to the cabin other than what you've told me about, photos, and reports of some type?"

"That is correct."

"All right. With respect to any photos or reports that you have in your possession—that relates to utilization by defendant Kaczynski, turn that over to the defense."

Freccero nodded, and Judge Hollows asked if he had any questions.

"No, Your Honor. And the scope…I'm just trying to understand the scope pertains to those locations they've tried to describe in their motion?" The prosecution was still playing technicalities.

"No," the judge answered. "It refers to any locations that the Government has knowledge of from its report, from its interviews, from its confirmation process that there's a shack out there that may have been utilized by defendant Kaczynski. *I don't care if they've used the right gulch annotation in their motion.* If you've got some information that relates to that, turn it over. [emphasis added]"

"Okay. Okay. I guess my hesitation…I just want to make sure it's not a problem; I want to make sure we comply with the court's order."

"Correct," Judge Hollows answered. "That's what they're looking for, correct, Mr. Balazs?"

"Yes, Your Honor," Balazs answered.

Judge Hollows concluded, "All right. Thank you. Do the initial disclosure by the end of today; and by Wednesday of next week, everything else."

Of course, Freccero knew he needed to be cautious here. He said, "…I would just note that we may not have copies of the photographs so we might have to show the photographs and make arrangements for copies, if they actually…if any of those photographs are relevant. I can't make copies by the end of today, is what I'm saying."

"Right. Make a Xerox by the end of today. If they need something better, they'll tell you."

As the hearing ended, despite all its hedging, the prosecution had managed to pacify the judge. But it wasn't over. I suspected they soon would be trying frantically to get my pictures, negatives, and the evidence list.

It was a sure bet evidence from the secret cabin and caches would become a focal point during court proceedings. The prosecution wasn't out of the woods yet, because the judge surely would come down on them even harder when the court discovered there was a fingerprint, evidence, and even handwriting from the cabin wall that hadn't been produced.

It was turning into an awkward eleventh-hour situation at best. And there was no chance all this would be missed by the press.

The hearing had barely adjourned when the ringing of my phone became as constant as the cooing of my wife's white dove, peacefully caged nearby.

When I came in from working, the answering machine tape was full and the phone was still ringing. By now the late-afternoon winter sky was dark, a harbinger of things to come.

Among the messages was an ominous one from Dave. He said the motion to disclose had contained the names Diagonal Gulch and McClellan Gulch.

I knew there was no such place as Diagonal Gulch; that was just a code name used by Ted to conceal the location of his secret cabin. It was more a geographic description than a name, one that Ted used to mask his hideaway in the journals. What he meant was that his secret cabin was situated in a gulch that ran diagonally off the main gulch, which was McClellan. It was a clever way to disguise the real name of that gulch. McClellan was a different story. It could be found on virtually every map.

Dave's message went on to say that Jerry Burns at the Forest Service had just called and said his office was being flooded with media calls asking about the location of McClellan Gulch.

Almost everyone in Lincoln could give directions to McClellan and my home, so about the only thing I could do was brace myself for the fury that would soon be headed up the Stemple Pass Road.

Looking out the window, I could already see vehicles driving slowly past the entrance to my gulch.

Dave ended by saying, "I'm sure that you have the weather on your side now to help keep those folks out. Good luck with the media— I feel for you."

I decided to call Bobby Didriksen and see what he knew.

He had successfully run cover for me so many times in the past that people often called him to find me.

Bobby said he had been trying to call me.

He said there was a man from ABC at his house, eager to talk to me; they had flown into Lincoln by helicopter and landed just west of town.

Bobby said they wanted to take me for a ride in the helicopter to get some pictures at the secret cabin site.

"Why don't you talk to him, he's a nice guy," Bobby said. "His name is Mike and he's sitting right here."

With that Mike took the phone.

He had been on assignment in Seattle when the call came in that Ted's secret cabin had been the topic of a court hearing. He was told to get to Lincoln without delay.

Mike asked if I would go up in the helicopter with them, take them to the site and help them shoot some video.

"You don't know what you're asking," I said.

Even though I would have enjoyed a helicopter ride, there was no way I'd divulge the location of the secret cabin to the media, or anybody else for that matter.

"The mountains are steep, rugged, and covered with timber, and there's no place to land either," I explained to Mike. "The cabin can't be spotted by air, even with a helicopter."

I wasn't lying. Dave and his pilot were unable to spot it from the air even after they were told exactly where to look.

I knew it was only a matter of time before other media people approached me.

I told Mike I'd tell my whole story to someone soon, depending on the trial, and wondered if he was interested.

"Very much so," he said.

I told him I owed it to both Betty and me to carefully weigh how the story would be handled before I talked to anyone. Then we talked about some of the pictures, evidence and other items I had in my possession.

We decided to meet that night or the following morning.

"I'm in room number seven at the Sportsman's Motel," he said.

That evening among all the messages was one from a reporter at the *Sacramento Bee*. I knew they were the paper of record for the trial, so I wanted to return the call. They had called several times since Ted's arrest.

The reporter said my name kept coming up in conversations with different people, and he wondered if I could tell him about Ted's secret cabin.

Just the day before, I had refused to let the same reporter quote me, but today was a different story. Everybody in the media knew about McClellan Gulch and that I owned it.

I told him that he could print a quote from me in the paper. I said, "The rumors about a secret cabin are true. There is a secret cabin. The FBI did not find it. I did, more than a year ago." I explained that I did live in McClellan Gulch, how long I had known Ted, that I had taken the FBI to the cabin the previous summer, and that I had worked closely with the FBI. That was all I wanted to say at the time.

The phone rang into the night, and began again the next morning.

I told Betty I was going to Lincoln to visit Bobby and to see what was happening in town.

At least one or two mobile satellite uplink trucks were already setting up for on-the-scene reporting. The town was crawling with reporters, every motel and room was booked, and out-of-town vehicles were everywhere. I decided to take a back route to Bobby's house.

He met me at the door and said many people were looking for me. "Really, I would have never guessed," I replied.

We laughed and then both noted the town looked similar to the way it did when Ted was first arrested.

I told Bobby I was headed down to see Mike from ABC.

"Mike has already called to see if you were in town yet," he said, and added, "NBC has called, too. The woman you and Betty know is also in town and would like to see you."

I called Mike and told him I'd be over shortly. He said the story was far bigger than he would have believed and told me an ABC crew was working in Sacramento on a documentary. He felt that type of format would best cover my situation.

I agreed. I appreciated how ABC's *20/20* had handled my earlier interview. But I told him I had to leave for a minute. I promised I'd be right back.

In the few minutes while I drove to the NBC crew's motel, the trial effectively ended.

Court had convened in Sacramento at 8:01 A.M. Pacific Time, almost an hour ago. Just now, the defense had proposed a plea agreement.

When I arrived, the NBC crew members already were talking about the plea and advancing theories about what it meant to their Lincoln story. Essentially, they decided the plea agreement had diminished the importance of my story.

I was amazed, but at the same time relieved. First, I wouldn't get caught up in a long, drawn-out trial; second, a lot of information that I was privy to wouldn't make it into court proceedings and become a matter of public record; third, I felt liberated from the shroud of secrecy. I could talk now!

I favored the longer documentary type format and I decided right then to go back to ABC. Mike had me talk to a producer named Peter Bull, who said he would come to Montana soon, and I agreed not to make any commitments until he arrived.

I left for home, anxious to tell Betty of the new developments. She would be very glad to hear I wouldn't be stuck in Sacramento for the trial, and I knew the ABC proposal would please her. And, indeed, she was as relieved as I to hear the case was over.

At 3:22 P.M., January 22, 1998, as the court adjourned, the criminal case of the United States versus Theodore John Kaczynski was in the history books.

Ted had pleaded guilty unconditionally to all offenses, in both the California and New Jersey cases. He would spend the rest of his life in prison without the possibility of parole. All that was left was the formal sentencing, which wouldn't occur for several months.

As Betty and I talked about the sentence, and how we were glad Ted wouldn't be put to death, we thought our lives might start to return to normal. I had lost my ability to discern normalcy, whatever that was.

ABC producer Bull arrived in Lincoln the following week, and we met for lunch at a local cafe. We worked out the details and by the end of the week his film crew was in Lincoln. They wanted to air an hour-long *Turning Point* documentary on the day of the sentencing. We had mixed weather for the taping, but it was nice enough to do some outside work. Things went well, and Peter and his crew packed up and left Lincoln. He told me it was going to be a tough squeeze, considering the amount of footage he had. I told him I understood and was confident they would do a good job.

Betty and I were more relaxed during the next couple of months than we had been in two years.

I had sent the last batch of photographs to Dave before the end of the trial. His wife, Sue, left a message that he received the package and would call at a later date. I was going to miss talking to him, but I knew they would return sometime for a vacation and we all could have a reunion along with Jerry Burns and his wife.

Dave shared a funny story during one of our last conversations about Ted.

Prisoners are not normally taken to court together, but on one particular day Ted was forced to ride in the back of a vehicle with another prisoner. The driver sternly told Ted and the other inmate that he didn't want to hear one word from either of them.

Sitting there quietly, Ted was obeying the command when the other prisoner started talking softly to him. Ted turned and whispered very seriously to shush, he didn't want to get into any trouble.

He didn't want to get caught talking, against orders, but he had no problem sending lethal bombs to people.

Actually, the story spoke volumes about how Ted would get along in prison. He'd be just fine, would keep to himself and not cause trouble.

On May 4, Ted was given an airtight sentence. For the five counts of transporting and of mailing his bombs that caused three fatalities, he received five life sentences, to be served concurrently. Also concurrent would be four twenty-year terms for transporting and for mailing two bombs that resulted in injuries. Following these were three life sentences to be served consecutively: two for carrying firearms while committing a crime and the third for transporting one of the bombs that resulted in injury. Consecutive to those life sentences came a thirty-year term for carrying a firearm while transporting one of the bombs that resulted in injury.

He was fined $650.00, but the fine was waived because Ted was "without the ability to pay." Any proceeds Ted received from books, articles, or films about him would be paid to the United States Attorney General. Finally, he was ordered to pay restitution to victims in the amount of $15,026,000, and allowed no possibility of parole.

The reign of the notorious Unabomber was over.

Many factors came into play in the government's decision to do what it had sworn not to, and that was plea-bargain the case.

Dr. Sally Johnson's psychiatric report certainly played a pivotal role in the decision. Johnson spent twenty-two hours interviewing Kaczynski in his Sacramento County jail cell and also studied his writings. She concluded Ted was paranoid schizophrenic, but competent to stand trial.

Theodore J. Kaczynski
c/o Michael Donahoe
P.O. Box 258
Helena MT 59624 - 0258

The Independent — Record

Editor:

    I am now leaving for Sacramento. I have been very well treated at the Lewis and Clark County Jail, and I would like to thank all of the jail staff publicly for their kindness and consideration.

Theodore J. Kaczynski

Ever aware of his public image, Kaczynski sent the Helena newspaper this gracious note in 1996.

With Johnson's report, the government realized that if tried and found guilty, Ted might not receive the death penalty anyway. But when the defense demanded disclosure of the information about the secret cabin and evidence included therein, the government surprised everyone by accepting a plea bargain the very next day.

Prosecutors at once saw how much the secret cabin buttressed the defense's portrayal of Ted's isolationism in a mental-defect defense. Weighing the odds of obtaining a death sentence considering those factors made them realize the whole process wasn't worth it.

The plea bargain appealed to Ted. It was a sure way to save his life, but equally importantly, to prevent the court and the nation from learning all the sordid details of his acts.

He could also avoid being further embarrassed before the public, especially the people of Lincoln, who would have learned about all the "unchargeable offenses": acts of vandalism, thefts, shootings, etc., which might have been part of a trial.

Ted always had and continues to have a great concern for the public's perception of him.

As one reporter asked me, "Why would Ted's public image even matter to him? He's admitted to the bombings."

The reason is Ted, in his own twisted way, could justify the killings to save the planet from the evils of technology and satisfy his need for revenge.

It was an evil means, but in his mind it was justified by the end.

But how could he justify the vicious, selfish, and criminal acts he committed right here in the Lincoln area? Those acts had nothing to do with his cause of saving mankind from technology.

Ted will spend the rest of his life in prison, but he didn't have to go to trial and face the public he had terrorized for two decades.

A Closer Look

Ted Kaczynski's life was, is, and always will be an enigma to anyone who studies it. Even though I knew Ted for nearly the entire twenty-five years he lived in Lincoln, I really didn't know him.

I have many regrets regarding my relationship with Ted. Perhaps nothing would have slowed his pell-mell charge toward infamy. But everyone who ever knew him must have the same thoughts as me, that somehow we could have sidetracked him and helped him solve his problems short of violence.

In Ted's journals he said he made a conscious effort to overcome his middle-class inhibitions, becoming free to commit crimes without the burden of guilt. He deprogrammed society's norms and the training of his early years. He then reprogrammed his mind so he felt satisfaction from violence, even murder, acts that seemed to cleanse his mind and ease the hatred temporarily. His reprogramming, which crystallized around ideas developed early in his life, led him to adopt a twisted logic and situational ethics.

His primary reasons for committing crimes were hatred and revenge. But in later years, as he tantalized the media and the FBI with his letters and manifesto, he found it advantageous to advance a more acceptable justification for his crimes, i.e., saving the world from the evils of technology in order to preserve individual freedom and the environment. Even if he were captured and threatened with the death penalty, Ted could then become a martyr for his cause.

KACZYNSKI JOURNAL, APRIL 1971
My motive for doing what I am going to do is simply personal revenge. I do not expect to accomplish anything by it. Of course, if my crime (and my reasons for

committing it) gets any public attention, it may help to stimulate public interest in the technology question and thereby improve the chances of stopping technology before it is too late; but on the other hand most people will probably be repelled by my crime, and the opponents of freedom may use it as a weapon to support their arguments for control over human behavior.

I have no way of knowing whether my action will do more good than harm. I certainly don't claim to be an altruist or to be acting for the "good" (whatever that is) of the human race. I act merely from a desire for revenge.

Twenty-five years later, just before his arrest, Ted again wrote that his personal resentment of the technological system, not the good of mankind, was the motivating energy behind his actions.

JAN. 23, 1996 (RECOPIED BY TED FROM EARLIER ENTRIES)
I now have more of a sense of—mission—a concern with issues wider than personal resentment of the technological society. Never the less, it should be made clear that the motivating energy behind my actions comes from my personal grievance and personal resentment of the technological system. I certainly wouldn't take such risks from a pure desire to benefit my fellow man. I imagine that anyone who ever makes great efforts or takes great risks on account of social issues has some powerful personal motive, even if he persuades himself that he is actuated by pure altruism.

Ted's personal motivation was reinforced further by his sense of superiority over most everyone else.

UNDATED JOURNAL ENTRY
I believe in nothing. Whereas I don't even believe in the cult of nature-worshippers or wilderness-worshippers. (I am perfectly ready to litter in parts of the woods that are of no use to me—I often throw cans in logged-over areas

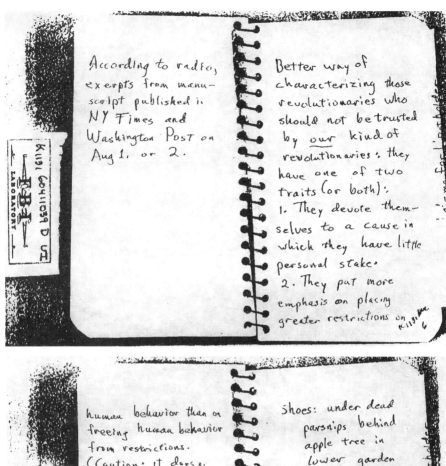

According to radio, excerpts from manuscript published in NY Times and Washington Post on Aug 1. or 2.

Better way of characterizing those revolutionaries who should not be trusted by our kind of revolutionaries: they have one of two traits (or both):
1. They devote themselves to a cause in which they have little personal stake.
2. They put more emphasis on placing greater restrictions on

human behavior than on freeing human behavior from restrictions. (Caution: It does no good if they seek to free behavior from restrictions in areas where we already have almost complete freedom anyway, e.g. sexual freedom, religious freedom, etc.)

Shoes: under dead parsnips behind apple tree in lower garden
9 items in shed
2 items by black raspberry bushes

Two rifles, with scope, .22 pistol, package of ammunition, hat.

Kaczynski's pocket notebook: news of the manifesto's publication, philosophy, and key to caches.

or in places much frequented by people; I don't find wilderness particularly healthy physically; I don't hesitate to poach.)

The fact that I was able to admit to ~~myself~~ that there was no logical justification for morality illustrates a very important trait of mine. I have always had a strong tendency to admit an unpleasant truth to myself, rather than trying to push it away with self-deception or rationalization. I am certainly not claiming that I've never indulged in self deception—I only claim that I have much less tendency to self-deception than most people.

This requires an important qualification....

Thus I tended to feel that I was a particularly important person and superior to most of the rest of the human race. Generally speaking, there was nothing arrogant or egotistical in this feeling, nor did I ever express any such feeling outside the immediate family. It just came to me as naturally as breathing to feel that I was someone special.

In Ted's early writings he tried to justify his need for revenge within the parameters of the fading influence of his middle class morality and his past experiences, until he made a breakthrough.

UNDATED JOURNAL ENTRY
I'll just chuck all of this silly morality business and hate anybody I please. Since then I have never had any interest in or respect for morality, ethics, or anything of the sort.

Ted's ideas of revenge and his ability to carry out terrorist acts fit neatly with this belief that it was all right for him to hate anybody, but he was angry that he required further "deprogramming."

FROM KACZYNSKI AUTOBIOGRAPHY
The reader must realize by now that in high school and

college, I often became terribly angry at someone, or hated someone, but as a matter of prudence, I could not express that anger or hatred openly. I would therefore indulge in fantasies of dire revenge. However, I never attempted to put any such fantasies into effect, because I was too strongly conditioned by my early training, against any defiance of authority. To be more precise: I could not have committed a crime of revenge, even a relatively minor crime, because my fear of being caught and punished was all out of proportion to the actual danger of being caught. I could have much more easily risked my life in a lawful way, then [sic] take an equal risk of spending 30 days in jail for some minor crime. Thus, when I had a fantasy of revenge, I had very little comfort from it, because I was all to [sic] clearly aware that I had had many previous fantasies of revenge, and nothing had ever come of any of them. This was very frustrating and humiliating. Therefore I became more and more determined that some day I would actually take revenge on some of the people I hated.

As those thoughts matured, Ted planned, but couldn't quite follow through with, his first attempt to murder a scientist.

CHRISTMAS DAY, 1972:
About a year and a half ago, I planned to murder a scientist—as a means of revenge against organized society in general and the technological establishment in particular. Unfortunately, I chickened out. I couldn't work up the nerve to do it. The experience showed me that propaganda and indoctrination have a much stronger hold on me than I realized. My plan was such that there was very little chance of my getting caught. I had no qualms before I tried to do it, and thought I would have no difficulty. I had everything all prepared. But when I tried to take the final irrevocable step, I found myself overwhelmed by an irrational, superstitious fear—not a fear of anything specific, merely a vague but powerful fear of committing the act.

268

I cannot attribute this to a rational fear of being caught. I made my preparations with extreme care, and I figured my chances of being caught were less than, say, my chances of being killed in an automobile accident within the next year. I am not in the least nervous when I get into my car. I can only attribute my fear to the constant flood of anticrime propaganda to which one is subjected. For example, murderers in TV dramas are always caught.

Shortly before his mail-bombing began, he wrote:

FALL 1977

The technological society may be in some sense inevitable, but it is so only because of the way people behave. Consequently I hate people. (I may have some other reasons for hating some people, but the main reason is that people are responsible for the technological society and its associated phenomena, from motorcycles to computers to psychological controls. Almost anyone who holds steady employment is contributing his part in maintaining the technological society.) Of course, the people I hate most are those who consciously and willfully promote the technological society, such as scientists, big businessmen, union leaders, politicians, etc., etc. I emphasize that my motivation is personal revenge. I don't pretend to any kind of philosophical or moralistic justification.

The concept of morality is simply one of the psychological tools by which society controls peoples' [*sic*] behavior. My ambition is to kill a scientist, big business-man, government official, or the like. I would also like to kill a communist.

Ted coolly considered the consequences of being caught. At first he planned one violent act that would result in his death. In his autobiography, he looked back on a session with a psychiatrist he saw while contemplating a sex change operation; he changed his mind while still in the waiting room, yet directed his disgust at the doctor.

As I walked away from the building afterwards, I felt disgusted about what my uncontrolled sexual cravings had almost led me to do and I felt humiliated, and I violently hated the psychiatrist. Just then there came a major turning point in my life. Like a Phoenix, I burst from the ashes of my despair to a glorious new hope. I thought I wanted to kill that psychiatrist because the future looked utterly empty to me.

I felt I wouldn't care if I died. And so I said to myself "why not *really kill that psychiatrist* and anyone else whom I hate." What is important is not the words that ran through my mind, but the way I felt about them. What was entirely new was the fact that I *really felt I could kill someone*. My very hopelessness had liberated me. Because I no longer cared about death. I no longer cared about consequences, and I suddenly felt that I really could break out of my rut in life and do things that were daring, "irresponsible," or criminal. My first thought was to kill somebody I hated and then kill myself before the cops could get me. (I've always considered death preferable to long imprisonment.) But, since I now had new hope, I was not ready to relinquish life so easily. So I thought "I will kill, but I will make at least some effort to avoid detection, so that I can kill again." Then I thought, "Well, as long as I am going to throw everything up anyway, instead of having to shoot it out with the cops or something, I will go up to Canada, take off into the woods with a rifle, and try to live off the country. If that doesn't work out, and if I can get back to civilization before I starve, then I will come back here and kill someone I hate."

What was new here was the fact that I now felt I really had the courage to behave "irresponsibly." All these thoughts passed through my head in the length of time it took me to walk a quarter of a mile. By the end of that time I had acquired bright new hope, an angry, vicious kind of determination and high morale.

Ted's feelings at the time on preserving his life and finally being able to place his first bomb are also reflected in his autobiography, started in 1978 and finished in 1979, written while Ted was in Illinois.

FROM KACZYNSKI AUTOBIOGRAPHY

It's not a question of preserving my life and health; getting out of the power of civilization has long since become an end in itself for me. By now I have practically lost all hope of ever attaining this end. There my happiness in my Montana hills is spoiled every time an airplane passes over or anything else happens that reminds me of the inescapability of civilization. Life under the thumb of modern civilization seems worthless to measure and thus I more and more felt that life was coming to a dead end for me and death began at times to look attractive—it would mean peace. There was just one thing that really made me determined to cling to life for awhile [*sic*], and that was the desire for—revenge—I wanted to kill some people, preferably including at least one scientist, businessman, or other bigshot. This actually was my biggest reason for coming back to Illinois this spring. In Montana, if I went to the city to mail a bomb to some bigshot, [driver's name] would doubtless remember I rode the bus that day. In the anonymity of the big city I figured it would be much safer to buy materials for a bomb and mail it. (Though the death-wish had appeared, it was still far from dominant, and therefore I preferred not to be suspected of crimes.) As mentioned in some of my notes, I did make an attempt with a bomb—whether successful or not I don't know. In making a second bomb I have only barely made a start…

Even though Ted had a few guilty feelings in the beginning, those faded as he continued on his quest for revenge.

SEPT. 15, 1980 [CODED JOURNAL]

Since committing the crimes reported elsewhere in my

notes I feel better. I am still plenty angry, you understand, but the difference is that I am now able to strike back, to a degree. True, I cant strike back to anything like the extent I wish to, but I no longer feel totally helpless, and the anger duzzent gnaw at my guts as it used throughout. Guilty feelings? Yes, a little. Occasionally I have bad dreams in which the police are after me. Or in which I am threatened with punishment from some supernatural source. Such as the devil. But these dont occur often enuf to be a problem. I am definitely glad to have done what I have.

Even though this coded entry showed a flicker of guilt, it was doused in his final statement.

A year earlier, after his first bombing and just two months before his second, he had written:

FROM KACZYNSKI AUTOBIOGRAPHY

One thing that our society demands is that you have a recognized place in the system. By quitting my job [at Prince Castle Spice Packing Plant], I've made myself again an outcast, a good-for-nothing, a bum—someone whom "respectable" people can't view without a certain element of suspicion. I can't feel comfortable in this respect until I get away into the hills again—away from society. Besides, in quitting I feel as if I have signed my own death-warrant. Drifting along indefinitely in that job would have been the path of least resistance—and that, in a way, was the only thing remaining between me and the finish of everything. Now the path of least resistance is simply to go back to Montana, and once I'm there, I'll kill, because, as I decided before I left Montana, if I ever went back there I'd have to kill, because I had too much accumulated anger over the inroads of civilization. I'm not likely to change my mind and go looking for another job—job hunting, going to sleep, and getting up for work again the next morning. (Maybe there would still be something better I could still strive for, some corner of the world where there's still some wilderness, or other things, but again, I'm so terribly—tired—of struggling.)

For those reasons, I want to get my revenge in one big blast. By accepting death as the price, I won't have to fret and worry about how to plan things so I won't get caught. More over, I want to release all my hatred and go out and kill. When I see a motorcyclist tearing up the mountain meadows, instead of fretting about how I can get revenge on him safely, I just want to watch the bullet rip through his flesh and I want to kick him in the face when he is dying. You mustn't assume from this that I am currently being tormented by paroxysms of hatred. Actually, during the last few months (except at a few times) I have been troubled by frustrated hatred much less than usual. I think this is because, whenever I have experienced some outrage (such as a low flying jet or some official stupidity reported in the paper), as I felt myself growing angry, I calmed myself by thinking—just wait till this summer! Then I'll kill! Thus, what I've been feeling in recent months is not hot rage, but a cold determination to get my revenge. But I want to be in my home or hills in Montana, not here in the city. Death in the city seems so sordid and depressing. Death in these hills—well, if you have to die, that's the place to do it! However, it would have been very tempting to just hang onto my job at Prince Castle indefinitely, even though I have nothing to look forward to.

The truth is, I don't want to die!

When Ted returned to Montana in 1979, he had resolved his inner battle over whether he wanted to live, or die in one glorious burst of revenge. He had committed felonies by placing two bombs and he was a month away from planting another by mail aboard an airliner in November 1979.

His previous successes brought him newfound confidence and boldness, reflected in the acts of vandalism carried out in the Lincoln area and his escalating bombing campaign. He did consider himself slightly vulnerable and occasionally considered the possibilities and ramifications of capture.

> Oct. 23, 1979 [Kaczynski journal]
> I am about to stash these notes in a hiding-place, so I will record now some things that I didn't like to write here when the notes were not hidden. Before I left on my hike this summer I put sugar in the gas tank of one of [name]'s snowmobiles. So hopefully [name] will have some trouble with it this winter. When I went out on my hike this summer I was planning to lie in ambush by some roadside (dirt by-road) a long way from home and shoot some trail-bikers or other mechanized desecrators of the forest, without too much regard for consequences. But once I was out in the woods I started to reconsider, for two reasons. One was that once I was out in the woods I felt so good that I started to care about the future again—I wanted to have more years to spend in the woods. The other reason is that I thought of an excellent scheme for revenge on a bigger scale and didn't want to screw it up by getting caught for something else before I had a chance to carry it out. Considering technological civilization as a monstrous octopus, the motorcyclists, jeep-riders, and other intruders into the forest are only the tips of the tentacles.
> I was not really satisfied with striking at these. My other plan would let me strike perhaps not at the head, but at least much further up along the tentacles.

Ted now seemed set. He had overcome his inhibitions and his early social indoctrination. He had also successfully tempered his desire to die in one big showdown. And the early bombings remained unsolved.

The only flaw holding him back was the weak performance of his early bombs. That was something that could be overcome easily through development and testing. He would create lighter, deadlier and more easily hidden devices. The time needed wouldn't be a problem for Ted, who could apply himself as he had during all those years of schooling. Ted had infinite patience.

The winter before he went to Illinois, and just before and as the bombings began, Ted regularly complained to his journals about jet planes flying high over the Montana mountains, and of how the noise of loggers or helicopters, and small airplanes spoiled his hikes. He wrote:

> MONDAY, JAN. 23, 1978
> Yesterday, Sunday the 22nd, was a very happy day.
> Only a few jets passed over, and mostly there was peace and quiet.

While on a 1979 trip in McClellan Gulch, Ted recorded his deep hatred of aircraft. Ted couldn't enjoy the secluded forest if there were any noise or other signs of man's intrusions. And even the most idyllic and private areas Ted knew in McClellan Gulch were not immune to the noises of man in some form or another. This drove Ted to spend less time enjoying the very thing he loved most, and more time and energy working on his plan of revenge against a technological society and its human creators and devotees.

Soon after he mailed his first bombs, his language changed dramatically:

> JUNE 6, 1979
> The only disruptive sounds this morning have been caused by the 9 evil jet planes that have passed within my hearing.

> JULY 24, 1979
> Yesterday was quite good—heard only 8 jets. Today was good in early morning, but later in morning there was aircraft noise almost without intermission for, I would estimate, about an hour. Then there was a very loud sonic boom. This was the last straw and it reduced

me to tears of impotent rage. But I have a plan for revenge....

No one who doesn't know how to appreciate the wonderful peace and satisfaction that one can get from solitude and silence in the woods [*sic*]. In Lombard, Illinois there is far more jet noise, and at times it is very annoying, but it does not disturb me nearly as much as does the lesser jet noise here, because here the noise destroys something wonderful; while in the city there is nothing for the noises to destroy, because one is living in a [expletive] pile anyway....

By silence I don't mean all sound has to be excluded, only man-made sound. Most natural sounds are soothing. The few exceptions, like thunder and raven cries, are magnificent and I enjoy them. But aircraft noise is an insult, a slap in the face.

It is a symptom of the evil of modern society that few people today even understand the old-fashioned proverb, "Silence is golden." Yet where today can one get silence? NOWHERE—not even up here in these mountains.

JULY 25, 1979

In this trip I had been sort of putting aside my anger at the jets, in order to enjoy this wonderful forest.

But that solid hour of aircraft noise (partly jets and partly light planes) yesterday, capped by a startling sonic boom, brought up all that anger. Things are spoiled for me now, so I will go home today. Then I will work on my revenge plan. I feel very melancholy about leaving this camp. I was so happy here. I had looked forward to staying out in the woods much longer than this. Isn't there any place left where one can just go off by oneself and have peace and quiet?

Three months later, Ted was still lamenting how that July trip in McClellan Gulch had been ruined by aircraft noise.

*   *   *

Oct. 23, 1979

Now, ever since that last day out when I was upset by the almost solid hour of aircraft noise, I have never taken any full or unalloyed satisfaction in the woods, even on those days when there are few aircraft, motorcycles, or other disturbances...In fact, I have made a conscious decision not to let myself have that feeling of wilderness freedom anymore in this [Lincoln] area, because it is just too miserable when that satisfaction is shattered by planes or the like...You understand, it is not the noise in itself that bothers me, but what that noise signifies. It is the voice of the Octopus—the octopus that will allow nothing to exist outside the range of its control. Now with all the planes and so forth, this area makes me think too much of those miserable remnants of prairie that one sees in the Chicago area around airports and in suburban factory districts, or of the smog-choked Cook County Forest Preserves. Just sad reminders of what once was; though I no longer find satisfaction in this mountain country, I still love it. I suppose it is the same way a mother loves a child who has been crippled and mutilated. It is a love filled with grief.

On November 15, 1979, Ted's bomb mailed from Chicago set fire to the cargo aboard American Airlines Flight 444 as it took off from Dulles International Airport. The plane made an emergency return to Dulles. Several passengers were treated for smoke inhalation.

When Ted arrived in Lincoln, purchased his small plot of land and built his cabin, he immediately started exploring the country. He began with areas adjacent to his home cabin and then spread out from there.

After the first two or three years he had covered nearly every area within a ten-mile radius. Though he wandered much farther at times, hiking almost twenty-five miles to the north into the backcountry of the Bob Marshall Wilderness Area, he concentrated mainly on the areas to the east and south of his home cabin in Florence Gulch. These areas he thoroughly explored were the ones where he could live off the land, the areas that would sustain him and his way of life.

As time passed, new roads were built, timber stands logged, and mining claims staked. That, coupled with the increase of cabins, homes, and campsites being built and developed on nearly every available piece of private land that ran along Poorman Creek and near his home, dramatically cut into the wild areas available to Ted. And made him angry enough to take chances.

> OCT. 23, 1979. [KACZYNSKI JOURNAL]
> ...I wanted to shoot some of those miners who were [expletive] things up down around [name] Creek, if I could get an opporunity that the looked [*sic*] safe from the point of view of not getting caught. One day I went down there and watched, from cover, a guy with a bulldozer who was tearing a hung chunk out of a hillside that was otherwise very beautiful....It made me sad to see a big old Douglas fir that this fool had torn up by the roots with his machine. But I didn't shoot at him after all. In part this was due to the inhibitions that are trained into us in modern society, and which are very difficult to overcome. But I have advanced far enough now in that respect so that I might have been able to overcome the inhibitions except for the fact that...I had thought-out as well as instinctive reasons for not wanting to get caught; and I was afraid this guy might have a partner somewhere. Through the trees I had only a very fragmentary view of the site; the guy running the bulldozer might not be the only one there; if I crept close enough for a clear shot at the bulldozer-man, I might have been seen by another man who was nearby in another place without my knowing it. The woods were quite open—no good hiding. So I satisfied myself by going back a couple of days later when I correctly figured no one was there, and sabotaging the bulldozer. It was hard to do any thing to it because of its sturdy, tank-like construction, but I cut the fan-belt, cut some tubes, put dirt in the place where oil goes in,

and a few other such things. Besides that, there was a nice new pickup down by the road, I think belonging to some of these mining-fools, and I smashed the windshield and cut some belts and tubes on it....

CODED JOURNAL

...SUMMEROF1981IBEGANHEARINGDISAGREABLE [*sic*] NOISESOFMACHINERY,SOMETIMES SURPRISINGLYLOUD,DEPENDING APPARENTLY ON METEOROLOICAL[*sic*]CONDITIONS.-OFTEN BUT OTHERWISEBEAUTIFUL,SILENTMORNINGWAS-RUINEDFOR MEWHENTHESENOISES STARTEDUP.THEFOL-LOWINGWINTER MANY OTHERWISEPLEASANT EXCURSIONS-WERERUINEDFOR ME BYTHE MOANING AND HOWLINGOF-THOSE IRONMONSTERS,AUDIBLEBUTOFTENLOUDLY)[*sic*] FOR MILES OVERTHE HILLS.MADEUP MYMIND TO GET REVENGE,-BUT IT WASDIFFICULT TO DETERMINEJUSTWHERE NOISE-WASCOMINGFROM.HADTOWAITFORSUMMER ANYWAY,SINCEMY TRACKS COULDEASILY BEFOLLOWED IN SNOW,BUTNOISE SEEMEDTO STOP INSPRING.THENIBEGAN HEARING IT AGAIN IN LATESUMMER,1982.ITHINKITWASINSEPTEMBERTHAT-ITOOKBLANKET,PISTOL,1DAYS RATIONS AND FOLLOWED-NOISETO FIND IT CAMEFROM A LOGGINGOPERATION IN [*name*]CREEKDRAINAGE,LOGGINGOFF ONEOFMY FAVORITE-WILDSPOTS.THEIRMETHODWASHORRIBLE.ASFARAS I COULD-TELL WITHOUT GOINGCLOSE ENOUGH TO RISKBEING-SEEN,THEYWEREJUSTPUSHINGTREES OVERWITHBULL DOZERS INSTEADOFCUTTINGWITH SAWS.WHENTHEY LEFT FORTHEDAY I WENT IN ANDFOUNDTHE WHOLE SURFACE OFTHEGROUND STRIPPED RIGHTOFF LEAVING UGLYTANGLE OF LIMBS,UPROOTEDTRUNKS,ANDDIRT.THEY LEFT A 5GALLONCAN OF OIL SITTING ON THEIRMACHINETHAT THEY USE TO PICKUP LOGS ANDLOADTHEM ON TRUCK.I POUREDTHE OIL OVERTHE MACHINES ENGINE AND SETFIRE TO IT.I BET ITCOSTTHEM OVER1000BUCKS TO FIXIT.SPENTPLEASANTNIGHT SLEEPING OUT ONTOPOFTHE MOUNTAIN ANDCAMEHOME LEISURELY INTHE MORNING.I FELT SO GOOD AFTERHAVINGDONE THIS.THOUGH A MITE

Besides the timber burned in Ted's fire, the cost to the logging contractor to replace his equipment was $75,000—far beyond Ted's thousand-dollar estimate.

He would write about each area as the changes took place and how they affected his way of life.

[FROM KACZINSKY'S SPANISH-LANGUAGE JOURNAL, TRANSLATED BY LANGUAGE SERVICES UNIT]
JAN. 31, 1982
This winter, hunting in the long hill which extends towards the south from the first peak to the east of Baldy, I have seen many colored stripes on trees. I think that this means that they will cut wood there, which will ruin the area. That one is my favorite area which can be reached easily from my ranch without staying in the woods overnight. Besides it is also the best area to hunt for rabbits on this side of Stemple Pass Road. The ruin of this area will make it more difficult for me to get enough meat during the winter.

Further encroachment on Ted's own side of Stemple Pass Road led him to state: "I have practically written off the entire area around my home as a total loss."

The south side of Stemple Pass Road, my side, was another story. He knew my large block of land was protected, no matter how many people moved into our area, no matter how many new roads or logging sales. I would keep it a safe haven, the one place where Ted could be assured of privacy, the one place he could freely hunt year-round without the danger of being caught.

Ted wrote extensively in his journals about how much he valued this gulch, extolling the silence, the total privacy, the mountain grouse that were so tame since they were never hunted, and the beauty and unspoiled nature of the area.

He used words like "special," "magical," "most favorite," and "most secret" to describe the camps and his secret cabin there. He also used poetic and romantic words and phrases to describe his feelings: "tranquillity," "sensitive to the silence," "beauty and mystery of the wild," and even "sacred."

All these places he described were located in McClellan Gulch and the small tributaries that flow into it from the east and west. In fact, within ten pages of his Spanish-language journals, Ted described fourteen of his most special, secret, and favorite places, excluding his home cabin. Twelve were located within my drainage.

[FROM KACZINSKY'S SPANISH-LANGUAGE JOURNAL, TRANSLATED BY LANGUAGE SERVICES UNIT]
JULY 25, 1982
I first went to my camp in the dry and open slope that faces McClellan's stream. Since the weather appeared to be good when I was going to bed, I did not unwrap my coat cloth. It rained during the night; I had to get up, make fire, and unwrap my cloth; and I was wet nevertheless.

JULY, 1982
...Another following day, the day appearing much better, and I having found that it was possible to bring my bundles with less difficulty then [sic] before, encouraged myself and went to my high camp over McClellan.

OCTOBER 1982
In the first half of October, feeling nervous and tired due to difficulties and anxiety that had to do with my cellar to store roots, and other anxieties too, I picked up only the more essential things and I took off for my favorite place: the stream that flows into the McClellan Stream...

NOVEMBER 15, 1982
... I headed south walking...across the slope of the mountain, on top of McClellan, very high. The morning was very beautiful and I was very happy...Afterwards, I walked a little bit down to the stream, so as to enjoy the

wonderful and dark beauty of the place...I wish I could express the wonderful mystery of that stream.

AUGUST 1982

The weather still looked bad in the morning; I was discouraged because of this and because of the difficulty of bringing my bundles and as a consequence I went to my most secret camp...McClellan; when it makes rain this camp is much better than the other one....

Another following day I took a stroll uphill on the opposite side of the camp. By good fortune I was able to kill a blue partridge. I picked up a few wild onions too. For me that place is somewhat sacred, because it had not been touched too much by the hands of men.

JULY 29-30, 1982

Another following day I went to my high camp over McClellan; it turned out to be hotter than the day before and even though I had with me approximately half a canteen (or a "quart") of water, I still suffered from more thirst and tiredness than the day before.

NOVEMBER 1982

Upon arriving to my old camp in that place near the stream that flows in the McClellan Stream, I began to feel the tranquillity of the forest. I did not care that the forest was cold or wet, with an inch of snow that covered the ground. As always, I enjoyed the wild beauty of that area.

NOVEMBER 29, 1981

In my earlier notes I mentioned that I built a very small cabin in an isolated site several years ago. Near my cabin was a favorite place of mine where I would usually camp out. Here an owl would usually sing for me at night...It is tranquil here; there is peace here. The soft sound of the wind in the pines increases the feeling of peace.

APRIL 29, 1983

The twenty ninth of April the sky was clear and the weather was pleasant, and I transferred my [secret cabin] camp out to the next cliff [direction] from where the [cabin] is. After raising my coat and making a layer of branches to protect myself from the wet floor, I ate and went to sleep on the slope that was up higher from the camp. (This slope provided me with an abundance of herbs). [sic] The view seen from this slope is extremely beautiful. I enjoyed being there very much. After resting for a while, I walked barefoot from one side to the other of the hill and forest that borders with it, in a very silent way. I like very much to walk slowly and silently through the wild. The following day I went up the mountain at daybreak. I felt very happy and energetic. I walked on top of the mountain…It was a magical morning; I was very sensitive to the silence, to the beauty, and to the mystery of the wild. I was very happy.

MAY 1983

When the sun was setting towards the west, I went down to the Barranca Soslaya (slanting cliff) and then cliff up to the fountain [sic] to get water to drink. On the way, I stopped to dig some Lomatium roots. I got some big ones. I was tired when I arrived to camp. By the way, this camp is on a beautiful cliff, with a beautiful clear water stream. Up higher, the cliff is narrow and the slope is strong; further below,…the cliff is narrow there too and not too easy to access, so that it does not invite whoever passes through the Barranca Soslaya to go up there.

Ted caught a last glimpse of the country he loved as he rode hand-cuffed in the dark along the gravel Stemple Pass road toward Helena, knowing he would never again see the small cabin he had called home for twenty-five years.

He was carried over the rutted road that led across the Continental Divide he had explored so many times, into the Helena Valley and

Helena Federal District Court, then to Sacramento, and finally to federal prison. There would be no "plan B."

The freedom and personal autonomy Ted so adamantly sought were the same freedom and personal autonomy he chose to take from others. The rules Ted laid out for everyone else did not apply to himself.

But as he pleaded guilty in exchange for life in prison, society finally gained the upper hand.

The former resident of Montana's Florence Gulch boarded a small aircraft that transported him from Sacramento to the maximum security facility in Florence, Colorado, where he would be spending the rest of his life.

As he entered the prison he paused and took one last long look at the Rocky Mountains, the northern part of which he had called home for nearly half of his adult life.

The cell that was to become his home would have no window to the surrounding mountains. A skylight to the outside world would be his only view; the small window directly overhead would offer him only a glimpse of the clouds and sky, not the mountains he had loved.

Ted had used the freedom our Constitution guarantees every citizen to carve a path of violence and hatred, a path that led him to a small cell in a facility that epitomizes the very technological society he loathed.

JAN. 21, 1978 [WRITTEN AT SECRET CABIN]

Our Society allows us great freedom to do nothing or to dream or to play games. But I consider these trivial freedoms and have little interest in them. What I want is the opportunity to make the practical decisions affecting the physical conditions of my own existence. For example: consider the risk of worldwide famine. Probably a small risk at present, so that modern society probably gives me better assurance of food supply than I could give myself as a primitive hunter-gatherer. But that's beside the point. As a primitive I would have the right to deal with the problem myself and make my own decisions regarding it.

As it is, the system makes all the decisions for me and I can do nothing about it. Another example: the system makes all the decisions influencing air pollution (and noise pollution!) and it galls me that I can do nothing to change these decisions. All practical decisions are made by the system. I want personal autonomy in making such decisions. But that is impossible in a technological society.

By his own hand, Ted destroyed his own personal autonomy— but what a wasteful wreckage he had made along the way, of himself and so many others.

The Authors

As you turn off Stemple Pass Road and head up the lane that parallels McClellan Gulch you see a scattering of old vehicles and parts and—most imposing—an assembly of heavy equipment that includes giant Cats, semi-tractors, road graders, draglines, and gravel conveyors. It's obvious these are tools of the trade for a man who makes his living off the land.

Chris Waits (left) and Dave Shors.

A pack of curious dogs greets a visitor before an official welcome is offered by Chris Waits—mechanic, road builder, welder, well digger, logger, contractor, and hard rock miner—a man who's practiced just about every trade and skill known around Lincoln, Montana.

As you enter the hand-built house of Chris and his wife Betty, it's quickly apparent that you're not visiting the typical single-minded Montanan. First to catch your eye is the massive bookcase, a 30-foot wall, ten feet high, stuffed with a library ranging from Old Testament translations to textbooks on metallurgy. Then there's the computer workstation with all the latest accouterments. Just across the room is a grand piano with classical music scores marked and dog-eared from hours of practice.

"My pride and joy is the piano," Waits says. He's played since the age of three, mentored by his mother, a musician and piano teacher, who lives close by. To the musically inclined families of the greater Blackfoot Valley, Waits is known fondly as piano teacher, church organist, and host of recitals held at his converted auto repair shop he called the Lincoln Center for the Performing Arts.

"I don't know anything he can't do and do well," says close friend and Lincoln patriarch "Bobby" Didriksen, who serves with Waits on the local historical society board. "He can remember everything that's ever said. You can have a conversation with Chris and then he can sit down and write it out, word for word."

Waits' intellect sneaks up when you least suspect it. In a discussion about Ted Kaczynski's Spanish-written journals, Waits offhandedly mentions that he too is a student of Spanish...as well as of Hebrew, Greek, and Latin.

As you become acquainted with Waits it becomes clearer how for twenty-five years the brilliant, hermit math professor time and again gravitated toward the wealth of knowledge and thought that resides at the mouth of McClellan Gulch.

As an associate editor of the *Independent Record*, the daily newspaper in Helena, Dave Shors coordinated coverage of the Unabomber story when it broke in April 1996. His staff's reports helped give the world its first view of the reclusive hermit.

Fascinated with Montana mining history, Shors had kicked around the Lincoln backcountry for years, photographing what's left of the gold and silver mining era. These days he spends his weekends operating, with his wife Crystal, a quaint Helena antiques store that specializes in Montana lore and historical books.

A loyal customer of old books has been a colorful character from Lincoln named Chris Waits, who shares Shors' interest in Montana history, particularly mining. In the spring of 1998, soon after Kaczynski entered his guilty plea, Waits was buying some books from Shors when their conversation turned to the Unabomber and the ordeal Waits had endured in helping the FBI with its investigation.

Talk about publishing a book ensued—Shors had just co-written and published an autobiography of a legendary Montana fly fisherman, Pat Barnes. Waits wasn't much interested in working with a big city publisher, and he and Shors seemed to hit it off.